THE DEVIL

Also by Graham Johnson:
Powder Wars
Druglord
Football and Gangsters

THE DEVIL

BRITAIN'S MOST FEARED UNDERWORLD TAXMAN

GRAHAM JOHNSON

MAINSTREAM
PUBLISHING

EDINBURGH AND LONDON

First published in Great Britain in 2007 by
MAINSTREAM PUBLISHING COMPANY
(EDINBURGH) LTD
7 Albany Street
Edinburgh EH1 3UG

ISBN 9781845961787

This book is a work of non-fiction. In some cases names of people,
places, dates and the sequence or details of events have been changed to
protect the privacy of others. The author has stated to the publishers that,
except in such minor respects, the contents of this book are true.

A catalogue record for this book is available
from the British Library

Typeset in Dirtyhouse and Palatino

Printed in Great Britain by
Clays Ltd, St Ives plc

Dedicated to Abbey, Connie, Dionne, Emma,
Raya and Sonny

ACKNOWLEDGEMENTS

First of all, a massive thank you to Stephen French for telling his story, because, after all, this is *his* book. He gave up his time for hundreds of hours of interviews, and travelled up and down the country to ensure that this book could be written. Thank you to my copy-editor Emma Murray of Editing and Beyond for her eagle eye, suggestions and advice. Her efforts often went way beyond the call of duty. Also, thank you to Anna Hunt for proofreading and Rohan Tait for picture editing.

Honore et Integritate

CONTENTS

PART THREE – THE STRAIGHTGOER

AUTHOR'S NOTE

This book is based on a large number of interviews with the main subject, Stephen French. Other research materials included press cuttings, criminal records and interviews with witnesses, criminal or otherwise. However, the story is mostly reliant on Stephen's personal testimony.

I decided to write the book in the first person, using 'I' instead of 'he', so that the reader would get the story from Stephen's perspective and not mine. I decided to do this in an attempt to bring the reader closer to the action and to give a direct insight into what Stephen French did, thought and felt, with as little spin, analysis or journalistic input as possible.

There is a glossary at the back of the book if you're not familiar with some of the slang used.

Graham Johnson
August 2007

PREFACE

THEY CALLED ME THE DEVIL

You may think that my life is a doddle, what with the luxurious flats in Canary Wharf, the penthouse apartments in Liverpool city centre, £70,000 cars, Christmas in the Caribbean, and the five-star hotels in Las Vegas, New York, Florida and the Indian Ocean. Well, let me share with you a strand of the rope that gives me strength and makes me who I am. From my earliest memory to when I was 15 years old, I was bullied on a daily basis. During that period, I was stabbed with scissors, hit with a poker, lashed with curtain wire, scalded with hot water, and punched and kicked endlessly. Pain became my best friend. But then, when I was 16 years old, my balls dropped and I began to man up. I stopped the bullies with a well-aimed and even better propelled everyday house brick. Yeah! Leave me the fuck alone.

At 17, the bullies were back, this time with a concealed blade: a steak knife homing in like an Exocet missile for my throat in a deceptive and lightning attack. I was unarmed, lying down on my mother's couch, maxing out. A nanosecond somehow became an eon, and I managed to get my left arm between my throat and the grim reaper. The blade was violently plunged through my arm, midway between my left wrist and elbow. It pierced my skin, its serrated edge scraping across the bone and completely severing three tendons, pinging them like overstretched rubber bands. I was left with the use of my left index finger and my left thumb only, but I could still make a fist. I weighed around 175 lb, but I was on my feet. My throat was not cut, as had been my assailant's murderous intention.

In the melee that ensued, my bright-red blood sprayed my mum's front room, and I knew without being told that I was in a fight for my life. As I subdued my armed assailant with my bare hands, I knew instinctively that I would find myself in this situation many more times. And as my assailant passed into unconsciousness, I also knew – with a heightened, almost primal awareness – that I would always win and never lose a death match. That was the first attempt on my life, thirty years ago in 1977, and from that day to this there have been several more attempts to assassinate me – my enemies have tried to burn me, melt me with acid, shoot me or kill me in any way possible. This is my story . . . THEY CALLED ME THE DEVIL.

My name is Stephen Thomas French, and I grew up in Liverpool 8 during the 1960s and '70s, becoming a man in the 1980s. The narrative that follows could be superimposed onto the lives of any number of black males born of a mixed marriage in 1960s south Liverpool. When I first decided to help Graham Johnson write this book, I knew I had a good story inside me, but I also knew that I should take advantage of the life experiences of the people I've known throughout my life – including 25 years security experience and 30 years as a martial artist, man and boy – and the thousands upon thousands of individuals I've met during my pursuit of health, wealth and happiness.

The tile for the book is *The Devil*. There was much discussion about this between me and Graham Johnson. Initially, the working title was *Tall, Dark and Dangerous*. During the course of his research, Graham discovered that some of my enemies referred to me as the Devil. He became very interested in this and said that this must be the title of the book. I tried to compromise with him and suggested *They Call Me the Devil* as an alternative. I reneged after discussion with him, because I understand the commercial grab of the *The Devil* as a title, but I would like to go on record and say that I am a true and devout Christian and I believe in the Holy Trinity. I hate and loathe the Devil. The greatest trick the Devil ever pulled was to convince the world he did not exist. Where there is good there is bad, where there is ying there is yang, and this a belief that I hold very, very strongly. So, to my mum, wife, sister and daughter, the women that are really important to me, I apologise for the title of this book, but it's for reasons of sensationalism and commercialism, plain and simple, and has nothing to do with my faith. And if there are any objections of a divine nature, I assure you, Lord God in heaven, that the intentions behind this book are based on honour and integrity.

Stephen French
August 2007

PROLOGUE

The Tefal steam iron was red-hot as I pressed it hard onto the top of the man's back, just below his shoulder. He jolted violently, but the silver duct tape wrapped around his mouth muffled his screams. I gave him a squeeze of steam from the power jets, just for good measure. The acrid fumes of burning flesh whooshed around the basement room, carried by the plumes of vaporised water, tinged by the sulphur-like smell of charred hair. There were pools of piss, shit and blood already on the floor, so it didn't really matter. Yet the victim still refused to give up the location of his drugs or money. I temporarily removed his gag, and he blabbered that he didn't have the goods. When I put the gag back on, he begged for mercy using his hands and eyes.

The man taped to the chair in front of me was one of Britain's top drug dealers, worth between 30 and 40 million pounds. He had boasted about fearing no man and was responsible for the murder of many – mainly his enemies – during his underworld reign. Amongst his peers and rivals alike, he was feared like a death-camp commandant and revered like a dictator. No one had ever dared touch him. Me, personally – I couldn't give two hoots.

Forty minutes earlier, my partner Marsellus and I had burst his ken: a spartan, suburban mansion in a commuter town, just outside London. Our aim was to 'tax' the drug dealer – that is, to steal his drugs and money. Mucus now dripped from the man's bloodied nose, the detritus of kidnap and torture soiling

15

his Lacoste T-shirt and pastel-blue tennis shorts. The steel plate of his wife's state-of-the-art iron was now smeared with the sludgy, brown mess of burned human matter, mostly skin and follicle.

Using the same controlled, monotone voice – which I had learned from the psychological warfare manuals now used in Guantanamo Bay and Abu Ghraib – I whispered into the godfather's ear, 'Tell me where the pound notes are, and I'll turn the iron off. You'll never see me again.' But he refused to play ball, shaking his head desperately.

There followed a few seconds of struggle, while Marsellus kicked the chair backwards and wrestled the detainee's shorts and boxers off. Within the same motion, I thrust the near-melted-hot Tefal onto his naked bollocks, ramming it home hard for full effect, following it through with multiple blasts of steam.

Within two hours, I was on my way back to Liverpool with £320,000 in the boot of my Lexus and 20 kilograms of cocaine secreted at a safe house in Walthamstow in east London. Before I left the drug dealer's mansion, however, I wasn't able to resist going back for the biggest thrill of all. As he lay semi-conscious on the floor, coated with a thin film of vomit and bile, I lifted his head up and looked into his defeated and terrified eyes. Now I would show him just how bad I *really* was. *I took my balaclava off.* His eyes screamed in horror as he recognised my features.

'Yes,' I told him. 'You've just been taxed by the Devil. I really do exist. Now, what the fuck are you going to do about it?'

In my game, revealing your identity to a victim was a cardinal sin, but I couldn't resist this encore: showing him who had done this to him, challenging him to seek revenge. Of course, I knew that he never would. I was just testing myself, and, with that, I disappeared into the night.

PART ONE

THE RISE

1

BETTER THE DEVIL YOU KNOW

I was born in Liverpool on 8 October 1959, the son of a flame-haired white woman of Irish immigrant stock and film-star looks, and a black West Indian seafarer who was on the run for killing a man. Now, I am not going to bore you with a long family history, save to say that I am the product of the Irish potato famine and the African slave trade. I know that you want to get to the guns-and-drugs bit real quick, so I'll keep it brief.

My dad, Thomas Benjamin French, came to the UK aged 26 in 1955 from Trinidad as part of the 'Windrush' wave of immigration overseen by Enoch Powell. A year later, he married Vera Hughes, my mum. But it wasn't long before he fucked off – with the babysitter, in fact – leaving my mum with five children from three different fathers. There was my elder sister and brother Carol and Tony Desson, my middle brother Shaun Deckon and my full sister Helen French, shortly followed by yours truly. Having an absent father had a profound effect on me and was one of the main reasons I fell into a life of crime.

My mum sacrificed everything to bring us up. For a long time, I thought she was a vegetarian, because she would give us children the meat at teatime and go hungry herself. My first experiences of violence came from within the home – from my sister Helen. She tormented me physically, mentally and emotionally with fists, bats and knives from the age of three. That was probably the second reason I became a gangster. Helen gave me an incredible ability to tolerate pain, for which today I give thanks to her, for it has saved my life on many occasions.

At the age of six, I experienced racism for the first time. It was 1966, and I was keen to buy some World Cup Willy football stickers from the local sweet shop. My mum had hidden us under her coat to keep us out of the rain, but when she took it off in the shop the whole world stopped. The shopkeeper was disgusted that the white woman in front of the counter had slept with niggers. But it taught me an invaluable lesson. From that day on, I would not let prejudice and bigotry bother me.

Though my mum had a fierce love for us, she sometimes broke down under the pressure of trying to raise five children – every colour of the rainbow – without any money or support. I first went into care in North Wales with Tony when I was seven. On every occasion after that, I ran away. One time, I sneaked back home to discover that my dad had returned – to have an affair with the social worker, who was supposed to be looking after us. He had sex with her right on my mum's bed.

I picked up my first conviction for robbing cars at the age of 11, fuelled by the high-speed chases I had seen on *The Sweeney*. But I soon realised that nicking cars was not going to make me money. Enter George Osu – a real-life black Fagin. He was only 16, but he was a movie star to us all. Tall and slim, with the neatest of neat afros, he wore a long, black leather midi coat just like Shaft, and he always had pound notes on him. George's bag was house burglaries. It all came down to one thing – small windows. Only kids could get through them. At one time, George himself had been a house burglar – the kid who squeezed through those windows – but now he'd grown too big, so he was looking for others to recruit. George took me under his wing because I was skinny and nimble. He showed me how to get into a house and trained me how to systematically clean a place out. Soon, I was screwing two houses a week, and we made lots of cash. In no time at all, I was dressing just like George.

Meanwhile, the violence and racism of everyday street life were turning me into a world-class athlete. Every day I had to run the gauntlet of older skinheads who wanted to beat me to within an inch of my life. Skinheads were fierce-looking individuals – bright red 'ox-blood' Dr Martens, Fleming jeans, braces, Ben Sherman shirts and Crombie overcoats lined with red silk to soak up a nigger's blood. My nickname soon became Frenchie Lightfoot, because I could move like the wind and was as slippery as an eel. My body was like a reed: no meat, just tall with long legs. Sometimes the skinheads came to our house, and we had to barricade ourselves in while the windows were smashed and the door was booted in.

Not only was I fast, but I was also becoming a champion fighter in waiting. My sister's beatings had made me immune to pain. Most people are not hurt when they're hit, they're just shocked because they've never been hit before. However, I was so used to getting battered that I was able to strike back immediately. I also took up boxing, perfecting my natural ability for street combat, and was soon cock of the school.

To complement my physical prowess, I started honing my intellectual capacity by questioning everything going on around me. Come the early 1970s, we were the first generation of post-war British-born blacks. It wasn't like we were just off the boat – we felt that we had a right to be here. Black people had been in Liverpool in one form or another for 400 years, and this gave us a deeper sense of heritage and connection with the UK. The upshot was that we were militant and the first minority to fight back. At the age of 12, I joined the Young Black Panthers, a fierce black rights group based on the one in the States. The *Observer Magazine* – the colour supplement of the Sunday broadsheet – came to do an article on us. They took a picture of us climbing the wall outside the Anglican cathedral. The bit in the text below about the skinheads was spot on:

> The Great Wall of Liverpool surrounds the cathedral and is
> a conveniently situated training centre for Young Panthers.
> Getting up to the top is what matters. Going up fast and skilful

like a novice commando gives you new confidence, prestige and sinew. Qualities that are going to be tested in your next encounter with white skinheads. The inner city district of Liverpool 8, near the cathedral, has appalling housing, bad schools and chronic unemployment. Whites and blacks are trapped together in the same vicious cycle of slumdom.

What made us fierce was simple. Unlike previous generations, we had no fear of the English lads. We went to the same schools and shit in the same toilets. One day, in a history lesson, I saw a picture of a pre-war pope blessing the Italian tanks, howitzers and machine guns that were going to Africa to fight the Abyssinian men on horses. I remember thinking, 'Here's a priest who preaches love, forgiveness, honour and to worship thy father, and he's blessing these weapons to fight against black people in their own land.' It made me question my faith. Up until then, I'd been an altar boy.

In the course of time, I realised that it wasn't God's fault, and, instead, it was man twisting God's word. One day, I got thrown out of a class by a teacher who informed me that South Africa was a white country. When I put him right, he punished me for it.

Then came the tremendously hot summer of 1976, when race riots raged up and down the country. The National Front had been to Bradford and some of their thugs had set houses belonging to the Asian community on fire. Then they had gone to Leeds and set houses on fire there. Now they said they were coming to Liverpool to set *us* on fire.

George Osu's brother, Willie Osu – a stalwart of the community – went around rallying a demonstration with a loudhailer, saying, 'The fascists are coming! Are we going to take it? No we're fucking not, so get out onto the streets and fight back.'

Sure enough, Colin Jordan turned up with a column of NF storm troopers, all wearing Nazi uniforms and jackboots. They walked tall because they were expecting another easy victory. In Leeds and Bradford, they'd faced the new immigrant population fresh from India, Pakistan and Uganda. This generation still had a fear and respect for the 'Motherland' and for the white people in the country. So they took it up the arse and just let the NF do what they wanted.

Consequently, Jordan thought they were coming to Liverpool to do the same thing. But, fuck, was that a miscalculation. We ambushed them at the Pier Head and threw them into the River Mersey. The rest ran for their lives. We left them with a message – Liverpool blacks are militant. We don't take shit.

Meanwhile, I was still learning the ropes as a villain. At the age of 13, I was getting too big to fit through small windows. So, I recruited an innocent 11-year-old boy called Curtis to take my place. Curtis was reluctant at first, but I simply forced him through the windows. One crisp November evening in 1974, we picked him up from his mum's in George's stolen Ford Cortina. To make himself look older so he didn't get a tug, George wore a black false moustache that was in stark contrast to his ginger afro.

Now, our bag was this: Curtis had the face of an angel and was so light-skinned that he could pass for white. We'd find a big house in the country, get him to knock on the door with a kind of lost-babes-in-the-woods routine, and if someone answered, he'd innocently ask for directions home. If nobody was in, he'd come back to the car and give us the green light to go to work.

That night, after Curtis had established that no one was in the mansion, George turned to me and said, 'Frenchie, get in the house with him, put the stuff in boxes in the hallway, open the door, then I'll come and pick the stuff up.' I was a bit scared, but George spat on me, hit me in the face and told me, 'Get your fucking arse up there, open the door and stop making excuses.' That was the nature of our relationship.

As Curtis and I were creeping up the path like commandos, we suddenly heard a little noise. To make absolutely sure there was no one home, Curtis gave the door a loud rap and shouted through the letterbox, 'Is anybody in? Is anybody in?' Even at that age, he had an incredible nerve, unshakable confidence and an ability not to panic – whereas, on the other hand, my nerves were already beginning to jingle.

We quickly got the goods: a portable TV, a radio-cassette player, jewellery, silverware – anything that could be carried and sold quickly. As George was loading the things into the car, he said, 'You haven't done the kitchen yet. Get in there and see if there's any cash.'

So Curtis and I went back into the house. We opened the door of the kitchen, and there before us was the biggest fucking monster of a Rottweiler I had ever seen. Curtis flew into the car, leaving me to cop a terrible bite on the arse. That pretty much marked the end of my burglary career.

Curtis, however, stuck with it and went on to bigger and better things. The grounding we had given him must have stood him in good stead, for he went on to become the richest and most successful criminal in British history, worth – by some newspaper estimates – £250 million. According to the authorities, he became the most prolific drug trafficker in Britain, the most wanted man in Europe and an underworld figure revered like a modern-day Robin Hood. Such is his current standing that there are kids on council estates up and down the country named in his honour. He is Curtis Warren. Our paths would continue to cross for many years to come.

Although I had been a juvenile criminal for many years, I remember having a crisis of conscience at around this time. At school, I fought the urge to be bad, excelling academically, at maths, history and sciences. I used the phrase 'the poet and the pain' to describe how I was feeling. My essays always got read out in English class, but one lad thought that the flowery metaphors I used made me a puff. Later, he teased and goaded me in the bogs and a rage blew up inside me like I had never experienced before. This guy hurt me in a different way from the violence I had suffered: by destroying something good in my life, something I was proud of. He evoked a new type of pain inside. I got hold of his head and cracked it against the porcelain bowl of the toilet. His head split like a grape, but I continued to pound his skull until it was a mash of blood and bone.

The beast within me had been released.

2

GOOD VERSUS EVIL

After watching my hero Bruce Lee in the film *Enter the Dragon*, I decided that I wanted to channel my energy into something positive, so I took up karate. But there was only one problem – I had no dough. I had stopped robbing houses and couldn't even afford to pay for classes. One day, I heard of an instructor at the Liverpool Shaolin Karate Club who let poor lads train for nothing. His name was Ronnie Colewell, and despite being five feet ten inches and weighing just over ten stone he was one of the most dangerous men on the planet.

Over the next 15 years, he became like the father I never had. Ronnie had trained at a top martial arts academy in Japan and had decided to return to the inner city to give something back. Astonishingly, he had also managed to entice one of the world's masters to come back with him – 9th Dan Sensei, Keinosuke Enoeda.

Ronnie took me into his office and said, 'I can see something in you, Stephen, but I'm either gonna make you or break you getting it out. It's up to you which.' That was the first time that anyone had ever spotted potential in me, and I was determined not to let him down.

I got my yellow belt within a year and left school at 15 so I could sign on the dole purely to get money for subs. By that time, we were taking our martial arts all over the country to tournaments, so it would've been unfair not to pay my way. One day, we went to fight the England international coach's club team at Crystal Palace in London. The refereeing was bent as fuck. We scored our points clean, but the markers made out they hadn't seen our world-class jabs and kicks and ripped us off left, right and centre. In desperation, Ronnie turned to his five sons – that was me and the team – and said, 'We can't win here honourably, so I'm instructing you to forget the rules and attack them full on. Take them out in the next round. You follow? Let them have it.'

We knew what he meant: forget about no contact, just knock the other team out, full stop. At the end of the tournament, we five fighters stood proud and bowed to the other side. On the other side, only two men just about remained upright – the rest ended up in casualty. Needless to say, we got disqualified.

The club quickly became famous for its toughness and its trophies. Our bright-red tracksuits, emblazoned with the Toxteth LSKC on the back, struck fear into the hearts of our opponents. It wasn't long before news of our infamy got into the newspapers and the magazines.

Ronnie found me when I was a boy and turned me into an adult. I had been brought up by women, but he taught me how to be a man – how to confront my fears and walk tall. He also had a knack for turning out trained killers. The club was inadvertently responsible for creating a generation of super gangsters who would later impose a reign of terror on the world. However, that was not its main purpose, and the club also acted as a sort of social centre where he taught us life philosophies – paradigms I still use today. He gave me the equipment – physically, mentally and spiritually – to deal with anything that life could throw at me. He taught me well. He must have done, because I'm still standing today after seven assassination attempts.

The club was also the place where I met a lad called Andrew John, who would prove to be another great influence in my life. From the first moment we met, we became more than mates – we became brothers, siblings and soul mates. He was an incredible martial artist and the only man I have ever truly feared. From then on, rarely a day went by when we didn't hang around together.

Soon I was eager to move from no contact to full contact – this meant that you could whack a geezer out and draw blood, so it was as close to reality as possible. Intuitively, I knew that's where I would come into my own and become a champion fighter. But I still had a long way to go. I was six feet three inches tall but still rake thin. One night when I tried to get into a nightclub called The Timepiece, a bully doorman called Tommy Wall stopped me and said, 'You're not 18. My daughter's got a bigger chest than you.' He then gave me a slap, and I fell to the floor. I can remember looking up at him from the gutter, knowing that there was nothing I could do, as he was a giant of a man with a legendary rep as a street fighter. Nonetheless, I felt the rage burning and the evil building up inside me. I swore that one day I would get revenge.

Though I was desperately trying to be a good boy, it wasn't long before the dark side came for me again. Me and a karate mate called Liam became street robbers. As well as a way of getting money, it was an opportunity to practise our kicks and punches on real people. It was kinda like when surgeons practise cutting up dead bodies instead of drawing diagrams.

At that time, all the lads in the neighbourhood were becoming muggers. It was all the rage. According to police records released later, Curtis Warren was also snatching purses on the same circuit. Liam and I started off by 'queer bashing': simply waiting near men's toilets and robbing the 'cottagers' who hung around such places for sex. We knew they wouldn't report it to the police, as it was too embarrassing for them. This taught me the first golden rule of taxing: unreported crime is the best crime, because there is no punishment.

Then we started rolling three or four punters a week. Our secret weapon was a nine-feet-long leather Comanchero whip. Liam would sneak up on a victim from behind and lash the whip – like in a cowboy movie – so it wrapped around the legs and pulled the target down. One night, we attacked an Irish brother who wasn't a stranger to hardship or street life. He was a man who had evidently decided that he wasn't going to be robbed by a couple of boys. The fight that ensued eventually became too much for my cohort Liam, and he soon deserted me, leaving me to deal with this raging bull on my own. Once it was one-on-one, the Irishman's adrenalin kicked in – as is nature's way – converting him from victim to attacker. The bull rushed me. Time slowed down. A second became a minute. As he charged towards me, I assumed my fighting stance and shaped my fist into a 'ram's head' – I protruded the knuckles of my index and middle finger so they stood out from the rest like two antlers. This uranium-tipped apex – known as the *Sekon* in Japanese – became the focal point of all my power, and I channelled all my inner chi into this deadly spearhead. Like an arrow from a bow, like a bullet from a gun, I fired a straight right-hand punch to meet the oncoming juggernaut. On impact, the blow landed on the point of his jaw – the target area – at the moment that he was accelerating to his optimum speed. An immovable object meets an oncoming force and collision occurs. As my knuckles crashed into his jaw, his eyeballs rolled to the back of his head. He was unconscious before he hit the ground.

This was the first of what would eventually become a total of 39 victorious street KOs. As the Irishman lay on the ground, I took his watch and his wallet, making £17.50 that night – a good score. In 1977, that bought me a shirt, pants and a pair of boots.

Later that night, I caught up with Liam, who asked me for his share. I looked him square in the eyes. 'Sorry, mate, you haven't earned it,' I said, refusing point-blank to hand over any of my hard-gotten booty. For the second time that night, I took up my fighting stance, daring him to challenge my decree. He was a martial artist like me, and deep down I knew I was pushing the boat out by not handing over any cash. But he hadn't acted honourably during the robbery, so I didn't feel he deserved a share of the stolen cash. Anyway, he didn't challenge me or look me straight in the eye. I knew I had won a silent battle. He accepted his defeat and moved on, and we are still friends to this day.

Again, I had learned an important lesson that I would later put to good use: never to think that fellow warriors were of the same calibre as me. If they were not of my ilk, they shouldn't be rewarded. If they had been soldiers in arms and had left their posts in the heat of battle, they would have been branded deserters.

When I began to run nightclub doors later in life, certain individuals – who shall remain nameless – deserted their posts during engagements. Come pay time at the end of the night, I adopted exactly the same method I had used with Liam all those years before. I would look the culprit right in the eyes and say, 'There's no money here for you tonight. Instead, those who have earned with honour are going to share your pay.' I would take up my fighting stance in my office in the bowels of the nightclub, ready to defend my position. No one ever tried to fight me, and I went on to be a multimillionaire.

Despite committing over 200 street muggings, I was still battling with my conscience. It's hard to believe, but I didn't really know that any of this amounted to serious crime, not even the burglaries. To me and my friends, this was just the norm. Therefore, I was still unsure whether I was *really* cut out for a life of *hard-core* crime. In a last-ditch attempt to save my soul, I signed up for the Job Creation Programme as an apprentice painter and decorator, along with my oppo Liam. However, it wasn't long before the temptation of easy money lured us back to our urchin ways. We started robbing the council houses we were supposed to be decorating.

After I qualified, I decided to get away from Liverpool and all its scallywag temptations. In 1978, I got a job as a live-in painter with Grand Metropolitan Hotels in London. It was a good screw, well paid and there were lots of opportunities for skiving. I'd simply find an empty room in the hotel – preferably the penthouse – and pretend it needed a new roll of wallpaper or a lick of paint. Then I'd lock myself in and watch telly all day. In the evenings, I worked a second job as a cleaner in a Blackfriars office block, mopping 13 floors one after the other. My plan was to get enough money to start a new life back in Liverpool – maybe start a decorating business or open a shop. My dream was to move out of the ghetto.

Two months later, I returned to Liverpool with £1,000 in my pocket, the equivalent of about £2,500 today. Sixteen hours after jumping off the rattler at Lime Street Station, my ambitions to start over were in the dust. I was penniless, having blown everything that I made playing 79 kalookie in an illegal gambling den. I'd gone in there wearing rows of gold sovereigns on my hands and come out in my slippers. They had even taken my brand-new adidas trainers. Years later, I found out that the old card sharks – with names such as 'Leadbelly' – had cheated the naive young mark who had wandered into their lair. Once again, all of my hopes had come to fuck all – and this time it was mainly down to me. I was angry and bitter. In the maelstrom of confusion, I decided that going straight simply didn't pay. I could feel the beast reawakening inside me.

Gutted with my loss, I went straight into town to mug someone to make up for it. This was the point, I think, when I went over to the dark side for real. The beast had forced his way to the fore and was looking for an unsuspecting victim to prey on. I went into Flannigan's Irish bar, full of rich Irish punters on their way to the Grand National. I joined the ranks of muggers, prostitutes and pickpockets who had descended on Liverpool to take advantage of the flush racing fans that flocked to Aintree annually. It was like feeding time at the watering hole – lions on the hunt for antelopes. I stood at the bar until I saw a guy pull out a nice enough wad, waited for him to get pissed up and then followed him into the toilet. I gave him a few licks, took his wallet off him and got out of there. I got about £350, which was enough to see me through. That day in 1980 was the last and only time I would ever be flat broke.

After that, all I ever wanted to be was a hard case – to be feared rather than loved. However, I was always generous with my family. When I ate, everybody ate. When I made a packet, I made sure it got whacked out on my family. You could say that's the penance I paid to appease my own conscience.

Even though I was well and truly on the road to hell, the internal battle between good and evil never really left me. On the one hand, I still had the urge to be a good man and to stop fucking evil things happening, but, on the other hand, temptation was getting too much for me.

3

RAISING HELL – THE TURNING POINT

For a man to truly achieve his destiny, his life must not be lived in isolation. It must be wrapped up with important events going on in the wider world, on a collision course with history.

For me, *the* point of impact occurred on 3 July 1981. Britain was in the grip of a massive recession, nobody had a job and I was fighting grinding poverty. I had just settled down with a girl I had met about a year before, shortly after I got back from London. Her name was Maria Sampson, and my first son, Stephen, had recently been born. I was trying to get work, do the right thing and fight against the evil inside me, but it was a dustbowl out there.

Beneath the surface of the city, incredible tension simmered between the police and the black community. False arrests were run of the mill. This was before racism became a mainstream issue, and I knew, like every other black lad, what it was like to be on the other end of a policeman's boot. I was 11 the first time Merseyside's finest assaulted me and 42 the last, with at least a dozen incidents in between.

It was a summer's day in 1981, and our Stephen was a month old. I was out with my brother Andrew John. We were at the stage of trying to physically outdo each other. We were T-shirted up, it was warm and we were hanging around on a street near the perimeter of the ghetto. Suddenly, a police officer my age – thin, naive and wet behind the ears – stepped out from one of two police cars and attempted to physically and verbally abuse us. He told us to move on, when there was clearly nowhere else to move on to. Babylonians they were, flexing their muscles.

Another police officer said, 'Monkeys, get back to the zoo. Go on, get your arses back to Granby Street,' meaning that we were to get back to the heart of the ghetto and stay there.

A lad called Leroy Cooper was with us. Leroy was the most eloquent lad I knew and today is a well-published poet. He verbally slaughtered the bizzies, and they retaliated by resorting to their old stalwarts of, 'You dirty black bastards! You nasty niggers, get back to Africa!'

At this, Leroy became incensed. Andrew and I, accompanied by another mate called Ivan Freeman, watched as he rammed the police car with the bicycle he was riding. Three policemen came at him and attempted to arrest him. At this point, Andrew gave me 'the look' – one that painted a thousand words. We were veteran martial artists, in complete control of our bodies and minds, and we were prepared to step into the arena of combat – even if it was against the storm troopers of Margaret Thatcher's establishment. Leroy cried out, 'Enough is enough!' Thus, the touchpaper had been lit. An uprising had begun. The rest, as they say, is history.

Though the papers called it the Toxteth riots, what happened next wasn't really a riot; it was a rebellion against oppression and injustice. One of the police cars, a Panda or Rover, I think, was pushed into some roadworks, then down a hill, before being set alight. The three injured officers escaped in the other car. The ferocity of our retaliation swept through the ghetto like a whirlwind; never before had such a force been seen in the UK. Leroy marched through the streets, like Spartacus through the villages, as the ranks rapidly swelled behind him.

Andrew John and I fought side by side against the pigs. Terrified Merseyside police were forced to bus in officers from outside the region to put on the front line. The poor bastards never knew what hit them. However, it was not about race: both black and white joined forces in the battle against oppression and police brutality.

I ripped the stripes from a sergeant's arm, took his helmet and wore the spoils of victory like a Zulu warrior wearing a British red coat at the Battle of Isandlwana. They were badges of honour: proof of my courage and valour in the face of the enemy. Then I took a bin lid as a shield and broke off a table leg as a weapon. The army of people around me followed suit. I started to rhythmically bang the bin lid on the ground to warn my attackers off. Soon enough, my soldiers in arms began to do the same, making an unholy racket. Our aggressors turned heel and fled.

There is something about watching the sight of your enemy flee that gives you a feeling higher than any drug. Although it was short-lived, I will never forget the glory of that victory for as long as I live – the screams, yells and dances of celebration. I was 21 years old, and for the first time in my life I felt truly free. I was the all-conquering lion of my tribe. I raised my head up to the blazing sky, let out a primeval roar of victory and felt a wave of sensation go through me that was better than sex.

Nothing I have achieved since that moment comes even close to the feeling of power and strength I had that night in 1981. I felt like a Roman gladiator who had won his freedom in the arena. However, that was not the end of the battle. Full-scale rioting blew up over the next nine days, in which the police used CS gas for the first time in mainland Britain. The resulting damage amounted to 468 injured police officers, 500 arrests and at least 70 demolished buildings.

Like a phoenix from the fire, I rose from the ashes of the riots a different man – the first of many epiphanies. It was then that I was reborn as the Devil – officially. I won the title off a guy called Lloyd Johnson, who had been the Devil before me. Amid the smoking ruins and tensions of the post-riot landscape, he had abused my sister in the street, because he thought she was white. Me and my brother rounded their whole family up, and I presented Lloyd 'the Devil' Johnson to her, like a dog at her feet. I told him to kiss her feet and apologise. So, it was from that day on that the name the Devil passed from him to me. He was evil and dark, but now I was the new 'King of Hell'. Power, domination and control would be my watchwords from then on.

But, as always, I faced a dichotomy of feelings. Kindness and love sat beside hate and violence in my soul. At the same time as being christened the Devil, I took it upon myself to adopt a poor orphan child and bring him up as my own. The baby's name was Danny, and his dad – a wanted man – had been forced to flee abroad after the riots. Later on, his dad was killed in tragic circumstances, so I vowed to look after his son as if he were my own.

After the riots, we in the black community wanted to appoint our own leaders. However, Militant-controlled Liverpool Council and their leader Derek Hatton wanted to parachute their own man into the job – a black race-relations expert from London called Sam Bond. Needless to say, we were having none of it. Everywhere Bond went, he was attacked and abused.

Like many radical parties, Militant relied on muscle to help impose their influence behind the scenes. Enter Stephen French – or 'The Frenchman' as I was sometimes known – a young, up-and-coming hoodlum who was getting noticed by the white chieftains who controlled the levers of power. One day, I was secretly approached by some rogue Militant members, without the knowledge of Hatton and co., who wanted me to do their dirty work. Thanks to my flair for martial arts, I had a bit of a reputation as a hard-hitter. They paid me £500 to protect Sam Bond at an upcoming meeting at Toxteth Sports Centre. The way I saw it, they were bribing me to turn against my community and endorse their man.

I agreed to the job, but when I got to the meeting I stood up in front of Bond and the crowd and tore up the £500. I told someone to turn the lights off, and Sam Bond and Derek Hatton were assaulted in the ensuing chaos. At that time, I could've done with that £500, but I also knew that some rogue Militant members were as bent as a nine-bob note. They had the working man fooled, and they had just tried to have the black community off as well, by forcing a leader on us whom we didn't want.

But none of this really mattered in the greater scheme of things. As the politicians busily rearranged the deckchairs on the sinking ship, they failed to notice massive and sinister changes taking place in Toxteth, as well as in the wider world. The post-riots landscape was becoming a breeding ground for organised crime on an industrial scale and was nurturing some of the biggest gangsters that the UK would ever see. Several factors relating to habitat and lifestyle came together by chance, creating a unique environment that allowed crime to thrive.

First, you had a group of black lads, aged 14 to 24, who were physically fit and strong – they trained, played football and did boxing every day. They had no opportunities and no money, but they were clear-headed and they banded together because they had to. Second, there was a police no-go area, where dealers could sell drugs with impunity. This gave the dealers on the front line an area of incubation where they could grow as big as redwoods without fear of being cut down. The mentality was very much anti-police and anti-establishment – one which justified crime as a political action and a form of self-help for an oppressed minority.

Simultaneously, there were macro changes in crime outside the ghetto. You had a group of white, middle-aged former armed robbers who wanted to invest in a more profitable type of crime. In addition to this, there was a new generation of leaders who were taking control of old crime families: young lads who had none of their fathers' hang-ups about selling drugs. For the first time, they wanted to make strategic alliances with black gangs, who had the 'narco' expertise they were looking for, in order to distribute drugs on a mass scale.

Geography also played a vital role. Liverpool was a port where the crime gangs were world experts in trade-based crime. They had been smuggling contraband and robbing the docks blind for centuries. The docks were controlled by them – an advantage that would allow them to steal a march on rival gangs in the UK and the rest of Europe.

On a world level, there was an explosion in the production of cheap drugs, due to mass-production farming, and the Colombian Cali cartel was looking to open up new markets in Europe. This dovetailed nicely with a general increase in the spending power of the ordinary consumer, who could now afford to buy drugs. New technology could also be added to the equation: mobile phones, faxes and cheap international air travel all helped to facilitate the life of the drug dealer. And the 'Big Bang', financial deregulation and the property boom of the 1980s made it easier for drug barons to move money across the world and launder their profits.

The success of Liverpool Football Club in Europe in the 1980s also provided a good cover for scallies who travelled far and wide across the Continent without raising suspicion. They consequently made contacts in cities such as Amsterdam and settled in all the major distribution hubs, such as Rotterdam, Paris and Hamburg. The bottom line was this: Liverpool had become the number-one drugs capital of the UK and was starting to give even Amsterdam a run for its money. At its centre were the black gangs, who for the first time were able to take control and get more than just a few crumbs of the cake.

All the variables fell into the same orbit at the same time. The scene had been set, and a new type of graft had changed the criminal landscape for ever. Bag robbers would become multimillionaires within months. Armed robbers that owned fruit-and-veg shops on the boarded-up streets of Liverpool would soon have enough money to buy oil fields in the Caspian basin, banks in the Far East and football clubs.

However, before you could enter the super league, you had to pay your dues and get a kitty together to fund the drug deals. This was commonly called armed robbery. In 1984, a job opportunity came along. The Solid Gold Posse was Britain's first all-black gang of armed robbers. The head of the SGP was a mate of mine called Edgar. I had already done a little bit of work with him on a security van at a cash and carry. He liked my style, because I'd hit the guard so hard that his visor had come off his face, and we'd got away with all the money. On just that little stunt, we had made seven grand, worth about £20,000 now.

Edgar would spot a security van, rip out his notebook and log the date, time, location, registration number and details of the business that the van was servicing. Then he'd return the next week to see if the van came back, to determine if it was a regular pickup or not. He'd do this for a month until he got a complete picture of the routine. Using this intel, he'd plan to rob the van around that scheduled time. He planned everything down to the last detail, even the getaway. Usually, this consisted of a quick burn away from the bank in a car to a pre-assigned safe house, where we changed our clothes and left the money. Then it was out of the back door and we were gone. We never had the problems of street cameras or high-tech surveillance. It was all pretty basic back then, and if you got away from the scene, you got away with the robbery.

Edgar's firm was difficult to get into, and there was a kind of waiting list. Nonetheless, Andrew John had started doing jobs with them. One day he was caught during an armed robbery and remanded to jail so a full-time spot became available to do another job with the SGP.

To join the SGP or not to join – that was the question. I wrestled with a devil on one shoulder and an angel on the other. The stakes were high, but so were the risks. I knew it was a step up the ladder, possibly even a route map to the big time. So, who would triumph? The angels of my better nature or the infernal serpent?

4

THE DEVIL MAKES WORK FOR IDLE HANDS

It was 1984. I was 25 and about to pull off a series of high-profile armed robberies. As you may have guessed, the temptation to earn my stripes was too irresistible to turn down.

The first one was with the SGP. Four or five of us went into a bank armed with pickaxe handles – I don't even think we had a gun. We went in – masked up and wearing balaclavas and boiler suits – smashed the counters and robbed the money in broad daylight. Game over. Now, during that type of job, I always made sure I had a little trick up my sleeve – literally. I wore a jogger's kit underneath my overalls: shorts, a vest and a pair of trainers. It was a simple stunt that saved my bacon on many occasions.

As we got in the car and pulled away from the scene of the crime, a police car suddenly appeared behind us. But it was just a coincidence, and they had no idea what they had stumbled into. All of a sudden, the people in the street who had just watched us run out of the bank started making signs to the policemen in the car, trying to get their attention. They were pointing at us and shouting, 'Get on them, they've just robbed the bank.'

The alarms were going, and there we were, five gangsters with masks on in a high-performance car. The chorus of have-a-go heroes who wanted to get us nicked had now reached a crescendo.

Twenty people were now shouting, 'They've just robbed the bank.'

Our driver was called Val, a phenomenal jockey who did his stuff under pressure and got us away. Soon we ditched the car and found ourselves in a railway station. We got on our toes, and I ran down onto a railway embankment. By then, the bizzies had tippled and were in hot pursuit. All I was thinking was, 'Where's the best place to hide?' So I jumped into a load of nettles – dense and jungle-like – thinking that there was no way the bizzies were going to follow me in. But when I rolled over and looked up, lo and behold, a police officer was standing there at no more than an arm's length away. 'How the fuck did he get there?' I thought. Although he was onto me, he was stuck in the nettles, hassled and half-trapped, so I decided to put some space between me and him as quickly as I could. However, I was running out of options. The only way I could get away from him was literally to throw myself down the embankment. In one bound, the Frenchman was free.

I bumped into one of my crew called Peter Lair, who was also busily looking for an outro. Peter Lair was one of the main players in Curtis Warren's crew. He was an incredibly violent street fighter, and though we had grown up together there was always a simmering rivalry between us. Other members of the gang were here and there, so I quickly rounded them up before confusion set in and said, 'Look, gentlemen, it looks like it's time to get off. We need to split up.'

Lair scrambled up the embankment, another lad called Nogger dipped into a tunnel and I ran up the line into a cargo station, hiding myself in a shed. I soon heard the cackle of police radios getting nearer and thought, 'They're going to search this shed, so I've got to get out of here.' I took off my boiler suit, ditched my balaclava, climbed on top of a railway carriage, jumped a wall and landed on a main road.

This was where my little disguise came in. I began to run along the road wearing a red pair of Nike trainers, a red athlete's vest and a bright-red pair of silky adidas shorts. Pure 'Marathon Man'.

By then, the police cars were flying past. But the fact that I was out of breath and sweating profusely from the armed robbery and my recent wrestle with the nettles didn't mean anything to them. I was just a jogger. My cold, concentrated nerves of steel had kicked in and had given me the bottle to pretend that I was just out for a run – subterfuge and misdirection. The police posses were steaming towards me in a blaze of blue lights and noise in their riot vans, patrol cars and motorbikes, and I was just running past them in the opposite direction – sweating but calm as you like. In their urgency to get to the scene of the action, they had to give me a pass.

Later that day at about 5 p.m., I heard the customary whistle that we all used at the door of our gang's HQ. I looked out and there was the rest of the gang. Edgar had got away, as had Peter Lair, but Val had the most interesting story to tell. During his Hoffman, he had found himself exposed, running along a deserted road with bizzies all around him. So, with lightning wit, he had climbed under an articulated lorry at a set of traffic lights and grabbed the axle, hiding in a box of dead space close to the exhaust. The truck had driven for several miles, and he had rolled out from underneath just as it had stopped at a junction – pure prisoner of war stuff. His face was covered in fumes from the exhaust. He reckoned he had looked like Sooty on his walk back home.

So, everybody escaped and we got about £20,000 in the robbery – £4,000 each. The story of the job was even on the telly, which was always a buzz. It described how we had all escaped, how much money we had nicked, how daring the raid had been and how close the police had come to catching us. It was a great thing at that time – if you were a firm – to appear on TV for something you'd done. We would all sit down afterwards, watch it, have a good laugh and say to each other, 'Yeah, that's our graft. We actually make the news in our graft.'

The point of the armed robberies was that they provided the little bit of wealth you needed to start off your drug kitties. But apart from the business purpose, they were always intensely emotional experiences as well. Let me just outline the process we went through when we committed a robbery. To begin with, we would have a designated area where we were going to meet before the job. When we all met up, everybody would have their own ritual that they went through. I always went very quiet and very insular before kick-off. There was a possibility that we could get caught and killed, and all kinds of different scenarios went through our minds. But one thing you can be sure of, everybody was there for the same reason – the money.

Let's say we were doing a job for Edgar. We'd go to the house where we were supposed to meet. Edgar always took charge from the outset, always knew how to calm people down. He'd say, 'Come on, time to put your kit on.' This meant it was time to put your boiler suit on, your boots, your trainers, whatever you were wearing underneath, get your clothes on and get your bally in your pocket. There might be four or five of you. If there was five, that meant there was a driver and four of you in the car who were going over the pavement.

The car was always stolen, and there were sometimes two. We might drive from the robbery to a second prearranged stashed car and drive away in it, because we knew that the first car we were in was going to be on top. It would have been outside, revving up waiting for us to run in and out. All hands will have had a good vidi at it – all these things are smash and grab raids.

So, we'd be in the vehicle on the way to the job, and when we got to within 100 yards of where the work was going to take place, the order would be given: 'Mask up.' We were now in game, because we were five guys driving along the road with masks on. There was no turning back, and we were all on offer. The adrenalin would begin to pump. The best way I can describe it is to compare it to the moment just before you start a fight. Your heart's pounding, your palms are sweaty and you don't know what way it's going to go. But when it actually kicked off, it was surreal. Sometimes things moved in slow motion. Then other factors would start to come into play – the buzz of knowing what we were about to do when nobody else in the street did. The pack mentality would kick in, together with a desire not to let any of our comrades down. We would begin to move swiftly and panther-like, and crash the gaff, making as much noise as we could, because noise frightens people. We'd bark instructions at the terrified staff, 'Nobody fucking move. This is a robbery,' and lace it with as much aggression and power that we could muster. If it was my job to smash the glass counter, then I'd do it like the SAS bursting a ken.

This was the early 1980s. There were screens in banks at the time, but they weren't bulletproof, reinforced or shatterproof. If I had a good heavy tool, I could fucking smash them to pieces. The adrenalin rush I got was phenomenal in these types of robberies; concentration in the extreme was required, enough to create a ballistic force to remove any obstacle between you and the prize.

I remember one robbery carried out by some of the boys of a rival crew, who were later convicted for it. At the time, they had their own little firm doing the same kind of robberies as us. They just drove a lorry into the wall of the bank, smashed the concrete, made a hole, ran through the hole, grabbed the money and ran out. It wasn't rocket science. Smash and grab – same methodology, different application. Later, the police said that Curtis Warren was involved.

After the screen went in, we'd go over the counter first, ignoring all the staff and not looking at anybody so as to avoid eye contact. We had a job to do: to fill our bags, taking the path of least resistance.

In those days, there'd be about four or five tellers, and they'd have the day's money in their tills. So we would smash into the bank, grab the money and load it into our bags. There was no feeling in the world like that moment. This was the actual fight taking place. It's like when you hear boxers talk and say, 'I was nervous, but when the bell sounded I was all right.' Once we'd gone over the counter, the bell had sounded. We'd rehearsed enough, and we were determined. We'd done this a million times before in our minds. We'd go on autopilot, just looking for pound notes. We'd be running along the counter from till to till, looking for those nice bundles with the pink wrappers on them that say £1,000 or £5,000. We'd bundle as many of these as we could see into the bags we were carrying. I usually used a kit bag or an adidas bag, one with a big flap on it, so I could fold it back and just throw everything in without trying too hard, throwing the flap over quickly again once I was done. It was important to have the right kind of equipment for this purpose. I saw many a robber lose all their loot on the jump back over the counter because they were using the wrong kind of bag. Then they had to waste precious seconds picking it all up again.

The alarms would now be going off, ringing in our ears. There would be people screaming and women would be lying on the floor – bloody, fucking mayhem. But if we could remain calm, we would win. How right Rudyard Kipling was. That was my forte – being cool under pressure. That's why Edgar had chosen me.

So, we've crashed the gaff with no ifs or buts, just speed, aggression and mobility, like in the paras. We've got the money, so it's time for the outro. We've got a guy sitting outside revving the car with a mask on. Next, we'd pile back into the car and drive away from the scene, looking behind to check that nobody was following. We're away, and from then on it would all be at high speed. We were hardly going to observe the speed limits, were we? We'd want to get away as quickly as possible. We'd have a predetermined route to follow and would know where we were going to get out of the car and what we were going to do with the stuff. It was all sorted out in advance.

So we'd be in the car, rallying along the planned route – left, right, left, U-turn – along backstreets and one ways, the works, losing any cars that might be on our case. At the point when we realised we were not being followed, we could take our masks off. Then everybody in the car would begin to laugh. Whether it was nerves, success, tension or whatever, it was funny. It was a relief. We'd got the money, and it was over. The feeling was euphoric. If you're a footballer, it's like scoring a goal. If you're a boxer, it's like knocking out a guy and winning a title fight. If you're in a nightclub, it's like chatting up Beyoncé Knowles and you're on the way to the hotel room. It doesn't get any better. We'd done what we set out to do, and we'd got our bacon. We were on our way home.

If the job was a switcher – when you swap into a second car – then there would be a clean-up operation in which every piece of clothing would be put into a bag and set on fire, something that was usually sorted by a pre-elected clean-up man. This sort of thing is pretty run of the mill now – you see it all on TV programmes, clothes getting covered in petrol and torched – but back then it was the difference between success and 12 years in the jug. It was all about not giving away any forensic evidence. When we'd smashed a counter, there would be fragments all over us. All the police needed was one piece of debris to match to the scene and that would be enough to put a bloke in prison. Kids' stuff. Even schoolgirls know about all this now, because they've seen it on some crime programme on Five. But I've seen hardened villains get slovenly.

For instance, one of the lads got a piece of glass caught in his trainers on one job, but he wouldn't throw them away because a pair of trainers to a Scouser is like the Victoria Cross to a war hero. He ended up doing six years for a £90 pair of adidas. Fucking six years. What's that? Fifteen quid a year? Come on, let's have it real, use your fucking brain.

The very best part of an armed robbery was when it was time to count the spoils. I'd usually know exactly what my end was going to be in advance, cos Edgar's intel was mostly spot on. But let's say I was expecting 20 grand and I ended up with 38 or 39 grand, it was brilliant. However, if I was expecting twenty grand and only ended up with fucking three grand, it was anticlimactic to say the least. It's like scoring an own goal or winning a fight by disqualification. It sullied the feeling; it emptied me. I'd take my share, but it wasn't what I was expecting. It was not what I was prepared to take all that risk for. Of course, there's the steward's and all that. The whys and wherefores would be debated and blame would be apportioned if someone had fucked up. The research was wrong, but the job was done and the crew would be sad.

That was when everyone would start looking at each other, getting bitter and twisted, wanting to search everybody. It was the old 'stick-down' syndrome. Members of the crew would start to think that there must be some devilment to explain why the take was down. Someone would then turn and blame someone else for creaming a bit off the top. The actual phrase was, 'Do you know what? I'm sure that cunt's stuck down on me.'

If you were supposed to get thirty grand and there was only twenty-four grand, then it stands to reason that six grand has gone missing somewhere, and someone would be suspected of hiding it by sticking it down their kecks. The stick down would usually happen as the guys were getting into the van after the robbery. During the confusion, when all eyes were distracted, someone might use this opportunity to put a bit of the winnings away on the sly.

I remember coming back from one robbery to the rendezvous point – after we'd all had to split up during the getaway – and the first thing my mate Peter Lair did was put his hand in my pocket to see if I was hiding something.

I said to him, 'You know what, you're just not that bright, are you? If I was sticking down on you, do you think I'd come into this meeting with it on me? Let's have it real, now. What do you want to search me for? Cos I would have stashed it before coming here.' Peter Lair resented me for my intelligence, like a lot of people do, because I point things out that are basic common sense. I continued, 'If I want to stick down on you, I'm not going to come to you knowing that you're going to search me. I'd leave it outside, wouldn't I? So what are you searching me for? Do you think I'm stupid?'

And that's the way I talk to people. I don't suffer fools, and I don't suffer them long. Sometimes it can get up people's noses.

5

DEAL WITH THE DEVIL

As an armed robber, I had built up a serious reputation. Not only that, but I had also become known as someone who would never leave his men behind on the battlefield. If you got stuck in a building during a heist, I'd come back in and pull you out – even if I was carrying the money or it meant getting collared. I was a man of honour, loyalty and integrity.

One time, one of the robbers I was with got wrestled to the ground during a getaway. I gazelled it back down the street to rescue him. He was being slaughtered by two cowards that had set about him; however, I had a ting on me. I pointed it at them, and they fucking ran. I saved him.

On another occasion, I went in and saved a guy who had been injured, despite the fact that he'd already turned the robbery into a nightmare by scheduling it wrong and missing the money. I risked ten years' jail for the pittance that we stole, but I rescued him anyway from the jaws of certain capture. I was pissed off and annoyed, but I still went back for him – like a US marine.

I was also getting a rep as someone who could tolerate pain. One of my most defining features is my unbelievable ability to endure horrific personal injury. Whenever I had to have stitches, I refused to take anaesthetic. I could feel them sewing through the skin, but I'd smile. It was a macho thing with me. I wanted my tolerance of pain to be known.

The next robbery involved a wages van for a huge factory. The security guard got out of the van, and I ran over and punched the guy so hard in his visor that it smashed into his face, just as I had done on my first job. He immediately went down. The visor had cut into his face and blood poured out of his nose. Edgar grabbed the bag, and we made off with the booty. When we got to the safe house, I pulled off my mask and subsequently hit the roof. In front of me was a girl I knew; in fact, it was her place.

'I don't want nobody knowing what I do,' I said.

'Well it's her house, and she wanted to be here,' the others replied.

A bit of pandemonium broke out. I got about £7,000 from that rob so gave her £500 to keep her mouth shut. She never, ever said anything, but she always looked at me funny afterwards.

I was getting a good rep, so I was recruited by another gang. The first robbery with them targeted the monthly wages for a shoe factory. The intel reports said there would be £100,000 to £250,000 in a little glass office inside the plant. This time Johnny Phillips, Curtis Warren's right-hand man, was on the team, as well as two white guys called Smith and Jones. My job was to stop any potential have-a-go heroes in their tracks. We gave little 18-year-old Jonesy a shotgun; he was only a baby, but the gun would be enough to persuade the cashiers to hand over the money. First, it was Smith's job to get us into the glass office by any means necessary.

Our problems started as soon as we got to the office. The cashier wouldn't let us in, knowing she was protected by a big glass partition and wooden frames which supported the conservatory-style structure. Smith screamed, 'Open the door, open the door,' but she held firm, thinking she was safe behind the bulletproof glass. However, when it came to security, they clearly hadn't catered for the powers of a world-class athlete. So I stepped up from behind and kung-fu kicked the structure on the right angle of one of the joints. The whole partition came crashing down. It was an absolutely fantastic noise. Everybody in the factory then knew we meant business.

We got the money and got in the car. Suddenly, we realised

that Smith wasn't with us. To give Jones his due, he said, 'We're getting out the car, and we're going back in to get him. He's me mate.' We couldn't leave a Spartan behind, no matter how fucking stupid he was.

Back inside, we found Smith still looking round for more money, trying to redeem himself for failing to get the door of the office open. He was running round terrorising everybody, the fucking idiot that he was. We grabbed him, took him out and drove off. When I counted up the loot, I realised we had only ended up with £2,000. I was fuming – absolutely livid. I had risked myself for a measly two grand. I never worked with those fools again.

However, one good thing did come out of this incident: the importance of forensics and how dangerous they were to a criminal was reinforced to me. For instance, Smith had refused to burn a new Berghaus jacket that he had been wearing underneath his boiler suit that day. The bizzies went to his house and matched up fibres from the partition that I had smashed down with those found on his top. He ended up getting a nine-year stretch. I laughed my cock off when I heard about it. From that day forward, I always made sure I got rid of my clothes – no matter what job I was doing. I reckon that saved me 100 years in jail time. So, I guess the job hadn't been a total waste after all. Every cloud . . .

According to the papers, Curtis Warren was doing armed robberies too, and he was a good blagger. However, things started to change when all of these guys started to go to prison. There's a scene in the film *Essex Boys* that illustrates the scenario perfectly. There's a couple of blaggers in jail, where they've come across nerdy student types on the prison wings. One of the armed robbers has got a picture on the wall of his cell – I think it was a Ferrari Testarossa, a car worth about £100,000 in the late 1980s. He looks at the car and says, 'This is my dream car. I'm going to have one of these one day.'

Then the weak student guy nervously butts in and says, 'I've got one of those.'

The hardcore blaggers reply, 'Shut your mouth,' meaning don't be fucking silly.

Nonetheless, he explains, 'No, no, no, I'm not bullshitting. I've got one of them. I'm in here for growing and bringing in weed, and I've got one of them as a result.' He was a Howard Marks type of guy.

So that was how those amongst the blagging community realised that drugs were the future. It was ironic that they had gone to jail to have their futures curtailed yet they'd found a better path within the four walls of their cells . . .

The bonus was that Customs weren't even switched on at the time, and it was a free-for-all. It was much easier sending a mule to pick up a parcel of drugs from some country than jumping over a counter with a shotgun. You could just go to wherever you needed to go by day boat – Holland, France, Spain – load your granny up with gear and send her back. If you actually had the foresight to have a false bottom in your suitcase, that was even better, and you could do what you wanted. It was hardly James Bond, but Customs were going for the obvious smugglers, pulling over the guys that stood there with their scruffy suits on with fags hanging out of their mouths; in other words, the ones who looked a bit suspicious. However, a pensioner wearing a floral dress and a twinset and accompanied by a few kids could walk straight through with ten kilograms of cannabis and even get a smile off the duty officer as she went by. Once again, our two friends – misdirection and subterfuge – came into play.

It was when the mainline hard-core criminal fraternity – not your burglars and your pimps but your armed robbers – piled into narcotics on a gold-rush scale that the drugs explosion took place. Armed robbers were the royalty of the criminal fraternity. They were the hard men, the violent men, the ones not to be messed with – the men that were supposed to be given respect. They were the men from the boxing and martial-arts fraternities who had the town halls to pioneer drug empires. Even if you traced the origins of families such as the Arifs and the Adams in London, you'd find that they were armed robbers before they became involved in drugs. If you traced their criminology and mapped out their criminal family trees, you'd find armed robbers at the core. It was where the initial funds came from – the first injection of six, seven, eight or ten grand that was needed to get from one continent to another and to pick up a shipment and get it back again. After that, when criminals saw the amount of money that could be made, they wanted more. Initially, everyone started off on weed – first one kilo, then two, then one hundred and so on. Back then, the main objective of every young ambitious gangster was to get a tonne of weed. If you could do that, you were a Hall of Fame guy. Then everyone started trying to outdo each other.

But, according to Customs and Excise reports, Curtis Warren took it to a different level – he bought a tonne of coke. He was buying a kilo for between £3,000 and £4,000 in Colombia, and selling it for £30,000 a kilo in the UK. The dealers were selling that for £1,000 an ounce. You do the maths. There was £30,000 to £40,000 clear profit for them on a kilo.

So, in the early to mid-'80s, all the conditions – environmental and personal – were in place for my entry into the drugs trade. However, I was holding back. Even though my peers were growing rich, I was trying to fight the evil inside me. Again, something inside me was telling me that it wasn't right. Instead, I threw myself into martial arts. It paid off, and I attained my first *dan* in Shotokan karate.

I'd have done anything not to sell drugs, so I kept looking around to see how I could make money from my fighting skills. Still, I couldn't even afford to go for a night out at that time. I took a job at Liverpool University as a community sports teacher, but I was trapped in a flat with Maria, my son Stephen and her three kids from a previous relationship. Deep down I knew that there was only one way to a better life – and that was education. I enrolled on an access course in the hope that getting qualifications would one day get me out of the mess I was in.

However, things took a different turn one measly pay day when I headed down to Kirklands, my favourite bar. This was a really cool place to go, where black lads used to meet white girls. There was a doorman there called Fred Green, who used to make life difficult for me and Andrew John whenever we tried to go in. He always tried to make us pay, knowing that we were skint, while all the time he was letting everyone else in for free. We wanted revenge, but we didn't think that we could take him individually, so we did what's known in the trade as a 'double bank' on him. I attacked him from the front, whilst Andrew came from behind, and we had it away with him. As he was rolling around on the ground, we both looked to the stars and had an idea. If we could actually defeat the man on the door, why couldn't we just take over the venue's security for ourselves? So we did. He was an old lion who was starting to lose his teeth, so he didn't make too much noise when we told him that the door was ours.

From the off, Marcello Pole, the millionaire owner of the bar, took a shine to me. He said, 'You've had the ability to remove Fred from the door. I'm going to give you a chance, cos I'm a believer in the survival of the fittest.' After that, to give him his due, he gave us the contract. Nevertheless, he still said, 'You've got to let me stay in charge of the bar and business.'

I find that when you meet new people in life, it takes between thirty seconds and one minute to find out whether they're good for you or not, and Marcello and I knew we were good for each other. Other young bucks with the taste of fresh blood in their mouths would have tried to take the whole club off Marcello. However, I knew that if I allowed him to give me instructions, he would always feed me when I was hungry. He was an experienced businessman and had been involved in clubland for over 30 years. He had seen it all before – the hard cases coming and going. He wasn't intimidated by me; he knew that I was just the latest in a long line of faces. It was a case of 'Here's the new guy I'm dealing with' as far as Marcello was concerned.

The door at Kirklands was like a crash course in drug dealing and our first proper entry into that game. In a way, the drugs came to me in the end. They always do.

6

THE APPRENTICE TAXMAN

The white customers who came to Kirklands smoked hash, and the
black guys liked bush. The dealers were doing a roaring trade,
knocking out £2 draws to the punters, so we told them that from
now on they were going to have to give us – the security – some
money if they wanted to serve up. They gave us between £20 and
£50, on top of our £30-a-night proper wages – an instant 100 per
cent pay rise. Marcello turned a blind eye to the cannabis dealing
as long as we stopped it every now and then under his instruction
– before a police raid, for example.

Meanwhile, I was picking up kick-boxing trophies at breakneck
speed – first by becoming the British champion and then by
winning the European title. I was using a technique called
'visualisation' to devastating effect. The first time I came across it
was in 1977 when I was listening to an interview with Wimbledon
tennis champ Björn Borg. He said, 'Before I start the tournament,
I see myself lifting the Wimbledon shield. I look in my mind and
visualise myself being a champion on centre court.' I was like,
'Wow. Fucking powerful stuff, man, powerful stuff.' I robbed his
idea and envisaged becoming the British champion. I fought a guy
called Nick North in Manchester for the title and battered him. To
this day, he's never forgiven me. Later, I won my European title
in Athens against a German guy called Carlos. I had also pictured
that victory clearly in my mind before making it an actuality.

I started applying my Olympian violence to the street. Following some brutal skirmishes with other gangsters, mine and Andrew's reputations as men not to be fucked with increased and attracted lucrative opportunities. And there was always barroom chaos to contend with. In the past, Andrew and I had fought and knocked out the same men, so we were well matched in that sense. One night, a black soldier who'd come from the Falklands suffering with that war syndrome thing came in. He stared at me all night, and then suddenly he started to run at me like he had a bayonet, screaming, 'Aaaaaagh!' He ran straight onto my Sunday punch – a right hand. His eyes rolled back, and he was unconscious before he hit the floor. He was still asleep 15 minutes later.

While we were getting our stash together, a break into the proper drugs game came from an unexpected source. A guy called Robin came to see me, saying that he'd had a kilo of cocaine stolen from him by a black guy in our community called Randy. Andrew and I found Randy at his mother's house. He'd gotten high on his own supply, been too fucked to sell the stolen kilo on and hadn't made much damage to it. There was still 35 ounces left, so we just took it back off him.

Robin was delighted when we called him with the good news. The bad news was that we were going to keep half as our payment. He said, 'No, well, look, that wasn't what I intended to give you.' Too bad. Then he added, 'I was going to give you ten grand for getting it.'

When he said this to me, I nearly fell over. I put my hand over the receiver and said to Andrew, 'We're keeping half this stuff and he thinks we're taking too much, but he's prepared to give us ten grand for it!' Only then did the figures start to compute in my brain – ten grand probably didn't even cover half the amount we had. 'A.J., we've got to find out what this stuff is worth,' I said.

At that time, I had no understanding of the amount of money involved in drugs, or the value of cocaine or anything like that. You have to remember that I was 23 or 24 years old, a member of the England karate team and I didn't drink much or smoke – I was a finely tuned athlete, whose body was a temple, and I usually only sipped orange juice. And I had fought all temptation to get involved in the business of Class A drugs – until then.

Strangely enough, we turned to my old mate Curtis Warren to value the stuff. He'd just been released from prison for holding up a security van. When inside, he'd become friends with Callum, an incredible, untouchable villain. Callum was from a dynasty of traditional gangsters who owned a snooker hall and gym and invested heavily in drugs. Today, the dynasty is worth tens, possibly hundreds, of millions of pounds. Callum and Curtis were only starting off then, but Curtis was still able to tell us that our kilo was worth about £1,000 per ounce. We found out we had £35,000 worth of gear.

Armed with this info, we phoned Robin back and told him that from then on we were his unofficial partners. I said to him, 'We've got your gear back for you. You wouldn't have had it if it wasn't for us. Whatever you're getting for it, we're having half. We're not looking to do anything bad, like kill you. But next time you get one, we'll come with you as your partners to make sure you don't get robbed.' Deep down, I think Robin was just happy to have two good enforcers on his side who weren't looking to rip him off or do anything bad to him.

Word soon spread that we provided protection for drug dealers, helping them if they had a problem. Drug dealers started flocking to us, saying, 'Such and such has robbed ten kilograms off me. Can you get it back?' Or 'One of my distributors took five kilograms on tick and has bumped me the money. Can you recover the debt?'

Commissions on recovering narco debts started flooding in. Then Andrew and I hit on a brilliant idea – we should be more proactive. Robin's problem had been a passive situation that involved us solving an existing drugs robbery through negotiation. He had come to us. Why not go out there and generate our own business? Why not simply rob the drug dealers directly? Why not use extreme violence to make them give us their drugs and money? After all, they weren't going to fucking snitch on us, were they?

Thus began my descent into drugs, organised crime and what

is now known as taxing. It was strange timing, because it was all completely at odds with developments in my family life, which had become more stable. After many years, I'd finally made peace with my dad for abandoning us. For the first time, we were doing the father and son thing and being friendly together. The reconciliation had started very tentatively and frostily more than ten years before when I'd been forced to go and visit him when I was aged about eleven. At that time, he was living with the same babysitter he'd run off with. When it was time for me to leave, he told me to give her a kiss goodbye. Fuck off. She was nothing to me, and as far as I was concerned she was the reason my dad wasn't at home with us. I've always had a fierce loyalty to my mother and anyone close to me, so I dodged under my dad's arm, jumped over the couch and ran out the house to avoid her.

When I got to the age of about 18 or 19, my balls had dropped, and I actually considered myself a man. Only then did I start to empathise with my dad. He had fought in the war for 'Queen and Country' and had been entitled to come to the UK. Yet Britain in the early 1960s was a cold and racist place. On top of this, he also had the added pressure of being on the run. He had entered a mixed-raced relationship with my mum, who already had three children by two different men, and had two kids with her. No wonder he had fucked off – the pressure was too much for him. After realising this, I began to make allowances and started to build a relationship with him.

However, it wasn't as simple as that. Though I'd forgiven my dad on a surface level, I hadn't realised the effect an absentee father was having on my life. Although I didn't fully understand it at the time, my violence, aggression and propensity to evil and crime were partly down to my dad having not been around. While I was growing up, I'd had a series of uncles – my mum's boyfriends – but I'd never had a father to teach me right from wrong and how to deal with certain situations.

I had been raised mainly by women, and that is why I'm now so in touch with my feminine side. Believe it or not, it's being so sensitive that's made me so harsh. You wouldn't believe how sensitive I actually am, because it's covered by layers and layers of socialisation process and attitude. In part, I blame my father's absence for my chequered history – car thief by the age of 11, burglar by 13, mugger by 15, urban ninja by 18, armed robber by 21 and on the verge of becoming a drug dealer and protection racketeer by 24. Still, to this day, my dad's the only guy that I've never confronted about the things he's done to me. We've got this father–son dynamic: I can't face him down and tell him about the pain he's caused me. It's the elephant-in-the-room scenario.

However, it wasn't all a downer in my personal life. At that stage, I had met the woman with whom I would spend the rest of my life. Her name was Dionne Amoo. I first spotted her walking along the street. Then I bumped into her at a birthday party and instantly fell in love with her. The only problem was her boyfriend.

She used to come into Kirklands, so one night I went over to her boyfriend and said, 'Dionne doesn't want to be with you any more. She's with me now. I'll give you the first shot free and after that it's all on.' He never fought me for her; he just walked away, and since that day we've been together.

As for Maria, I found out something about her that destroyed my trust in her. I moved out and left her to bring up my son Stephen, with my full financial support. Danny, my adopted son, was being brought up by my family.

Meanwhile, Andrew and I had decided to turn our business idea into a reality. There was certainly a gap in the market for something we called a 'taxman'. This was an individual who preyed on drug dealers, taking their money off them by any means necessary – in other words, an underworld extortionist. The plan was to learn where these drug dealers held their stash of cocaine, heroin or draw and anything else of value, such as cash, cars, jewellery or expensive assets. How? By kidnapping and torturing them and stealing everything they had.

The philosophy behind taxing was simple. As drug dealers

were involved in illegal activities themselves, they couldn't very well go to the police if they had been done over. Therefore, they could not rely on the biggest gang in Liverpool to protect them – Merseyside's finest boys in blue, the police force. As I had learnt before, unreported crime was the best crime, and the only recourse drug dealers had was the underworld. Gangsters were the only people that they could go to for help if they had been taxed – to ask them to threaten the taxman into returning their gear. However, at the time, Andrew and I thought we were invincible. We were fearless world-champion athletes and nobody could touch us. So that didn't fucking bother us.

PART TWO

THE PLAYER

7

FULL-TIME TAXMAN

My first taxation was on a heroin dealer called Brian Wagner from the Everton area of Liverpool. Me and my mate Marsellus conned him into thinking that we wanted to purchase ten kilograms of heroin – worth about £250,000 wholesale.

Strangely enough, he invited us to his mother's house to do the deal and took us right up to his bedroom. Here was one of the biggest Class A dealers in the city, taking us up to his room as though we were going to listen to pop records. I quickly came to realise that the majority of drug dealers weren't very smart guys. They'd put their most valued narcotics in their own houses, under their own mother's bed. How fucking daft is that?

I sat on his bed while he took out a blue Puma sports bag from his wardrobe and laid it on his Liverpool FC quilt cover next to me. Then he showed us a packet of the gear, containing about five kilograms.

I said, 'Well that's nice. But where's the rest?' He shrugged his shoulders and said that he couldn't show us the other five kilos, so I pulled a gun on him and pistol-whipped him across the mouth. We were in game now. He knew that this was no run-of-the-mill sale. He was bleeding, saying that he didn't have any more kilos, so I put the gun in his mouth and said, 'Tell me where it is, prick, or I'll put your fucking brains all over that Pink Floyd poster on the wall.'

He mumbled some bollocks about 'no more gear', so I rammed the end of the barrel further into his mouth, smashing his teeth.

Meanwhile, his mum was shouting up the stairs, 'Do you want a cup of tea, lads?' She didn't know what was going on, and there she was getting out the chocolate HobNobs for her visitors.

'No thanks, Mrs Wagner,' I said politely, pushing the gun further down her son's throat. I then said to Wagner, 'If you don't fucking tell me, I'll do your fucking ma as well, you fat cunt.' With that, he loosened up a bit.

'I've got it stashed close by,' he admitted.

'Good lad,' I said, putting the gun in my back pocket, like you see in the old films during a stick-up.

I marched him out of his house. However, as we were leaving, his mum spotted the blood from where I'd just hit him. She said to him, 'What's happened, Brian? Are you all right, son?'

Fair play to the lad, he just smiled and replied, 'We're just messing about, mam. Don't worry. Just wrestling and boxing and that. I'm only going to the car to get plasters. I'll be back in a minute. Put the kettle on.'

We all smiled, thanked her for her hospitality and got in the car to go and find the goods. Dickhead was in the back, I was driving and Marsellus was in the passenger seat. We were travelling north in the direction of the new cathedral when suddenly blue lights appeared behind us. Oh dear! The bizzies. I had a firearm on my person, five kilograms of heroin in the boot, a top drug dealer held under duress in the back and the police were about to stop us. Had his mum got suspicious and called 999? 'No,' I thought. 'It's too quick, surely?' I looked for other bizzy cars. 'If his mum didn't call them, what the fuck is going on?'

My brain started to work overtime as I tried to figure out what was going on. Suddenly, Marsellus interrupted my train of thought. He said, 'Kick it, kick it,' street talk for 'Foot down and get off'. 'Kick it, Stephen, now.'

He was panicking, but I said, 'No, I can blag this.' By then, I had concluded that it was a routine stop. Even back then, I had nerves of steel. I didn't want a chase all over the city. I knew my limitations behind the wheel of a car – I'm no getaway driver. In fact, I'm not even a very good jockey. 'No, it's OK, I can handle it,' I insisted.

Marsellus replied, 'No, Stephen, no. Take the chase. It's too on top.' But I wanted to see if I could speak to the police officer. If he intended to arrest us, we would have to take it from there, but there was half a chance I could blag it if he was just a traffic bizzy.

I jumped out confidently and said, 'Yes, officer, how can I help you? What is the problem?' I gave him my details, using a false name and address, and all the while I was lining him up for a good right hand, just in case. If he was to decide that he was blowing us through or calling for back-up, then it would all be on. The bizzy would get knocked out, and I would be getting off. Then again, why take that chance? For some reason, I had a sixth sense for that sort of thing. I didn't feel any danger about the tug. I didn't feel it was on top, despite the fact that Marsellus was still nudging me and telling me to, 'Kick it, kick it. We can do it! Take the chase. It's not too late.' No, I knew that my false details would match with my description, so I was going to front it out for the time being.

The bizzy started taking notes and going through the motions. It turned out that he didn't even want to search the vehicle, he just wanted to tell us about a broken tail light. 'Get it fixed,' he said.

Meanwhile, I was still lining up for a right hand, because I knew that it could go either way. If things went wrong, it would be a case of escape by any means possible. However, in the end, the bizzy drove off, and I got back into the car. Marsellus and I sat heavily into our seats. He turned his head towards me and said, 'You're fucking good, you. You are really fucking good. Now let's go.'

Meanwhile, Wagner was in the back, probably thinking, 'What's going on here?' He was one of the top grafters from one of the toughest barrios in one of the most on-top cities in the world. He was a pretty streetwise guy. Nonetheless, he had just watched a live lesson by a 'big-top operator' in action. I actually reckon he was half impressed – half rooting for me, even though we had kidnapped him. After all, he was also a villain at the end of the day.

Once we were on our way, he directed us to some lock-ups at the back of a school, where he had the rest of his gear stashed. We quickly relieved him of the other five kilograms, stripped him naked and let him go. That was our first tax – a quarter of a million pounds for a few hours' work.

Funnily enough, the same guy got taxed three or four times after that by different crews. He ended up – and I've got to be very careful about bandying this label about, because I've been tarnished with it as well – as a police informer, to get him out of a prison sentence later on in his life. I haven't heard much of him since.

The main lesson that I learned from my virgin tax was to trust my instincts. Some people have a sixth sense for danger – I am one of them. Some people call it instinct; in comic books they call it spider senses. Whatever it is called, this sixth sense is an intuitive early warning system that allows me to pick up on impending threats – even when there are no visible signs of danger. It required me being totally switched on to my environment so that when something was out of place my spider senses would tingle. Jails and cemeteries are littered with people who don't listen to their sixth sense. I was determined to keep my body free from stress and worry so that my spider senses were never dulled.

One of my heroes is Bruce Lee, who mastered the philosophy of Jeet Kune Do. Jeet Kune Do involves a fighter adopting any style or move that's good for him, discarding the rest. I put this into practice on a micro level with my taxing and widened the principle to apply to my whole life. I took on board what was good for me, what I felt worked, and discarded the rest. Nevertheless, it's a totally subjective thing. Jeet Kune Do – the way of the fist.

The other lesson I learned was: make hay while the sun shines. The drugs game was still in its infancy and ripe for exploitation. It was the early days of Class A, and the police weren't giving it the attention that I instinctively knew it would later receive. It was a free-for-all, a perfectly open market. For the importers, there weren't any restrictions on the ports. For the distributors, there wasn't any surveillance, no video cameras on the street. So, while I was driving around with kidnapped men in the car, I didn't have to worry about leaving a televised record of the journey. That would never happen these days. You'd be on the telly at 6 p.m., near-live, like O.J. in his infamous car chase. Security wise, it was a much easier and laxer time – but I knew that wouldn't always be the case.

The next bit of tax work to come my way involved five kilograms of cocaine and £20,000 in cash. This time the tip-off came from a 'cardmarker' – a third-party informant, close to the drug dealer involved. This meant that I would not have to torture the dealer in person, just go straight for the drugs. However, the downside was that the specifics were less reliable, because, at the end of the day, I was relying on someone else's information.

The cardmarker had told me that the gear was hidden in a mansion just outside Liverpool. I got my cat burglar gear on – black clothes and a balaclava – and put my experience as a juvenile housebreaker to good use. I picked the window locks and disabled the alarm, but when I got to where the gear was supposed to be it wasn't there. It was bum information.

I learned an important lesson from that: wherever possible, always get the drug dealer in person to tell you where his assets are, even if you have to burn him with a steam iron or razor his testicles to get him to fold under questioning. From then on, I would discard information given to me by third parties and go straight to the horse's mouth.

Although I had just started my new career, I had learned many important lessons, and unlike most villains *I took them on board*. The vast majority of criminals live random, ill-conceived lifestyles by the seat of their pants. Already I was applying science, martial-arts philosophy and business reason to get ahead. However, that was only the beginning . . .

8

RAISE THE DEVIL

Soon I had mastered the dark arts of taxing, robbing at least one big drug dealer a week. Drug dealers tried to freak each other out by whispering, 'The Devil's going to get you, the Devil's going to get you.' The prospect would genuinely unnerve them. I became the bogeyman of the underworld. A myth began to grow up around me, fuelled by my resolve and unshakable fearlessness in the pursuit of tax. I'd face any odds in order to get what I wanted. It's not being prepared to kill, but being prepared to die that provides the winning ingredient.

However, I had one golden rule: once I'd got the drugs, I wasn't fucking giving them back. A lot of taxmen had come to grief by being too keen to undo their own hard work. They would steal a load of gear but cave in to underworld pressure and end up giving it back. The victims used to send emissaries, mates of mates and all that lark, to talk a taxman around or, if that failed, to threaten him. But me? No. You could send who you wanted – the SAS, the fucking SS led by the mujahideen – but you were not fucking getting it back. You'd have to snatch it from my cold, dead corpse. And this wasn't just said for effect or theatricality. It was the god's honest truth. Even if a victim tried to get their gear back, the chances were that they wouldn't be able to find me. Nobody knew my address, I had no credit cards, no bank cards – the CIA couldn't trace me. I didn't exist except in a drug dealer's nightmares. And my family was always kept safe, so my victims couldn't get at me by kidnapping my loved ones. In a nutshell, I ran a hermetically sealed operation. It was watertight.

Before I went to work, I'd go into character, like a method actor. I'd immerse myself in a part. I'd get my game face on. I've seen that in films, such as *Pulp Fiction* in which Samuel L. Jackson and John Travolta are talking shit about Big Macs but go into mode before they bang on the students' door.

Nonetheless, when I came out of 'game', something inside of me raged against the evil. I knew that there was something better for me out there. I passed my access course, and in September 1985 I won a place at Liverpool University to study psychology. In the back of my mind, I hoped that I could give up crime one day and get a decent job.

In the meantime, I was leading a double life. By day, I went to lectures and sat in the library with blonde girls from the Home Counties. At night, the Devil would come out to play. Technically, you could say I was leading a triple life, as I was still training hard as a kick-boxer. I won my first world title at Wembley Conference Centre on 25 November 1985. I was the light-middleweight supreme champion of all four million members of the World All-Styles Kick Boxing Association. I was the only world champion the university had ever had, and they went cock-a-hoop over it, putting me in the campus newspapers.

I opened a sports management company called Wear Promotions. Between having a business to manage, drug dealers to rob and training to do, I found myself too busy to attend any lectures. When it came to my finals, I terrorised the lecturer into telling me what questions would be on the exam: psychological intimidation – the art of fighting without fighting.

In 1988, I graduated with a 2:2. Not bad. Although I was the only one out of forty students to get a full degree, I still couldn't get a job. So I decided that if no one would employ me, I'd employ myself and opened up my own security business, supplying doormen to nightclubs. Ironically, that later opened up a mass-market for me to sell narcotics, on a hitherto unknown scale, direct to the consumer. I was working front of house and controlled the supply into the clubs.

There was a bar on black lads at a nightclub called The Grafton, so I forcibly took the door off the gangsters who had it. The underworld didn't like a nigger getting uppity, so the threat of war went to DEFCON-1. To defend the club, I installed the fiercest crew on this planet at maximum-force readiness. We had Stephen French, British, European and world kick-boxing champion; Andrew John, of the British karate team; Jack Percival, Commonwealth boxing gold medallist; Brian Schumacher, captain of the 1984 Los Angeles Olympics British boxing team; Sidney Bulwark, an infamous local boxer but a terrible bore; Aldous Pellow, former British Army boxing team; Big Victor, a real heavy street fighter; and Gerry the Gent, the nicest guy you could wish to meet but a vicious cunt once he'd had one over the eight.

In our looming war, a racist hard case called Tommy Gilday proved to be the equivalent of Archduke Franz Ferdinand before the First World War – he was the trigger. Gilday was a fearsome heroin and cocaine importer who could punch like a mule. One night, Gilday came to The Grafton to reclaim the door. Andrew John fought violently with him. Just as Andrew was starting to overpower his opponent, Aldous interfered. He was afraid that Gilday's defeat would bring about serious, serious reprisals. I knocked out one of Gilday's gang in the same go-around, and Gilday was ushered off the premises, promising, 'I'll be back, don't worry.'

As a direct consequence, the top four crime syndicates in the city ordered a mob of three hundred men to lynch the six of us. I posted lookouts outside of the nearby Grosvenor Casino and at a club at the corner – I paid little kids on bikes a fiver each.

At 10.30 p.m., the lookouts came bombing over to me. 'There's vans and vans and vans of them armed with machetes, baseball bats, hammers, knives, the pure works.' I paid them and told them to get off. Apparently, a crime family connected to the IRA had been on their way to a completely separate incident when they had bumped into Gilday's chilling cortège by complete coincidence. 'Come with us,' he'd told them. 'We're going to sort out the niggers in The Grafton.' Filled with Nazi bloodlust, they had thrown in their lot with Gilday. Now the enlarged mob was throwing bins and bricks at the door, screaming like savages. I told my men, 'Steady yourselves. Wait until you can see the whites of their eyes.'

I had chained the front doors up to prevent them from being booted in. The mob, who were all wearing balaclavas, started rattling the chains. It was quite an ominous sound, like the French CRS riot police banging their shields together before an attack.

Suddenly, half a face came jutting through one of the gaps. 'Here's Tommy,' said Gilday, grinning maniacally, like Jack Nicholson in *The Shining*. 'I'm back. I told you I was going to have yous.' Meanwhile, the machetes were coming through the three-feet high, two-inch wide vertical slits in the door.

'Stand to,' I said to my lads, 'we're going to fight this battle to the death.' The punters were all screaming, and the assistant manager was beginning to panic. I could see Aldous Pellow also starting to fade quickly. Nonetheless, I turned to Andrew John, who stared into my eyes, giving me 'the look'. Then the doors caved in.

Now, the Frenchman, like all good field marshals, always has a secret weapon in reserve. To be fair, I had foreseen what was going to happen, so I had taken the precaution of concealing a 1940 German Luger in a Yankee shoulder strap over my left breast. So, as the ranks charged towards me, I took up my fighting stance, drew the weapon and let go a round over the oncoming stampede. Pow! Bang! Crack! I called my Luger 'the equaliser', because all 300 men about-turned and ran for their lives. Well, nobody wants to get shot, do they? This was before guns became standard, so it came as a bit of a shock to the gang and snapped many of them out of their lynch-mob lust.

All six of us chased the three hundred men up the street, shouting at them, 'You're a sad crew. There's only six of us. Come back!'

Within minutes, the police arrived on the scene. Cunningly, I reversed the story completely and said that Gilday's crew had shot *at us*. These were the days before they could dust you off for forensics. However, while I was blagging the bizzy, I noticed that other members of my team were not doing quite so well under the pressure of questioning. I could see that Aldous was faltering under his interrogation and was going to fold at any moment. I was afraid he would tell them that I had fired the gun. Aldous was frightened of authority, after being in the army, so I made up an excuse and got him away from the bizzies as soon as I could.

One of the coppers saw this and turned on me, 'You're lying French. You fired this gun. The shot's been fired from inside. End of story.'

So I said, 'Well, if that's what you think, you prove it, but I'm telling you they shot at us.'

The bizzy retorted, 'Well, why did all 300 of them run away, then?'

I replied, 'Well, I don't know. Maybe because you fellas turned up.'

This logic bemused him, and it also made the bizzies look good, a kind of reverse flattery, so he swallowed it.

Suddenly, the phone in the nightclub rang. It was Tommy Gilday. Aldous picked it up, and Gilday immediately started trying to rewrite the history of the rout. He said, 'I knew there were only blanks in the gun,' blah, blah, blah, trying to undermine our glorious victory.

Aldous was frightened of Tommy, so he was gibbering, 'Yeah, but, no, but, yeah, but,' and almost being nice to him. What I had come to realise in dealing with these guys was that you didn't give an inch. You didn't call them 'Tommy', and you didn't talk friendly with them. You let them start to doubt their own confidence. Let them start to worry. Let them start to think, 'Who the fuck is this guy Stephen French who they call the Devil?'

I snatched the phone off Aldous and said to Gilday, 'I've got a real fucking bullet with your name on it, so fucking come back.' Bam – I slammed the phone down. Josef Stalin-like – uncompromising.

Now, what you have to realise is that this guy was used to his peers and enemies – mainly other middle-aged, white gangsters – sucking his cock and telling him how big his muscles were, what a criminal mastermind he was and how they were not worthy to sell his kilos of brown and white. Like all godfathers, he was seriously fettered by his suck-holing crew. Now here I was, a young black kid whom he had never met, showing him no respect and what's more telling him to go fuck himself. For the first time in his career, Tommy had been confronted by a dark, animalistic force as unpredictable as nature itself. The result – his head was wrecked. The battle had been won in the mind – and I was the victor. End of.

Theatricality and dramatics – great weapons, man, great weapons. You've got to be able to back it up, mind you, if it goes to the wire, but a lot of my success was down to my invincible Japanese mindset – I had a siege mentality.

So, instead of trying to attack us on a different night – and with 300 personnel under arms, he would have been assured of total victory – he caved in. He called for a powwow instead – the underworld equivalent of the Paris Peace Accords. Now, what you've got to realise is that in the past these white gangsters would never have tolerated black criminals, never mind negotiate with them. However, the black community was becoming more powerful. Ebonics and little bits of our culture were finding their way into the mainstream. Suddenly, everyone was wearing tracksuits in the street. We started that. Saying 'Yeah, man' – again, a black thing. Even The Beatles were influenced by black culture. Before they played at The Cavern, they used to go and buy pot off a black barber called Lord Woodbine. He taught them the blues. So, subliminally, black culture was kicking in – and the ripples were being keenly felt in the underworld. We had finally come of age as a force to be reckoned with.

The mediators of the powwow were two well-known black

doormen from Toxteth called Smith and Suncher. Smith agreed that his house could be used for the sit-down. Because Gilday knew Smith, he would come under his protection. We only laid one ground rule. If at the end of the parley we couldn't find a solution, we had to agree not to engage in any violence there and then. However, the next time we were to see each other, no matter where, it would all be on. The beauty of the powwow was that everyone was searched before they went in. And I was confident that my kick-boxing skills would be enough to ensure that I came out on top, if it did all go off.

So, there we all were: me and Andrew on one side of the table; and Tommy Gilday plus one of his sidekicks on the other. There was a lot at stake. First, this was our title shot – our chance to leapfrog a rung on the underworld ladder into the big time. If negotiations went badly, we could lose the door on The Grafton, which would also lose us our other contacts. Second, we could lose some serious face and slide back into the criminal gutter.

I have an unnatural ability to read situations and get a feel for the way a thing is going to go. I was 99.9 per cent sure that this one was going to go in our favour, as I felt we had all the advantages psychologically. When Andrew John and I were together, we unnerved people. We were like a pair of panthers. Also, Tommy Gilday had already felt the strength of Andrew John in the fight that had sparked everything off and he'd faced a gunshot from me.

I did all the talking, whilst Andrew maintained a menacing silence. Everybody knew that I was the brains. I immediately went on the offensive, making out that it was all their fault. Then I said, 'We'll let your attack by 300 men go. We'll grant you a reprieve.' As a sweetener, I threw in a bone: 'We don't even mind if you go to the club when you want. You can come in for free.'

Finally, it was decided that we would work The Grafton. Then, in a unifying spirit of underworld togetherness, we also negotiated a little bit of a protection racket that would benefit us all. If the owner of the club tried to get rid of me and Andrew, Tommy agreed that he would come down, make some noise and smash up a few things. We would pretend to chase him and his crew off, and Mecca would be forced to keep us on as security and up the fee, which we'd then share with Tommy. Textbook protection.

There's a book called *The 48 Laws of Power*, which reinterprets for the twentieth century the teachings of such political thinkers as Machiavelli and Stalin. One of the main rules states that you must *use* your enemies. We hadn't even heard of the book at the time, but that's what we were doing naturally.

In the end, we became allies with Gilday, although Andrew wanted the last word: 'You've reprieved yourselves this time from some very serious violence, so you owe me a favour.' He was cryptically referring to Gilday's connections as a drugs trafficker. The favour meant that any time we wanted some large amounts of coke or heroin, Tommy would have to serve us up.

A few years later, Tommy fell out of a tree and died. I was genuinely upset, as I had got to know him well by then and thought that he was a very funny guy. I remember thinking, 'Isn't it mad? Tommy faced death in the underworld every day, but he died because of an act of God.' It reminded me of a story I'd read about soldiers in Vietnam who'd freaked out after one of their mates drowned while on R & R – despite having been shot at every day in the jungle. It was a lesson in our mortality. Every day before going to work, I'd ask Marsellus or A.J., 'Are you ready to die today, kidder?'

Without fail, they'd reply, 'At the drop of a hat, mate.'

9

THE HOUSE OF HORRORS

Andrew and I decided to make our taxation more systematic. Through The Grafton, we had met a drug dealer called the Blagger. The Blagger was unique in the narco hierarchy. Although he was black, he lived in a hard-core white area of Liverpool called Croxteth, where drug dealing was carried out on a similar scale to the boom in Chinese manufacturing. The inhabitants of the tower blocks in this decimated post-war wasteland consumed so many drugs that the area became known as 'Smack City'. Behind the misery of the whacked-out families, dealers were growing disproportionately rich. To us, that meant only one thing – potential tax victims. The beauty of it was that the Blagger knew exactly who to target. All that we had to do was devise a method of luring the dealers into our trap.

We quickly persuaded the Blagger to switch sides – from straightforward dealer to point man in our tax crew. His job was to act as the bait for our taxations, by posing as the front man for a fictitious gang of drug 'Mr Bigs'. He was to groom the dealers over several months by doing a few legit deals with them before the sting. On each project, we had a kitty of, say, thirty grand – ten grand each from Andrew and me, plus ten grand from a ruthless villain called the Rock Star, our new business partner. We'd give it to the Blagger, and he'd buy a kilo of cocaine from the latest hotshot drug baron. We'd turn that over quickly and then buy another kilo off the same dealer, which we'd also turn over quickly. This phase was all about setting up the victim, getting his confidence and making him believe that the Blagger was a valuable and trustworthy customer – always paying the exact amount in cash, and always with a chat and a smile. Most importantly during this honeymoon period, the deal would always take place at *their* venue.

Before we knew it, the dealer was ready to give the Blagger credit. This was our signal to start preparation for the sting. The dealer was thinking, 'Well, the Blagger is a great customer – buys loads, no gip and always comes up with the money. Everything's OK. Everything's straightforward.'

Once we had their trust, we'd start getting a few kilos on tick and repay the credit bang on time. Then we'd gradually start to introduce a few problems. We'd be deliberately late for a payment, for example, thus forcing the dealer to come out of his comfort zone for the first time – straight to the 'House of Horrors'.

I'll give you a real example. Our first victim was a red-headed guy called Kevin. Now, Kevin was making noise that the Blagger owed him £28,000, which was true, as we had deliberately failed to clean our slate after a handover. The Blagger said that he had the dough, so Kevin agreed to come down to the House of Horrors to collect. This house was purposely acquired for taxation torture. It was a Victorian property in probate, waiting to be repossessed by some mortgage company, but I had the keys. It was perfect for an ambush. The front door opened to the left onto a long, 16-feet corridor that ran straight into the kitchen. This open-plan effect lulled the victim into a false sense of security. However, what they didn't know was that there was a recessed alcove under the staircase on one side of the corridor: an ideal place for an assailant to launch onto unsuspecting prey.

As part of our drive for increasing tax efficiency, I had revamped our intelligence-gathering arm. Through research – one of the lads was fucking Kevin's bird – we found out that Kevin kept all of his drug profits in an army kit bag in his house. One night, Kevin arrived at the House of Horrors to pick up his dough as arranged. We positioned a girl in the kitchen at a wooden table, eating a bowl of soup. This was the first scene that Kevin was greeted with – a welcoming, non-threatening female. As a further distraction, she had great tits and was wearing a low-cut, tight-fitting top – a pure Sharon Stone-style decoy. Don't forget, when a drug dealer like Kevin is going to do a job, such as collecting dough, he's on point; he's on red alert, ready for danger. So, he clocked the juggling tits, and the girl smiled at him. Kev smiled back and bounced indoors, acting the rock-hard drug dealer trying to impress her.

Little did he know that the Devil was coiled up, ready to pounce from the alcove. As he idled past, I put a serious choke on him. After that, I got him in a grip that lifted him off his feet, while Andrew made sure that he had no weapons. Physically subdued, real quick. I used my favourite method on him: I grabbed his forehead and wrenched it back using my left hand, whilst putting my right hand on his throat. I snapped my right hand down and gave him a good punch on the windpipe. After three or four seconds, he was out cold. I had cut off his air supply, and he was rendered unconscious. He'd be bruised the next day, but that was all.

When Kevin woke up, he found himself blindfolded and duct-taped to a chair. I said into his ear, 'Everything can go OK if you just tell us what we want to hear.' I was following my usual script. 'If you want to come out of this situation unscarred and unharmed, just cooperate. Give up your money, give up your goods and everything will be OK.' I pressed a knife into his face and neck. 'Look, I don't want to have to cut you. I've cut a lot of people in the past, but all I want is your money.'

Then, to put him under further psychological pressure, I established a bit of moral superiority. 'You're peddling misery and death on the streets. You're selling drugs to kids, and you're not supposed to do that. So, I feel it's my responsibility to relieve you of the profits and redistribute the wealth.' This idea of playing a vigilante was so successful that I started using it as PR in the wider community. People on the street actually started to believe that I was on a crusade to stamp out drugs. It was good cover, especially in the newly politicised ghetto, where Malcolm X-style rejection of Class As was starting to be good currency. Cynical, I know, but true.

Despite all that has been said, the ideal taxing scenario is to be able to release your victim, if at all possible, without any physical marks on them. Let's say they choose to go to the Old Bill afterwards. Now, if I've actually sliced them on the face and given them seven stitches, that means that there's physical evidence. Pictures of the scars and the doctor's report can all be presented in a court of law. On the other hand, if I've only made the victim *believe* that he's going to be cut so that he gives up his money, then that's a different story altogether.

Let's just say that afterwards he thinks, 'Fuck it, I'm going to the police anyway.' The bizzies would then ask him, 'Where were you tied up? Let's see your marks. Did you get cut?' If he has no marks, it gives the Devil grounds for plausible denial. And plausible denial is one of my favourite phrases. It means that I could have done the crime, but I've got a plausible reason to deny it, because there's no evidence. A court won't hear it, because the British judicial system requires evidence. Praise be for plausible denial, because without it I would be in jail now on multiple life sentences. And villains facing some of the most serious murder and drug-importation charges have got off by using this gem of a loophole. When the going gets tough for the CIA and the FBI, what do they fall back on? Their old friend plausible denial. Those guys and the Mafia probably ironed J.F.K., but there's no evidence, so that one remains in its box. The grassy knoll? Triangulation of fire? Go on, you fucking prove it.

I had studied psychology at university, so I could talk in someone's ear and damage them more that way than by physically harming them. What's more, I could keep it up, Abu Ghraib-style, for two to three hours. Otherwise, I could keep a victim up for 24 hours without any sleep, drip-feeding fear into his head, Guantanamo-style.

Without screaming or shouting, I said to Kevin, 'It's nothing for me to cut off your ear, put it in your pocket and send you home with it. I've done it before.' Always precise and controlled, I continued, 'If you really think hard, you'll be able to work out who I am and who's doing this to you. You know who the Blagger's mates are. The Blagger brought you here. If any harm should come to him, even if he slips on a bar of soap in the bath, you'll have us all over you like a rash. You know what we're all about. You understand?'

I kept pressing home my motive of moral superiority. 'You were just hassling the Blagger for 28 grand that he didn't really owe you, you understand? So, now you're going to have to pay us a fine of 28 grand, cos that's what you were trying to con him out of.' I put the knife against his ear, and he started to weep uncontrollably. When they start to weep, that's usually the cue to ask the big question, 'Where's the money?' I said.

'My stuff's inside the kit bag,' he replied. Because we had prior intelligence, I knew we were on the right track and he wasn't trying to tell us lies.

'Where's the kit bag?' I asked.

'It's in the spare room, behind the kid's bedroom. My missus'll be there now.'

'Has she got a mobile number, yeah? Give us the digits?' I wrote them down carefully.

It was time for the pay-off. I gave Kevin a series of simple-to-follow instructions on how to organise the handover of the money. It was critical that his bird didn't twig that it was a tax situation. She couldn't be alarmed in any way. She had to be convinced that the handover was part of a routine drugs transaction that her beloved did ten times a day.

'You're going to get yourself together, and you're going to make that call to your bird,' I told him. 'You're going to tell her that a lad is coming round to your house in 20 or 30 minutes. You're going to tell her that she's got to get all the money out of the kit bag, because you're expecting a raid. Or that you need the money out of the house quick, because you've got a good deal on. Tell her not to panic, not to worry, just to get the money out of the house.'

The main thing for me was to get Kevin to sound normal. So I gave him a drink of water, calmed him down and said, 'Look, this ordeal is nearly over. You're worth the money, believe me.'

I was reassuring him because there was a chance he could get a bit brave as he calmed down and began to see the light at the end of the tunnel. People do – it's just human nature. He might also try to pull a fast one. Many drug dealers have worked out in advance a code with their wives and their stash minders to deal with exactly this type of emergency kidnap situation. For instance, say that Kevin's wife was called Margaret, he might have told her that if he ever called her 'Maggie' over the phone, it was bang on. So, my job was to convince him not to try any funny stuff.

He made the call and kept it simple: 'Look, love, just get everything out of the kit bag and put it in a bin liner. I can't come home and do it, cos I'm a bit tied up right now [how we laughed], so I'm going to send someone else. A lad called Jap will be around in about half an hour, so just give him the parcel.' His wife agreed.

Jap was our hand-picked bagman and a key player in the operation. Imagine what would have happened if I had gone around to see Kevin's wife to pick up the dough. If I had turned up at her door – 225 pounds of prime black underworld – she would have immediately thought that something was wrong: 'Aye, aye. What's Kevin doing sending this cunt to collect the money?' However, Jap was on hand. He was 17, had the face of an angel and a sunny demeanour like one of Fonzie's mates from *Happy Days*. He was skinny, innocuous and unthreatening.

Jap went to the house, and Kevin's wife said, 'You all right, kid? Are you sure that Kevin wants me to give you the money? You want me to come with you?'

'No, I'll be fine,' he replied. 'I'm going to meet him with the money. He'll call you when it's all sorted out. You stay where you are. You've got the kids to look after, and that. He just asked me to do it, knowworramean?'

Kevin's wife was cooing all over Jap: 'Aargh, aren't you lovely.' She was probably also thinking, 'Kevin must be on for a few quid here. Whoever he's with, they must have a deal going on.'

Jap was white. Well, he had to be white, didn't he? All of these scenarios had been carefully worked out by me. Years later, I would apply the same technique when borrowing millions of pounds from the banks for legitimate property deals. I'd do all the arse work on the deal – getting a site and planning permission – then I'd just put a squeaky-clean white guy in front of the bank manager to borrow £14 million. The banks would do the checks on him, and, boom, boom, boom, the money would be released. It's simple psychology: a white guy is someone the banks know, someone they can trust and are used to. Don't give them anything out of the ordinary. That's when the alarm bells start sounding.

I had a number of Jap-style bagpersons on the books, such as a half-Chinese bird who was brilliant for collecting money because she was pretty and ingenious. However, behind the babes-in-the-woods exterior, she had balls of steel – the only thing that stopped her from being a man was the fact that she had no dick.

Anyway, Kevin's bird left Jap on the doorstep, bolted upstairs and came back down with a bin liner stuffed inside a massive holdall. Jap thanked her, smiled and got off the plot. He then counted the dough, bringing in the tally at £68,000. That was over £20,000 each between the three of us – me, A.J. and the Rock Star. Plus a little drink for the Blagger. Not bad for the late 1980s. We booted Kevin out of the House of Horrors, and that was that.

The best kind of tax was when you got the money and nobody got seriously hurt – just like in Kevin's case. Of course, they all *start off* with violence, so the prey can be led into a situation where he can be held against his will. To get to that point, they have to be pounced on. Nonetheless, if you're a good taxman, you can quickly end the violence and extract the tribute through psychological intimidation.

Take, for instance, the next episode at the House of Horrors. The following week, we lured a 17-stone drug dealer called Dominic to our 'Inland Revenue' office. Dominic had three kilograms of heroin that he wanted to sell to us, and we were sitting on a sofa negotiating. I opened my briefcase, which looked like it was full to the top with £20 notes – all counterfeit, of course, a thin layer simply covering some newspapers underneath. I closed the case and put it on my knee. 'You've seen the money, now where's the heroin?' I asked him. Then, suddenly, I flipped over the case to reveal a dagger hidden beneath – a twelve-inch blade with a five-inch handle.

During the seconds in which he had been bedazzled by the dough, I had taken one step forward and had threatened to slit his throat with a blade. He literally pissed and shit himself. He was a big guy, and there were all kinds of problems with his motions. The smell and sheer volume of faeces was phenomenal. A pool of urine started to spread around his trousers. The guy was 17 stone and supposed to be rough as houses, but I overcame him with ease, partly because I had taken him by surprise and partly due to my use of overwhelming force.

I put the blade to his throat and said to Andrew, 'You control him and get the details we need.' He was crying, and tears were running down his face. He told me where to find the gear, and we sent the half-Chinese bird around to collect it.

Now, deep inside me, I felt a bit sorry for him, sitting there in such a totally humiliating position. 'Go and clean yourself up, lad. I won't send you home stinking of shit. Take them kecks off. There's a pair of jeans up in the bedroom.' I couldn't let certain geezers go upstairs, because they'd be looking for a weapon to come back downstairs to smash me over the head with, but I knew who I could turn my back on, and I knew the villains who were to be given no quarter. Again, it came down to my spider senses. Nevertheless, Dominic was a broken man. He had come into the house a giant and had left a midget.

Once he realised that he wasn't going to be physically hurt, his reaction was one of overwhelming relief. If we were that way inclined, we could have fucking messed around with him: raped him; sexually tortured him with a broom handle. I've seen it done – not for a turn on, though, just for effect. But Dominic wanted to be away from us in one piece. He knew he'd embarrassed himself. There was no reason for him to keep up any bravado in front of us. His whole demeanour said, 'You've seen me for what I am. I'm a yellow coward. You have robbed me of my wealth and dignity. Before you I stand humiliated.'

'You won't tell anyone that I shit my kecks, will you?' he begged us, sobbing.

Our reply was, 'Don't make any problems for us, and this is the end of the matter. You've been taxed. It's part of your game. Put it down to experience, and get on with your life. It's nothing personal. It's just about money.'

That was true. It was never anything personal, as I never ever taxed anybody that I knew. It was always strangers, always people I didn't know. Also, I always taxed white geezers. Now, readers, the cautionary tale to come out of all this is simple: don't get involved with drugs, because it's a horrible, nasty fucking world, full of nasty, horrible fucking people – like me.

By that point, I had learned that taxing was all about raising enough money to fund bigger and better drug deals. For instance, we got £68,000 from Kevin. To buy two kilograms of coke you needed £60,000. You might sell one kilogram straight away for £33,000, making a quick three grand on the deal. Then you ounce one out or keep an ounce for yourself and find someone who sells ounces for you.

Friday was pay day. You bombed round everywhere and got your kitty back together again. Class A drugs – it's all cash. I've seen bin bags full of £20 notes. You could select one in three £20 notes in Merseyside, subject it to analysis and you'd find traces of cocaine on it. The thing about Charlie – and I've had lots of cocaine – is that it really heightens sexual pleasure. It's a sex drug – and that's the key to its selling power, if truth be known. The downside is that Charlie can also give you a bit of a floppy dick. However, you can always trust the market to throw up a solution, and it has done so in the form of Viagra. So, you get the nice rush off the cocaine, a fucking big hard-on off the Viagra and you're banging away all night. That's what the nation is awash with now – shagging round the clock.

There is a well-known gangster called Dave Courtney, and he has actually given that recipe out on a TV travel programme. I don't know which one it was, but you won't get those kinds of tips off Judith Chalmers.

10

DEFY BEELZEBUB

In the tax business, everything is political and interlinked. Being on the ball 24 hours a day like the prime minister is critical, as illustrated by the following scenario. Andrew and I were a little bit at loggerheads, because he had started dealing drugs with Curtis Warren and Peter Lair – but they wouldn't let me on the firm because they feared I would turn on them. Curtis Warren had been doing a number on Andrew's head for a while, trying to lure him away from me. To divide and rule.

One night, Curtis came into The Grafton and used his favourite line on Andrew: 'Are you still taking all the lumps, whilst Stephen's taking all the money?'

Curtis feared my intelligence more than my physical prowess. He knew that I was a very intelligent guy, which is why he wanted to weaken me by turning Andrew against me.

Other than that, things seemed to be going pretty well. I'd even got myself a new lieutenant called Robin. This was the same Robin I'd rescued the coke for in the 'Case of the Missing Kilo'. He'd fallen on hard times and now drove me around in a silver Mercedes. Any time we were going to sort out some serious problems, he was the guy who'd carry the tools. Andrew, Aldous Pellow and I usually travelled point in one car, whilst he drove behind in a separate vehicle with the guns. To get him back on his feet, I made him a partner in my drug deals. I was selling Class As, and he was selling Class Bs, but we pooled the profits.

It was a good deal for him: I was splitting thousands with him to give him a little leg up, and he was splitting hundreds with me. But, as students of *The 48 Laws of Power* will know, gratitude is a burden.

Soon, I found out that Robin had been chipping me on the weed. He was actually making £250 on a kilo but was telling me that he was only making £200 and pocketing the extra £50. Now, people may say, 'Well, it's only £50,' but, as businessmen like Philip Green and Bernie Ecclestone will tell you, if you look after the pennies, the pounds will look after themselves. Robin's scam had me down by £5,000.

As well as the dough, this hurt me personally. The French philosophy on friendship is simple: friendship is like a clean piece of blotting paper with no marks on it – brilliantly white and unblemished. However, if you blot your copybook, even with a little black mark by chipping me, I will get revenge. I will cover the sheet completely and turn it into a sheet of black carbon paper. And just remember, when it comes on top and I'm standing in your bedroom at the witching hour sporting the Devil's horns and a sacrificial pentacle, that it was you who opened the floodgates. I didn't start it. Second, if you're doing me out of what's mine, I won't moan and I won't cry, but I will plot and scheme to get you back – behind your back, so you don't know when it's coming. This is something that I always tell anybody at the start of a business relationship or a new friendship – just so that they know the rules.

The following morning, I got up and went to Granby Street. Peter Lair walked up to me very purposefully and, completely out of the blue, said, 'Was that your weed last night?' I'd not long been up, so I was a little slow, but I quickly regained my street wisdom, realising that whatever he was talking about could be an earner.

'Yeah, it was my weed,' I replied, not having a fucking clue what he was on about. However, he knew by my delayed reaction that it wasn't mine. That just goes to show what a fraction of a second can mean on the street.

Apparently, the night before, Lair had robbed 150 kilograms of weed off a young guy called Nazim. Curtis had had something to do with it as well, and they must have done it after I'd seen them at the club. During the taxation process, Nazim had told them that it was my weed in a bid to scare them off, or at least to cause them to have second thoughts. Me being me, and them being them, if I had said yes that morning – 'Yes, that's my weed and you better give it back' – it would've been returned, no two ways about it. This was because we had a mutual, grudging respect. Even though the weed had fuck all to do with me, if I had been on the ball I could have convinced them that it was mine and got myself 150 kilograms for nothing. However, I was a bit slow on that chilly ghetto morning, and Lair had got one over me.

Nonetheless, this little scenario ended up putting me in touch with Nazim, who was always backwards and forwards between England and Holland. He told me that he could bring us over some Class A – some cocaine – from Holland, score it for 16 grand a kilo and split it into ounces when it landed here, selling each one for a grand – that's 35 grand for a kilo. As a result, we'd make 19 grand profit on a kilo.

I said to Nazim, 'That sounds all right. Let me get some partners to put together a parcel, and I'll be back.'

This was a good opportunity for me to bury the hatchet with Curtis and Lair. I thought that if I offered them a split of the profits of any deal I put together, we could be mates and they would let me join their firm. But as students of history will know – appeasement always leads to more war.

Enter the scene, Harry Sheen. Harry Sheen was an old-time wheeler-dealer who loved to make money any which way. Robin had told me that he was looking to invest a bit of graft, so, later that day, I met up with him and he introduced me to Harry. Remember, I was keeping my eye on Robin, because he'd been chipping me on the weed, but I had a little plan in mind. To be honest, I was gutted about Robin's betrayal, because I'd got close to him. When a mutual friend called Jimmy Fizz confirmed my suspicions, it was even worse. I knew I had to settle the score; at the end of the day, business is business and progress is progress.

We decided to put together a kitty of 100 grand – 50 from Harry, 25 from me and 25 from Robin – and do a little tester with Nazim. Immediately, Harry started to play the role of godfather, telling me how it was all going to go. Already, I was thinking, 'When this thing lands, I'm taking it all. Robin's been fucking me.' While Robin and Harry were playing the big-time Charlies, I was thinking, 'You think I'm a dickhead, but I'm going to show you what I'm all about.'

Ringmaster Harry decreed he would take 50 per cent, Robin would get 25 per cent and I would get 25 per cent. Even though I was the one that would be turning the merchandise into money – because I was good at selling it – he was still getting the lion's share. Listen to the deal that this fucker thought he could make me wear: it was my contacts that were bringing the gear over, I was putting up half the money, I was liquidating the parcel into gear and Harry wanted to give me 25 per cent, while all he was doing was sitting on his arse or taking his dogs for a walk. I thought, 'Yeah, right.'

Before long, the parcel arrived, secreted in a tyre. It got delivered to Nazim as per the plan. Then we switched to the secret phase two of the op. I called Andrew John in to tax Nazim, snaffling all the gear before it was handed over to Harry.

Phase three was down to me. I went to see Harry and said, 'Look, Nazim's been kidnapped again, and the money's gone missing. I'm not suffering a monetary loss. I want compo.'

I made Harry give me another £25,000. I can remember him sitting in my house in Garston. He knew that he was being had over, but he didn't want to make trouble with me, because he knew how it went. Later, I caught up with Robin in a flat we had and told him the same story. Of course, he didn't believe it, so I told him the truth: that I was taxing the gear and the cash, and I wanted some more money off him as a fine – again, £25,000.

As he was handing over the money, he asked me why. I said to him, 'Look, Robin. I've been splitting thousands with you on the Class As, but you've been chipping me, mate, and this is the payback.' I also explained why I had fucked Harry: he'd tried to take the piss out of me on the deal. I said, 'Do I look fucking stupid? My colour doesn't wash off. It's not fucking green underneath. It's black right through to the bones.' Harry just thought I was a knobhead nigger bouncer.

So, that night, I went to a meeting with my real partners – A.J., Curtis and Lair – to divvy up the loot, which was a gesture by me to win them as trustees. However, I sensed tension in the air. We had about £100,000 worth of coke and £50,000 in cash. Thirty-seven and a half grand each for a day and a half's work – not bad. Curtis was saying nothing but watching everything. Andrew was being half cocky, flexing his muscles to show off to Curtis and Lair, trying to prove that he was not just my underling. Lair was being neutral and civil but was carefully monitoring the play – to see which way it was going to go – so that he could jump on the winning side.

I had always given Andrew room to express himself. Foolishly, he'd made the mistake of misconstruing this love as fear. He suddenly made his bid for power and announced, 'Let's keep Frenchie's share. He's always taxing everybody else, and now we're going to do it to him.'

Lair and Warren didn't say anything to this. They were leaving Andrew to carry the lot. Andrew's contempt for me was partially down to the power games that Curtis had been playing with him. Curtis feared me because I was too similar to him. He didn't want me on his firm in case I usurped him from his throne. Curtis was also envious of my ability to read a situation and steer the outcome to my benefit. I was a past master – Tiger Woods. So, Lair and Warren were seeing if Andrew could *really* put me under manners. I had the ability to turn from happy and jovial to a cold-blooded, calculated killer in a nanosecond – from smiley to vicious in the blink of an eye.

So, I looked at Andrew and said, 'Do you really think you're man enough to keep my money? Do you really think you're man enough to take my goods? Cos if you do, feel free to do it.'

Unbeknownst to him and the others, I had taken the precaution of bringing my best friend with me – a gun, perched firmly in the small of my back. Before I'd got to the meeting, my spider senses had told me that there might be a problem.

This was also an opportunity for me to see if I was real or false. To this day, nobody has stood in front of me and called me a cunt. I had no worries about Curtis, because I knew he wasn't going to get physical. Peter Lair was an incredible street fighter, but I didn't have any fear in my heart for him, either. But I was actually *wary* of Andrew. Not scared, just wary. However, I knew that if Andrew started to get the better of me, Peter Lair would join in and kick me to death. They would actually kick me to death. Andrew had become caught up in trying to impress his new masters, cos they'd convinced him that they were going to make him a millionaire. They would think nothing of killing me. Shit like that happens every day.

I looked at A.J. again and said, 'If you take my stuff, you'll never live to enjoy it. You're a big, strong guy, Andrew, so I won't give you a chance. I'll come out of the shadows, and you won't fucking see me. You understand? I will not give you a chance. So, give me my fucking money, give me my fucking goods and I'll be on my way. Otherwise, let's do what we are going to do.'

Up until that point, Andrew and I had been brothers. You couldn't get a fiver between us. No good could come of this. He looked at me and gave me a cold stare. Our eyes were locked. By not blinking an eye, we were saying, 'Who's got the biggest cock here? Who's got the balls? Who's gonna be *the* number-one-all-the-way-negro here?' The true mark of a warrior is facing up to something that you're afraid of, something that evokes fear in you. If you don't face a moment like that, you're nothing but a coward and a bully. So, I was unflinching, and I could see he was realising pretty quickly that 30-odd grand wasn't worth going to war over. Suddenly, he said, 'I'm only joking, Ste. Here's your stuff, mate.'

However, we all knew it wasn't a joke – it was just a way out. I snatched the goods from him. It was all over, but I went away with a feeling of dread in my soul. Something had gone wrong in there. He had broken the brotherly bond, and I would no longer be able to protect him. What would become of him?

11

SATANIC VERSES: RULES AND POLITICS OF TAXING

If you are a tax accountant, you might join a professional body, such as the Chartered Institute of Taxation. They have rules to keep budding taxmen in line, such as client confidentiality. However, if you're going to be a successful taxman in the drugs world, you must learn the following.

THE CODE OF CONDUCT FOR THE STEPHEN FRENCH FOUNDATION OF TAX STUDIES

Rule 1 – Never tax the same person twice

If you tax a man once, he can wear it. He may well put it down to experience, an occupational hazard, a necessary evil. However, if you tax him a second time, he *will* get angry, and it's human nature that he *will* seek revenge. This is because a frightened man is a dangerous man. If you tax him twice, he's going to think to himself, 'Every time Frenchie is skint, he's going to take my money.' You'll force him into taking some action against you.

I had the monologue to deal with this: 'I've taken these goods from you, but you have nothing to fear from me ever again. Even if somebody asks me to do something against you in the future, I'll have to tell them that I can't do it because we have history – that I've already done something to you, and I don't want to evoke feelings of fear or panic. So, my advice to you is to wear this tax like a shirt that doesn't fit and just get on with your life.'

The psychology behind this rule goes back centuries to Machiavelli. He said that men would often put up with great tragedies befalling them. Nevertheless, the same men would explode with unpredictable fucking ferocity if you managed to slight them in the smallest possible way and, as a result, would spend the rest of their lives seeking revenge. That is what my victims would see a second tax as – a slight against their honour, dignity and self-respect.

Rule 2 – Never chase dead money

Dead money is simply cash that is difficult to retrieve. The best tax is when you get the goods first time – often by surprise. But if you learn of a particularly big stash and you go after it and fail, write it off. Don't bother going back for it, because you'll be going into a nest of vipers. Remember, it's only your greed that won't allow you to let go. If it's dead money, it's likely that *you* could die in the process of going back for it again.

Rule 3 – Never give the goods back once you've stolen them

This seems pretty self-explanatory; however, after you've taxed someone, 101 reasons to give the stolen goods back might present themselves. For instance, a gangster you know might also be mates with the victim, and he'll come lobbying to get the gear back on behalf of his pal. Or the victim or his allies might kidnap one of your gang and hold him for ransom until the goods are restored. Nevertheless, no matter what shit comes your way, *you must hold firm*, because thems your wages.

Rule 4 – Never tax someone you know

I'm not even saying for one minute that you'd do it deliberately. Sometimes it might be done by pure accident. For instance, you might not know when you tax someone that the gear is owned by a mystery third person in the background, who might turn out to be someone you know. Or you might be given some duff info about the ID of your intended victim, and when you attack the feller he turns out to be an associate. If so, you have to make amends. Crossing the line on this one can literally lead to murder, as will be later exemplified in a case study very close to home.

Rule 5 – Never leave physical evidence on the victim

Following a nice touch, the difference between jail and a £15,000 holiday in St Lucia can be as minute as a molecule. Don't leave any DNA on the victim. And remember, injuries are the most compelling evidence in court.

There are two other legal factors that are related to this rule, both of which are vital to a taxman – police intelligence and police corruption, the two being interrelated. It's not what the police *know*, it's what they can *prove*. All villains are aware of this. My police intelligence file consists of at least four to five boxes of shit that police claim I've been involved in. Nonetheless, it doesn't fucking matter, because none of it can be proven. The important fact is that my actual police record is only a sheet long. So, from four or five boxes of crime, they have only ever managed to boil it down one sheet's worth of convictions. That's because I make it a top priority never to leave physical evidence behind.

Now, police intelligence can work for you or against you, and this is where the police corruption comes in. For £1,500, I could find out what sort of investigations were going on in relation to me during my taxing days, especially out of one particular police station in Liverpool. In all fairness to the Merseyside Constabulary, Norman Bettison, appointed chief constable in 1998, later cleaned up the force. He was an honest man, and if you were in tune to the nature of the beast, you could actually feel it softening when Bettison came to power. You could actually feel the beast becoming more politically correct, because law and order and fair dealing all took priority over bent officers.

So concludes the Stephen French code of conduct. However, everyone who goes to work knows that the rules regulating behaviour don't just exist in a vacuum: there's something called 'office politics', a kind of invisible set of constantly changing rules that determine how we behave, and how the rules are interpreted and enforced, based upon our relationship with our co-workers. You'll be glad to hear that the drugs taxation industry is no different from working in an insurance office or a bank.

THE OFFICE POLITICS HANDBOOK FOR THE STEPHEN FRENCH FOUNDATION OF TAX STUDIES

A – *Choose your victim carefully*

Don't prey on criminal organisations bigger than yours. For instance, I once knew a drug baron called Jim, who was head of a powerful crime dynasty. If Jim phoned me up and said, 'Some nice Charlie there. I'm going to put a ki away for you,' I'd have to go down and see him, pay him for the gear and do a genuine deal. (Most of the time, the code he used was cars: 'A lovely ride. You'd love to drive this. Come down and have a look.') If anyone else rang up and said that to me, I'd simply steal the gear and get off without paying. However, you couldn't mess with Jim. He and guys like him were so cocksure of themselves. They had so much confidence in their own reputations that they would give out kilos of cocaine or heroin on tick, knowing that they would be paid. If they weren't, they would just murder the culprit. In the jungle, you won't see a lion trying to feed on a rhino. D'you get me? As a taxman, you look for an antelope that's come into the wrong part of the jungle or one who's come to the waterhole to feed. If you want to be involved in the nefarious world of drug taxing, you've got to make sure that you can hold your own.

B – *Draw up clear lines of demarcation in your business plan*

One day, I might be taxing someone, the next I'd be doing a legitimate drug deal with some proper dealers. But don't chop and change and confuse one with the other. Get this in your head: if you're doing a deal, do a deal. Don't suddenly think, 'I'm going to tax this person,' cos you're getting greedy. People will soon stop doing business with you, and your rep will suffer at the hands of the office politicians.

In these kinds of situations, it was useful to have a good 'checker'. A checker was a kind of bodyguard-cum-middleman-cum-referee who made sure that a drug deal went well between two parties who did not know each other and had yet to build up trust. Everybody and his brother wanted to sell drugs, but you needed a good checker to make sure that it didn't descend into anarchy. The minnows were scared shitless of doing business with the sardines. The sardines were scared to do business with the sharks. Then there were the killer whales who wanted to eat everything. With a checker, the minnows got themselves a net – an equaliser – to make sure that the bigger members of the ecosystem didn't start biting their heads off.

Because I obeyed rule A rigidly, I became a checker myself and made hundreds of thousands of pounds in commission. During these deals, some of the sharks would turn to me and say, 'What are you here for?'

'Well, I'm here to make sure that he doesn't get robbed,' I'd reply.

Of course, I could have turned Turk on the minnows and robbed them. However, I had to say to myself, 'When I'm taxing, I'm taxing. When I'm doing a deal, I'm doing a deal. If you double-cross the guy that paid you, you're not going to get any more work.' However, by remaining consistent and not betraying anyone, people started to say, 'Well, Frenchie had that £1 million in cash of my money in the room, but he didn't try and have me off.' Those jobs would then keep coming.

For instance, there was a gang from Huyton that was doing business with a black gang from my area. I got a call from Jim, and he said, 'Look, something's going on down there, Stephen, we need you around. Look after them lads. Them lads are all right.' It was a case of the old favour syndrome.

I said, 'Well, I was going to have them, Jim, but since you've given me a call, it'll go straight.' The lads from Huyton then knew that they had a checker. 'We can use this guy,' they were thinking. 'We can sell some stuff to the black geezers through this guy, because we've got a checker on them.' I did all this because I didn't want to upset my friends.

A lot of people thought that you could buy into being a checker full time: ensure someone's deal went OK, make a living and get a good drink out of it. But suddenly checkers became obsolete. This was because the minnows turned to another form of equaliser – the gun. This was why guns spread far and wide so fast throughout the drugs game – they levelled the playing field for the barnacles and crustaceans. The crustaceans could start trading with the crocs without fear. Look at all the shootings going on now. It isn't the crocodiles and the great whites who are doing it – it's the fucking plankton. The skinny teenagers in their 4x4s – armed to the teeth. The thing is, the killer whales can do fuck all about it. They've been rendered toothless because they've got a lot to lose, whereas the kids haven't.

C – Guard your reputation with your life

This is law five in *The 48 Laws of Power*, one of my favourite books. You've got to build your rep as a taxman with fear and violence, and then you've got to defend it. What I'm talking about here are the everyday slights made by your co-workers, designed to undermine your power. Everyone will understand what I mean when I say, 'Gossip is the Devil's Radio.'

I'll give you an example. In sobriety, Jim was fine. However, once he had had a line of coke and a few drinks, the horrible racist in him reared its head. His chat would be, 'Niggers this, and niggers that, and they can't come down here, and they can't do this and that.'

If I was out in his company, I'd say, 'You can't start that Jim, cos I'm a nigger.'

He'd then say something like, 'But I don't mean you, Ste.'

I'd reply, 'Yeah, but if anybody knows that I'm sitting here listening to you nigger this and nigger that and nigger the other, what does that make me? And I'm no fucking Uncle Tom. So don't fucking do that, mate. Curb that, otherwise I'll get off, understand?' You have to make sure you get on top of things like that.

D – Never show fear in front of the lads

If you crumble on the job, the lads will laugh at you. They'll say things like, 'Go and get the piece of wood out of that skip and strap it to your back. Get some backbone, lad, if you want to get involved with the graft.' There was a rice mill near the docks, and they'd say, 'If your arse is going to go, go and get a job in the rice mill and hump bags, don't sell drugs.' My fear was always under control, but I watched many fall by the wayside by lacking a good pair of town halls.

E – It's not all about race

The reason why I was always taxing white geezers was because I didn't really know any white people, and this made them practical, risk-free targets. (See the taxation code of conduct, rule 4.) Sure, it also made it easier for me to make them suffer, as I didn't trust any white geezers in the first place – I was brought up not to like Johnnys, as in John Bull the Englishman. However, later in life, my opinion changed. I never really had much time for white people until I met a white guy called Franny Bennett, who was a mate of the Rock Star's. And another white guy called Whacker, a really sharp young lad who was also a friend of the Rock Star's, had an effect on me, too. I really liked him. Unfortunately, he never realised that, because he was scared of me.

Then, finally, I met a white businessman and had an epiphany. I equate it to when Malcolm X went to Mecca and met white Muslims. Because he was so pro-black, he never wanted anything to do with white people. However, after Mecca, he realised that race and colour were just a construction of society, and it would only take two generations to breed racism out of us all. Two generations and it could all be gone. However, as it stands, the prejudice just keeps getting carried over and handed down from father to son.

Personally, I grew into a completely different person and was more successful than I had ever been before. I went legit and made much more money than I ever did as a gangster. So, my advice is don't let your vision be narrowed by your own prejudices.

In conclusion, I advise you to follow all these guidelines to the letter, as they might well save your life. Unfortunately, Andrew John ignored the rules. And he paid a very high price.

12

GATES OF HELL

One time, I went to prison to visit a friend and through him ended up making a useful contact. Pat was a baggage handler on the ferries between Hull and Holland. He had run up a load of arrears with the casino and had maxed out on his credit cards, so he offered to smuggle drugs for us to clear his debts. He had sussed out a fail-safe method: transport the drugs on a Sunday night. It was a no-brainer, really, because the security was so lax.

We started off small to see how it went, but I can't tell you how elated I was when it worked like clockwork – it was like finding a vein of gold in the Yukon. Every other Sunday, he brought in ten- or twenty-kilogram packages of cocaine. We would score it in Amsterdam for eighteen grand, Pat would get five grand, so that took our cost price up to twenty-three grand. We were knocking it out for £30,000 in Liverpool. So, on a twenty-kilo parcel, I was making one hundred and forty grand – every two weeks.

The downside was that Pat was earning so much cash that it didn't take him long to get himself out of the mire money-wise, and he decided that he wanted to put a stop to our smuggling operation. Oh no you fucking don't! I made him continue the scam for a further two years. Every fortnight, he'd come off the ferry with his bags, half pissed off. He'd be met by a van sent by me. Then it was a straight run down the M62 to Liverpool, where the bags would be distributed. We called the run from Holland through the Pennines to Liverpool the 'Ho Chi Minh Trail'. That was our code word.

Twelve hours after the gear had been scored in Holland, it was on the streets. Personally, I was strictly hands off – organisational only. My philosophy was to pay others to take the risk wherever possible. I took 80 per cent of the money pot and gave 20 per cent to joeys to do the serious work. They hadn't put up any of the capital outlay, so it was fair enough in my view. I would just remain at the back, not putting myself in any difficult situations. I had a man to pick up the stuff, a man for distribution and street soldiers to sell it to the users. It wasn't rocket science. It was pretty straightforward, but the return was fucking interstellar – thousands of percentages. Any businessman will tell you that a 25 per cent profit on a legitimate business is good – money for old rope compared with the drugs game.

However, wealth brings its own problems. I had loads of paper around that had to be laundered. I bought restaurants, bars, cafés – anything to make it clean and legal. There's a whole host of ways to launder money. For instance, a basic method is to give someone a grand in cash, and they'll give you a cheque for £950 back. But a personal favourite was the bookie scam we had going. We'd give a bookmaker we had on the firm £20,000 in cash every week. In return, he would give us a cheque for £18,000, saying that we had won it on a bet and that he had taken his 10 per cent. We could launder anything up to 100 grand on an accumulative bet. Then I found a similar scam. I'd go into a casino and change five grand of cash into chips. I'd play for a little bit, maybe losing about £500. Then I'd cash in the £4,500 of remaining chips and get them to give me a cheque, suggesting to the authorities that I'd won it.

When my profits got to a silly amount, I started doing computer transfers from abroad, moving money from offshore accounts into my UK account or sending a telefax to a shelf company. A shelf company was a company that could be bought 'off the shelf' from an accountant in Bermuda or the Cayman Islands. I would then hide my drug profits in one of these companies so that it looked as though the company had generated the profit itself. I'd then send a telefax to the bank controlling the shelf company's account, instructing them to transfer the money back to me. It was all just numbers.

Meanwhile, news of our success on the doors at The Grafton had spread, and new contracts started to roll in. A mate of mine called Panama Jones – on licence for double murder at the time – asked us to scare off some local bodybuilders who were hassling the owner of a club called XO's. Incidentally, Panama was the only security boss ever to stop Roger Cook from investigating him. I'm not sure how he did it, but his face never appeared on *The Cook Report*, that's for sure.

So, Andrew John, Aldous Pellow and I went to the rescue. We also took along a guy called Euan, who we nicknamed 'Clank' because he had so many tools on him that he clanked when he walked. Our first night on the doors was pretty eventful. A bodybuilder threw a heavy steel tyre-lever at me and another called Ergun threatened to throw me into hot fat. However, we soon saw them off, using a bit of the old 'ultraviolence'.

But it wasn't over yet. One day when we were on our way into the club, I looked up and saw five men in balaclavas coming towards me. Behind them, I could see people dropping out of the trees. There were about 30 or 40 of them in all. We took off, aiming to get inside the club, pull the drawbridge up and barricade ourselves inside. XO's was underground, and to get in you had to go down a narrow 45-degree staircase to a door at the bottom. To make sure that Aldous and Clank got safely inside, Andrew John and I mounted a formidable defence. At the top of the stairs, in a rearguard action, I pulled out my machete and performed some Errol Flynn-style sabre rattling to keep the attacking troops at bay. This gave Aldous and Clank time to get safely inside the club, arm themselves and institute a flanking manoeuvre to guard the next phase: *our* insertion.

Andrew and I then made a tactical withdrawal down the stairs with our backs to the wall so that we could join the others inside. However, the plan did not go well. When we got to the bottom, lo and behold, Aldous had shut the door and wouldn't let us in.

Clank was also stunned into inaction.

Something similar had already happened to me with Brian Schumacher in The Grafton. Some people react badly in the face of fear. Self-preservation kicks in, and they do some strange things for their own survival. They don't care about you – they just care about themselves. Aldous had lost his bottle and had left us to our fate. There was a little glass panel in the door, and I could see the whites of Aldous's frightened eyes. We banged on the door in desperation, but to no avail.

'Fuck it,' I thought. 'Whatever will be will be.' Andrew John and I gave each other the stare, steeled ourselves and prepared to stand to. We made an about-turn and faced the enemy. The hordes were now coming down towards us, like lava from a volcano or savages across a plain. They were baying like hyenas – they could smell the blood of victory – and were rejoicing in our hopelessness. Bar a miracle, it looked like the end of me and Andrew John. We were going to get chopped to death – no two ways about it.

Not so fast. Thank God for the narrow stairwell. As the stairs were only about four feet wide, the attackers could only come down two at a time. Their massive frames had been funnelled into a tight space. Luckily, both Andrew and I had our machetes and were fighting them off, making good work of their flailing arms and legs. We had our backs against the wall and a defensive shield of cold steel as our front line. As a result, they couldn't outflank us, and their tactical advantage of overwhelming firepower was gone. It was like we were the Spartans and they were the Persians coming down the mountain to get us. We were seriously outnumbered, but, because it was such a narrow pass, they couldn't get at us. The battlefield was just too small for them. The angle of the staircase also gave us a major advantage, as it meant our eye-level met with their foot-level and we were in prime position to hack into their shins and calves as they prepared their descent into the fray, cutting them off at their jump-off point. The two of us were holding off over thirty men – sounds mad, but it's true.

Suddenly, somebody called The Destroyer hurled an axe at us from the top of the stairs, trying to smash our defence. He knew that if he could take one of us down, our line would fold. I moved my head in the nick of time, and the axe went straight through the little glass window behind us. Smash! Like a gift from heaven, the crash awoke Aldous from his fear-induced trance, and he unlocked the door.

Once inside, there was no time for a steward's inquiry about Aldous's loss of bottle. I had the phone number of one of the bodybuilders' main men, so I called it and shouted, 'Come and do your worst! There's only four of us. Let's have it.'

After barricading the doors, I climbed up to a ground floor window to see what was going on outside. I was not prepared for the sight that greeted me: one of my top martial-arts instructors was flying towards the entrance. His name was Sensei Gary Spears, 7th Dan Goju-ryu and karate instructor. He was a giant six-feet-seven-inch Maori weighing about 24 stone, and he had a long flowing mane of hair down his back. His feet were so big that he could only wear sandals. He had been to Japan, where he had fought the masters and beaten them at their own game.

He shouted, 'I want to see the fucking black guy that's causing all the problems.'

This was the second miracle of the day. The martial-arts code dictated that I had to defer to and respect my *sensei*, so I immediately opened the door and walked up the stairs. My opposing warriors stopped in their tracks and parted. I walked over to the *sensei* and bowed to him. I turned to his men and said, 'I've got to respect this man. He's trained in martial arts. He's my instructor. Do what you will to me, but I cannot take up arms against him.' I'll tell you straight and honestly – he'd have ripped me to bits. He'd trained me to fight, and I was in awe of him, psychologically and physically. He would've just broken me up.

In response, Sensei Spears said, 'Fucking hell, guvnor, it's you! Come 'ere.' He got hold of me and said, 'Why didn't you tell me it was you?'

Relieved, I said, 'What the fuck are you doing here?'

'Have a look up there,' he replied and pointed to a balcony on a nearby house. I could just about make out a man holding a gun, trained on me. Sensei continued, 'Do you see him? He's an ex-army sniper. We brought him here to assassinate you.' Sensei waved his arms to the sniper to signal that it was all off. 'As it's you Stephen, we'll sort it all out,' he said. We shook hands, and that was that.

After that, the nightclub became a cash cow. We joined forces with Sensei and his gang, and did the old protection racket on the club. Any time there was a problem, the manager would give me and A.J. four or five nights' work at exorbitant rates. So, every few weeks, we'd ask Sensei and his mob to go in and smash a few plates. We'd get the contract and split the money with them.

This episode had taught me another valuable lesson: to abide by my own set of values. By staying true to the martial-arts code, I had saved my own skin and brought about a successful outcome. Unfortunately, this lesson proved to be short-lived, as I began to break my own rules – with devastating results.

13

PLAYING DEVIL'S ADVOCATE

The Hull connection and our protection rackets had taken off – but it wasn't enough. So, in 1989, I opened up another route smuggling cocaine. Andrew and I smashed it and made money hand over fist.

Then one day, a member of the gang called Romy Marion came to me and said, 'I need two grand out of the kitty.' I gave it to him, because it was fuck all to me.

A few days later, a woman came to see me and told me that Marion had been getting high on crack cocaine and that it had become a big problem for him. When I saw him next, I said to him, 'Where's the fucking two grand?'

Of course, he replied, 'I spent it.'

Now, in hindsight, I should have left it there. Trying to get £2,000 off a crack head is chasing dead money. Also, he was a mate, so it was against two of my personal rules to do him over for it. But I couldn't let it go: two grand is two grand.

After threats were made, Marion tried to make up the loss by offering a benefit in kind. He gave me a tip-off about some potential tax work involving a drug dealer called Samuel. Marion thought that he could get himself off the hook by returning the £2,000 commission on the money I was going to tax from Samuel. He reckoned I could score £100,000 off the guy. So, one night, I got my gloves and mask on, and went to Samuel's ken. A.J. wasn't around that night, so I took a lad with me who had been asking me for some tax work – his name will go with me to the grave. Inside the flat, we searched high and low but couldn't find the money. Me being the determined individual that I am, I decided to wait for this lad Samuel to come home so I could make him tell us where he had hidden his stash. I grabbed a big knife and a baseball bat, and crouched down in the dark, ready to jump on him as soon as he walked in the door.

One hour later, I heard the key in the lock and a shaft of light poured in as the door opened. I couldn't see who it was at first, because the figure was silhouetted. However, as he turned his head, I got a glimpse of who it was. For fuck's sake! It was Val the getaway driver from the Solid Gold Posse – my old crew. He was a very old and trusted friend. I'd been given jarg info by Marion – there was no Samuel.

Now, as you will remember, one of the golden rules was that I didn't rob anyone I knew. I only robbed strangers, so I couldn't do it – I couldn't tax him. What's more, I actually liked Val. I'd been in a lot of hairy chases with him, and he'd got me away on every fucking one, thus keeping me out of prison. *I was indebted to the guy.*

I lashed the tool and the bat on the floor in front of him and said, 'Don't move.' That was my signal to let him know I didn't mean him any harm and that I would not take up arms against him. If I'd been looking to rob him, I'd have whacked him senseless. Instead, I just wanted to make off without revealing my identity. However, he went for me. I didn't really want to fight back, so he was able to pull my mask off. 'Aaaahh, it's you Frenchie, it's you,' he screamed. Then, in a moment of panic, I whacked him once, knocked him out and got off.

Word quickly spread around the ghetto about what had happened. My name on the street was mud. Val was still part of the Solid Gold Posse, and they were still the main people from the black area. They were disgusted that I could do such a thing to one of our own. I was so enraged by the mess Marion had got me into, I decided that I was gonna kill him. I didn't mean just beat him up – I was gonna chop his fucking head off.

When I found him, I hit him on the back of the neck with a machete. He went down, stunned, and rolled over. I was now in prime position to chop right into his head. However, he suddenly got a second wind. It was like the crack cocaine was acting as an anaesthetic, making him immune to the pain and giving him the strength to fight back. He curled up on the floor and managed to put his leg up to protect his head, and I cut right into his flesh and bone. I kept on hacking through his arteries and sinews, but they wouldn't give way. The crack had got him bad, so I pulled back – breathless and covered in claret – and jumped into my car. As I got off, I ran him over for good measure. I thought he was dead – five chops to the head and neck and virtual amputation of his left leg. He'd ruined my reputation – I wanted him to suffer.

I then went to see Val, who was still in hospital after my attack, to argue my case – not out of fear, but because what had happened was a cunt's trick, and I didn't want my name associated with it. 'Val, I didn't know it was you,' I said. 'It was a genuine mistake.' By the end of the visit, I still wasn't sure whether Val believed me or not, but at least I'd got it off my chest and done the honourable thing.

Meanwhile, Marion had also gone into hospital with his savage, life-threatening injuries. He didn't fold under questioning, but the doctors reported the incident as a matter of routine. Before long, the police had launched a full-on attempted-murder investigation. It didn't take long before my name was thrown into the frame and the bizzies started to hunt me down.

As a result, Marion had realised that the situation had got out of hand and had checked himself out of hospital. He came to my house to make peace and have his say. At first, I didn't want to know, but he kept shouting through the letterbox, 'I know you're in.' Eventually, I opened up, and he started backing away from me, right down the path. I guess he didn't know how I was gonna react, so he was keeping his distance. He told me that he'd had a nervous breakdown, and was using crack to try and cope with it.

However, in spite of his explanation, I still couldn't forgive him for setting me up. 'You knew it was Val's flat,' I said, 'Val has got me away from several robberies, and the only reason I didn't twat him as soon as he came through the door was that it was him. All I was trying to do was get away, and I whacked him out of panic.'

Now, little did I know, Val had also checked himself out of hospital and was on the warpath. The drugs had worn off, and, in the cold light of day, he'd rejected the explanation I had given him at the hospital. He'd gone home to get his Magnum and had vowed to kill me. In fact, at that very moment – though I didn't know it at the time – he was sitting outside my house in some bushes, right next to where Marion was making his speech. Apparently, he'd been there for a couple of hours, lying in wait for me. He was gonna zap me right there and then on the doorstep. However, his plan had been thwarted when Marion had turned up.

Finally, my pay-off line to Marion was, 'You told me it was a guy called Samuel in the flat with the money, not Val. I wouldn't have gone into Val's flat, cos he's a mate of mine.'

When Val heard this, he was totally gobsmacked. Basically, he'd heard the non-partisan truth for himself and realised that I was completely innocent. He uncocked his Magnum – it's like a fucking hand cannon, by the way – and slipped back to the ghetto, piecing together the whole situation.

I know all this because Val caught up with me a few days later and said, 'You know what, Stephen? I was in the bushes. I was gonna smoke you, but I heard the truth. If you woulda said, "So fucking what about Val, blah, blah, blah, and I wanted to rob him anyway," I would've wiped you clean off the path.' He would have, as well, all Magnumed-up, Dirty Harry-style. Did I feel lucky? Yes, indeed I did.

Anyway, I soon got nicked for the attempted murder of Marion. I made bail, but the police banished me to Wales, banned me from Liverpool and prohibited any contact with the community. However, there was no way I was going to miss carnival weekend in August, a great time in the Afro-Caribbean community. Plus my brother was the organiser of the Merseyside International Caribbean Carnival, and I wanted to be there to give him some moral support. So I bought an afro wig with a beard on it as a disguise. I walked around and brushed past people that had known me for over 25 years, and they were none the wiser. I stood next to bizzies, but they didn't even notice. I then bumped into an old mate called Stephen Brown and said, 'Yo, Brown, what's happening?'

He gave me the strangest of looks, as if to say, 'Who's this guy? I don't even know him.'

Then, I said, 'It's me, man. It's me – Frenchie.'

Well, the guy fell on the floor and burst out laughing. That's when he told me, 'You look like "Afro Man".' If you remember the song 'I was going to do my work but then I got high', that's what I looked like.

This little charade taught me the beauty of disguise – the fact that you can be right on top of somebody who has known you from birth, but they won't even see you. I began to use this to great effect in my taxing by dressing up white men as police to gain entry into drug houses – my trusted friends: subterfuge and misdirection.

Anyway, it all got sorted. Someone had a word with Marion, and he withdrew his statement. He is actually my friend now, and I'm godfather to his 18-year-old daughter Rebecca. People are amazed that despite our history we're close. Nevertheless, I have two words for them: crack cocaine. This drug can turn the most normal of people into the vilest of creatures. It can turn a devoted schoolteacher into a violent abuser of his pupils, a priest into a molester of his own flock and a middle-class student girl into a prostitute.

A few days later, the wife of one of my friends came into the club. She was a lovely girl – a churchgoer and a model mother who'd never once been unfaithful. She wore floating floral dresses, had a severe bob and liked to bake cakes. Anyway, she had a line of Charlie on her birthday when she was drunk, and the next minute we caught her in a cleaning cupboard upstairs having a three-piper with some of the doormen – one up the front, one up the back and one in the mouth. A three-piper with her goody two-shoes dress in ribbons and her cotton panties in shreds at her ankles as these monster bodybuilders threw her about.

It is a demon drug in more ways than one, and it was about to get me into a hell of a lot of trouble.

14

THE PRINCE OF DARKNESS

Shortly after the Marion incident, a tax tip came in about some African drug dealer called the Chief, based on the south coast, so we decided to go down and rob him. It was the usual caper – I gave the Blagger ten grand to pose as a dealer and pretend to buy whatever so that he could see what the Chief's stash was worth and then call me in for back-up.

The Blagger went into the Chief's flat, while I waited outside. Sure enough, the phone call came as planned. He said, 'There's ten kis of cocaine, ten kis of heroin and a load of cash.' Within seconds of the call, I had burst into the ken. There were about 25 people in the flat. I quickly gathered about eighteen of them into one room to get control of the situation, while the Blagger stayed in the adjoining room with the Chief and his hard-core henchmen. The Blagger's job was to get him to hand over the gear and the money.

However, he was tough and refused to give it up without a fight. So, one of the lads with me called Johnny grabbed his baby and hung it out the window, which was about seven floors up. He threatened to chuck the baby out if the Chief didn't give him what we wanted. This is something that I utterly condemn and would never do. However, I didn't know that this atrocity was taking place, cos I was busy in the other room. Later on – because it was my operation – I would get the blame for the Blagger's action, adding to my reputation as the Devil.

Meanwhile, some of the neighbours had seen the baby dangling over the veranda – Wacko Jacko-style – and had telephoned the police. By that point, the Chief had given the bags of heroin and coke to the Blagger.

I told him I wanted the people in his room brought into mine, so that everybody could be brought under control in one space before we got off. Just as he was bringing the last person in, there was a bang, bang, bang on the door – police.

Immediately, the Blagger threw the heroin–coke combo out of the window, but, unbelievably, some of the stuff landed on a small ledge beneath it, and there was no time to brush it off before the bizzies came in. Within milliseconds, I'd taken my balaclava off, hidden my tool and mixed myself up in the room full of people. In the fray, I'd even grabbed a seat in front of the TV. I was totally confident that no one would grass me up, because that's a game of Russian roulette. Why grass me up when there is 20 kis of their gear in the vicinity? It was in the interests of all of the criminal fraternity in the room to get rid of the bizzies, so that we could sort it out between ourselves.

The copper said, 'We've just had a report of a little kid hanging out the window.'

I didn't say anything, just carried on watching *EastEnders*, keeping an eye on the door. Then, two more coppers came in, and I could hear more coming up the stairs. Some of the people in the room just said that it was all a domestic, a bit of a party that had got out of hand. The police were suspicious at first, but then they began to buy it – it was just a family squabble, nothing more.

Soon, to the collective relief of everyone in the flat, the bizzies started to file out. But as the last one was on his way out the door, something caught his eye. Suddenly, he turned around, his eyes fixed on a net curtain fluttering out of the window. I looked at the window and then looked at him. He moved his gaze down towards the ledge. 'What's this?' he blurted out. 'Whose is this?'

'For fuck's sake,' I thought. 'Here we go.'

He bolted over and scooped up a mash of white and brown

powder from the ledge. The hard-core users in the room baulked at the sight. He immediately got on the blower, and, within seconds, the bizzies filed back into the flat. They grilled people left, right and centre, but nobody claimed responsibility for the drugs, so they called for more back-up. We all got nicked and were taken to the police station. It wasn't long before they found my gun and my bally in the flat. Of course, I said fuck all. They also found the money – they found everything. Not good.

At the station, a bizzy came into my cell, 'One of the people in the room has told us everything. We know what happened. We know everything about you. You're that taxman from Liverpool, and you were down here to rob them.'

I replied, 'Nah, I don't know what you're talking about,' totally blanking the suggestion.

'Anyway,' he said, 'I'm not interested in you. You're just a villain from Liverpool. He's a major drug dealer. He's been a major thorn in my side for years, and I want rid of him. If you make a statement against him, you're home. End of story.'

I retorted, 'I don't believe you, mate. I don't believe a word you're saying.'

He then went and got the Blagger from another cell and shoved him in with me to let us conspire. This was against the rules, so, at that point, I knew the copper was serious. If we dobbed the Chief in, we would be free to go. Of course, no one wants to grass anyone up, but I said to the Blagger, 'It won't be like informing. We'll make the statements, and then we'll just fuck them off and hide when we get up north. When they try and find us for the court case, we won't turn up. We'll just give them a jarg statement for now to say that the drugs were in the flat but had nothing to do with us – we were just doing whatever. It's a win-win.'

This decision would later come back to haunt me, and I would get a reputation for being a grass.

Anyway, we got out, and as planned the Chief's court case later collapsed because we didn't turn up.

Now, that should have been that, but, me being me, I couldn't sleep at night knowing that I'd actually *lost* money on the venture. Remember the £10,000 I'd given to the Blagger? Well, that had gone skew-whiff in the scuffle during the police raid and had been confiscated by one of the plods. Knowing that it was gone for ever was niggling at me. I just couldn't live with myself, having not balanced the books. It was chasing dead money, and I told myself to leave it. Nonetheless, the darker angels of my nature got the better of me once again, and I phoned the Chief up, pretending to be the Blagger.

'I want my money,' I said.

'No,' he replied. 'I've done months of remand because of you making a statement. You can't ask me for that.'

I shouted, 'I don't give a fuck how much fucking jail you've done! If you don't give me the money, I'm going to fucking come down there and kill you. I'm going to burn you, set you on fire, do this, do that, do the other.'

Now, in the past, I've had some bad experiences with tape recorders, so I wasn't saying anything too bad – just telling him off a bit. It seemed to have the desired effect: he soon folded under pressure and agreed to meet me to return the money.

In November 1990, I jumped the rattler to meet him in Brighton station. The place was packed. As I was waiting, I gave a fiver to the tramp sitting on the floor next to me – the poor cunt. Still no show. I was there so long that the cleaner had to brush up around me. I bought a cup of tea for a beggar by the phones. The sheer number of tramps in the station got me thinking – there seemed to be a lot of homelessness down south. How could that be? Not that I was arsed. It just got me thinking.

Just as I was about to give up, I looked up from my copy of *The Guardian* and saw the Chief waving at me in the crowd. I bounced over to him. At that instant, everyone around me appeared to come to life: the tramp next to me, the skinny twat beggar by the phones, even the cleaner who had been pottering around me. Oh, dear! They were *all* fucking bizzies. And here I was, the voice of social conscience, thinking that Brighton was suffering from a plague of poverty and homelessness when the real reason was that the dossers were really undercover police. It was fucking horrible. Every one of them was a fucking policeman. A fake toilet attendant put the cuffs on me, and a phoney British Rail guy started to read me my rights. Pure cop-show fare.

The detective in charge said, 'OK, Blagger, you're nicked.'

Of course, they still thought I was the Blagger. However, the Chief soon put them right. He said, 'That's not the Blagger. That's his boss. He's the one – the taxman, the killer, the murderer. He is *the Devil*.'

The bizzies must have been thinking, 'This is great. We've got Mr Big. The Devil no less.' They were having a much better day than they'd expected.

That was just before Christmas 1990. How was that for a fucking present? I'd been a fucking fool, too right. Before I knew it, I was in a sweatbox – one of those long white prison vans with little windows for transporting inmates between jail, court and police stations. Each con sits in a little locker about 20 inches wide. It was very cramped and claustrophobic for a feller my size. I looked out of the window, and I could see the white facade of Pentonville Prison in north London.

I got put on the fours (the fourth landing) on C wing. The bizzies came to see me, and one of the detectives told me that my goose was cooked – that I was fucked. I was thinking, 'Well, what's the big fucking problem here. I've only told someone off down the phone. I'll be out of here once my briefs tie you in knots.'

However, he told me that it was serious and that they were going to charge me with two counts of blackmail. I said, 'Blackmail? Fuck off! What are you on about? I was only talking shit down the phone and that.'

However, there was a problem. This was around about the time of a famous poison plot involving Cadbury Creme Eggs. A man had been trying to extort money out of Cadbury by phoning up and pretending that he had spiked their chocolate eggs with poison. He hadn't actually done anything at all, but he still got ten years in jail for trying it on. The police were putting me in the same category. Blackmail was all the rage in the papers at the time. It was *the* de rigueur crime, and I was gonna get the full fucking *Daily Mail* pasting. The bizzies were gonna offer me up as a sacrificial lamb on the altar of public opinion and load me up with ten years – no back answers. All for talking shit down the phone. Can you believe that shit?

As if that wasn't enough, I then met my new prison guards. One looked me right in the eye and said, 'There's only one thing I hate worse than Scousers and that's black Scousers.' He then lifted up his lapel to reveal a National Front badge.

'That's all I need,' I thought. That was when I knew I was well and truly fucked.

15

THE GRIM REAPER

A lot of the top hard cases gave it the 'Big Time Charlie Potatoes' in the shovel. However, I kept my head down, didn't mention I was a world-champion kick-boxer and defo didn't mention I was the Devil. However, some inmates took my low-key demeanour as a sign of weakness.

As I'm a big, athletic man, the claustrophobia of prison soon started to wear me down. My only escape was the visits. One day, my mum came to see me and said, 'I'm glad you're in here.'

'What!' I gasped, hardly believing my ears.

'You're in jail for a reason, and I know it's for the good,' she continued.

No way. I couldn't believe it. My ma *wishing* the shovel on her son. Deep down, I knew that it was just the Irish in her – she's a bit of a psychic, and I think she said this because something inside her had told her to. *Her* spider senses had triggered for an as yet unknown reason. Nonetheless, for me, it was a sledgehammer. It robbed me of my only asset: hope.

When I got back to my cell, I started crying my eyes out, thinking, 'No one fucking cares. Even me ma's glad I'm in fucking jail.'

My cellmate turned to me and said, 'I thought you were supposed to be a hard-case Scouser. What's all the fucking tears for?'

Before he'd finished his sentence, I'd got him by the neck and lifted him so his feet were off the floor. It was only a bit of a go-around, but the NF guard ran into the cell, jumped in and immediately gave me a cuffing. He then got some other guards to bash me up, and I was subsequently moved to B wing.

After that incident, I decided that I was going to kill the NF guard. Luckily, I had fallen in with a lad called Dillon, who was connected to a big family of London gangsters. He persuaded me to lay off the bad screw. 'You don't have to have him,' he said. 'I'll get my family to sort it out.'

Three days later, the NF guard knocked on my cell door and said, 'Mr French, I won't give you any more aggravation. I won't ride you any more. I didn't realise . . . ' blah, blah, blah. True to his word, Dillon's family had boxed it for me.

One Sunday morning in early 1991, I was doing the 7.30 a.m. slop out when some lad on the fours shouted over, 'Frenchie, some lad's been killed from your neck of the woods. Do you know him?'

A murder still made the national news at that time. These days you'd be lucky to find a few lines about it in the *Echo*. I went back into my cell and listened to the 8 a.m. bulletin on Radio One, hoping that it was one of my enemies who had been ironed. There was nothing like starting off the day in jail knowing that great tragedy had befallen one of your rivals.

Suddenly, the relevant story came on and gave a bit more info – a karate champion had been gunned down. A feeling of dread came over me. 'What's his name?' I whispered into the tranny, biting my lip. The announcer shot back, 'Andrew John, shot dead in Liverpool.'

I looked at my cellmate and said, 'That's my brother.'

He said, 'What?'

I said it again, 'It's my brother. He's been shot.'

I was shocked and numb but not crying, as I hadn't taken it in yet. My cell door then opened, and the wing governor and a doctor walked in. The jail had already been phoned from the outside and told of the connection between me and Andrew. OK, he might not have been my blood brother, but everybody had classed us as siblings. We may not have come out of the same woman, but we had lived like brothers for a long time.

The doctor tried to give me some tablets. I said, 'I don't want no fucking medication.' A priest then came into the cell, but I fucked him off as well and said that I wanted to make a phone call. I phoned Stephen's mum and asked her, 'Who killed him?'

'Val, the getaway driver,' she said.

Val, who I had knocked out during the mistaken taxation of his ken. The same Val who had been waiting in the bushes for me with the piece. Maria filled me in on the details. After I had whacked Val and we had made up, I had given him two grand in compensation to see him all right. He had taken the money off me, saying, 'I now believe you didn't know it was me, which is why I didn't shoot you.'

That should've been the end of it, but, apparently, after I had gone inside, Andrew had reignited the dispute. He had said to Val, 'You fucking cunt, taking two grand off my mate in the jug after he didn't even know it was you.' Andrew had then made out that Val had threatened to go to the police if I hadn't compensated him. He said, 'You took two grand off him, otherwise you were going to the Old Bill. What kind of a fucking villain are you? Let's have it right.'

Anyway, he kept riding the guy and eventually got the two grand back off him. However, he then wanted more and more dough. He started taxing Val, taking a Mercedes from him. Val was terrified and humiliated. Even his family were ashamed of him. Apparently, Val's dad had wound him up even more by saying, 'Val, if you were back home in Jamaica, you would have to do something about him. Andrew John just thinks you're a bitch.'

So, Val had his dad telling him he was a bitch, and he had Andrew John pressuring him. He was coiled up in fear for his life – a terrified animal. So what did he do next? He lashed out and shot his tormentor. He sneaked up behind Andrew and put four bullets in his back. He didn't face him and shoot him from in front, because he was so scared.

At that moment, everything became clear to me – it was like a lightning bolt of truth, searing down from heaven. *That* was why my mum had said I was in jail for a reason. As I was the cause of all this, Val had more reason to kill me than Andrew. Also, if I had been on the outside, he would have assumed that I was pulling Andrew's strings, egging him on. The only reason I'm alive today is that I was safe in a prison cell.

However, I was in Pentonville, and my world had fallen in. I had been holding everything in since I'd been inside, but now I had a reason to let everything out, and I began to bawl and cry. When my brothers came to see me later that day, they smuggled in a two ounce piece of weed to get me through the mourning period. Usually, I'd have stuck the weed up my arse to get it past the screws. However, that day, my head was so up my own arse that I simply put the lump in my hand and walked brazenly past the screw. He spotted it immediately. 'What's that?' he growled.

I told him, 'I fucking need this. You're not taking it off me. My brother's just been killed, and that's that.' He looked at me and could see my head was done in.

'Go on, Scouse,' he said. 'You can go through with it, just this once.' He showed me some compassion that day, and I've never forgotten him for that kindness.

Back in my cell, I cut the toes off a sock to make a black armband in remembrance of Andrew. But, my God, you couldn't do fuck all in there without some shitbag trying to have a go. As soon as I came out of my cell, one of the inmates started sneering and jeering. 'What the fuck have you got that on your arm for?' he said.

Now, this prick had been riding me for weeks. Nonetheless, I'd kept my nose clean, saying nothing and not letting him know what I was really like. However, showing disrespect to the dead *and* the mourning was a different matter. I grabbed him by the bottom of his jeans and pounded him with my fists before throwing him off the fourth-floor landing. Luckily, the safety net caught him, but he had broken his arm. The screws came for me, but there were no witnesses. Then, some of the lads said to the top screw, 'Frenchie did what he had to do. The other lad was bang out of order.' As a result, the matter was dropped and nothing more was said.

Soon afterwards, I was called in to see the governor regarding my application to go to the funeral. When I got to his office, I saw that he'd drafted in a squad of muftis. Muftis are specially trained riot-control officers who specifically work in prisons. They wear crash helmets, black uniforms and protective gloves, and they wield batons to deadly effect. By bringing in the heavy artillery, I knew that the governor wasn't going to let me go to the funeral. The muftis were a precaution, in anticipation of my angry reaction. I had read the play, so I just wanted to hear what the chief was going to say, out of curiosity.

He immediately launched into a tirade. 'You've come to this jail and you haven't joined in any of the activities,' he said. 'You walk round this jail like you own it.' Apparently, when I walk, I strut. I've been told that it looks arrogant a few times. 'You're not going to your brother's funeral, and that's that,' he said.

At this, I launched myself at him. He was only a couple of yards away, but I only got as far as his desk before the muftis got hold of me. Greased lightning, they were. They fucking murdered me – they slaughtered me and knocked me unconscious for the first time in my life.

On the day of Andrew's burial, I was caged in a padded cell in solitary wearing a straightjacket with dried blood and mucus caked into my nose and my mouth – it was the lowest point in my entire life. 'It can't get any worse than this,' I thought.

I don't know whether it was the licks they'd given me, or whether it was the medication that they had pumped into me to calm me down, or if I was simply hallucinating through lack of sleep, but I heard a whistle from outside. It was the same signature whistle that Andrew and I had always used when meeting to go on an armed robbery or to go out on a tax. I manoeuvred my arse over to the window to hear better, but heard nothing but silence. There was no more whistling.

I'm intelligent enough to know that it could've been a combination of things – natural and physical phenomena – but I chose to believe that it had been a sign from Andrew. I put it down to him letting me know that he was OK.

Andrew gave me strength that day – the courage to have hope, even under the most horrible of circumstances. I was determined to get myself out of that hellhole.

16

COME HELL OR HIGH PURITY

When I got out of solitary confinement, my prophetic supernatural experience had fired me up to fight my case. As if sent by the heavens, a miracle revelation then fell into my lap. After I'd got nicked, I'd retained a firm of top accountants to look after some offshore financial affairs that I had going. During their visits, one of the tax assistants called Sandy took a shine to me. One day, Sandy was looking through my case notes when she came across the real name of the Chief. 'That name rings a bell,' she had muttered to herself.

I didn't really take any notice of her at the time, but a few days later she came to see me on a special legal visit. Breathless and excited, she exclaimed, 'You know that African guy who brought the charges against you? Well, I've done a bit of homework on him, and I've got some news for you – he's a well-known illegal-marriage fixer.'

I sprang out of my lethargic prison slump and said, 'What?'

Sandy went on to reveal how one of her wealthy foreign clients had once been so desperate to stay in the UK that she'd undergone a bent marriage of convenience. You'll never guess who the groom had been – the Chief. Sandy told me how he had caused all kinds of problems for her poor client – blackmailing her and the like – and she'd eventually hired Sandy to protect her assets and stop the extortion. What a stroke of luck! If it was true, the information was gold dust!

I got some phone cards together and called my people on the outside. Although most of the young lads in the ghetto weren't formally educated, there were some who were bright, organised and good with paperwork – good enough to be put on the payroll. I told one of them to go to the main registry office in central London and pull out all the marriage certificates that had the Chief's real name on them. They also started trawling the birth, death and marriage certificates at the main registry offices in Liverpool and Manchester, places where we knew the Chief had drug connections. You could bet your bottom dollar that if he had been selling drugs to little firms here and there, he'd also be involved in other dodgy dealings with them. If I could prove that he was a *multiple* marriage blagger, then I could use it against him.

While I was getting on with that, another stroke of good fortune came my way. There had been a recent explosion in the prison population, and Pentonville had suddenly filled up. One night, I was shipped out on STL11 remand – a special kind of custody – to a police station in Wimbledon in order to make some room for high-priority, non-remand prisoners. My solicitor decided to take advantage of the congested jail and punt for some bail, hoping that the desperate authorities would want to see the back of me for a while. Astonishingly, a judge in chambers agreed to hear the case, but he wanted a £100,000 surety to guarantee that I wouldn't abscond. That was some fucking money, mate, but I had it – no sweat.

I phoned up my mate back home who was looking after my stash of dollars. I said, 'Take a 100 quid [£100,000] out of my kitty and bring it down to London today.' There was a long silence.

'Oh, dear,' I thought. 'What the fuck has happened to my pound notes?'

'Stephen, I've got some bad news,' said the voice at the other end. 'All of your dough has gone.'

I was silent for a moment and then said, 'What? Can you tell me how and why please?' Cue lots of swearing, threats, banging the phone down, etc.

After I had been nicked for threatening the Chief, I had entrusted my money to certain individuals in Liverpool to try and make a bit of profit for me while I was in jail – in order to take care of my family. However, for better or for worse, they had invested it in a big drugs consignment, and the parcel had gone down. I had fuck all left. Can you believe that shit? I had the taste of freedom within my sights. I could almost smell the freshly cut lawns and the strawberries of the All England Tennis Club nearby – and now the rug had been pulled from under my feet. Nevertheless, there was no use complaining. Whatever the reasons, I was still in a cell, and it looked like I was going nowhere fast.

I hit a new low. I was resigned to never getting out. How was I supposed to dig the dirt on the Chief from behind bars? I could only rely on my oppos to a degree – there's no substitute for your good self, is there? Also, if I didn't get the Chief off my case, I was going the same way as the 'Creme Egg Killer', for sure. I knew I wouldn't get a second chance at bail; they'd soon clear the prison out and find a place for me again.

However, just when it was looking hopeless, a guardian angel came to my rescue. Eddie Amoo, my fiancée's dad, was a wealthy guy. He had been a singer in a famous pop group called The Real Thing in the 1970s. They'd even had a number-one hit in 1976, with 'You to Me are Everything'. You'll definitely have heard it at a wedding, and you've probably danced to it. It's a fucking good tune, I've got to admit it. Since then, Eddie had enjoyed a string of top-40 hits, and he'd built up a considerable business and property empire.

Of course, Eddie didn't have a clue what I did for a living. He never for one moment suspected that his future son-in-law worked for the unofficial Inland Revenue. All he knew was that I was devoted to his daughter – and he was prepared to give me a chance based on that. He stood bail for me. Can you believe that?

I phoned him from the court to say thank you. 'Eddie,' I said.

'You know what? You to me are everything.' We both laughed. 'Seriously, I won't let you down.'

If someone other than Eddie had bailed me out, I would have planned to abscond as soon as I was on the outside. Of course, I would have tried to discredit the Chief first, but that would have been a long shot, and I would have been straight on a plane to Holland or Spain or wherever if need be. But, of course, I couldn't do that. I couldn't let Eddie down. I couldn't even just disappear to some far-off place and secretly send him the £100,000 I owed him. I had to do the honourable thing: turn up for court and face the music.

When I hit the street in March 1991, there was no partying – it was straight down to business. Financially, I was down to my last 25 grand – my lowest net worth since 1980 when I had returned from London and lost all my dough to those card sharks. After Andrew had been killed, I'd bought his ride – a top of the range Saab – for sentimental reasons, but I had to sell it to get some money together.

When a professional criminal is facing a sure-fire spell in jail, he will do one thing: try and make as much money as he can to support his family in his absence. Up until that point in my life, I'd always considered myself to be on the periphery of the drug-dealing scene. OK, I'd imported and sold a lot of drugs, but I had never just been a *professional* dealer. I had always had other strings to my bow. The Hull connection had been so fucking simple, half the time I hadn't even touched the gear. I had never immersed myself fully in the drugs culture. First and foremost, I was a taxman.

Now I had come out of jail, was on bail and only had around 25 grand left to my name. I had mortgages to pay, families to keep and the possibility of six years of bird ahead of me. Thus, I made the conscious decision to become a full-time drug dealer – to live, breathe and sleep narcotics. I would personally bring it in by the armfuls if necessary. I would become a one-man drug-dealing machine on an industrial scale. I would flood the streets with as much heroin, cocaine and cannabis – not forgetting our old staple Ecstasy – as was humanly possible. Get paid – end of story.

I had made my decision; I just had to find a way of executing it. I am always planning ahead, looking 16 to 18 months down the road. On that occasion, my timing couldn't have been more perfect. My old friend and rival Curtis had gone from doing 50-kilogram to 1,000-kilogram shipments, making him *the* single biggest drug trafficker in Britain according to official documents which were later published. Warren had first been identified by the police as a rising star in the drugs game in 1991, according to their files, which later came out in the media. His name had come onto the radar during Operation Bruise, a crackdown on a Midlands-based smuggling ring. At that time, they had Warren pegged as a middle-ranking operator. Within months, he had shot up to become the wealthiest criminal in British history, worth an estimated £250 million.

As you may remember, I had started Warren off on his criminal career at the age of 11 when I'd recruited him into George Osu's burglary gang. From then on, we'd both drifted in and out of each other's lives whenever it suited us. Both of us were tough, bright lads, and neither of us wanted to play second fiddle to the other. So, for the most part, we ran in our own little separate outfits, bumping into each other from time to time around the barrio, doing business together when we had to. But there was always friction between us. Even so, deep down, I still wanted to be his partner.

According to the press and the police, Curtis Warren's official criminal history reads as follows: at the age of twelve, he picked up a two-year supervision order from Liverpool Juvenile Court for joyriding. Collars for burglary, theft, stealing cars (four times), robbery, offensive behaviour and carrying weapons were the highlights over the next two years. At the age of 16, he made the papers by mugging a 78-year-old grandma on the steps of a cathedral and was sent to borstal for 11 months.

At 19, he went to an adult prison for the first time for blackmailing a street hooker and her punter in a crude back-street extortion racket. Curtis, being the kind of person he is, used jail to his advantage by networking with senior villains. These white, middle-aged godfathers would come to be labelled the 'Liverpool Mafia' by the media. They were the founding fathers of Britain's drug explosion – men who would later go into business with Curtis and generate billions of pounds of drug money.

Following his release from prison, Curtis turned to armed robbery in order to bankroll his pioneering investment in drugs. He held up a Securicor van with a pistol and a sawn-off shotgun, bashed the driver up and got away with £8,000. However, he was soon nicked and got five years for that one. When he got out again, he still didn't have a kitty, so he went off to Switzerland to plunder sports shops for rare adidas trainers, Sergio Tacchini trackies and Ellesse tops. In 1987, he was caught robbing £1,250 worth of swag from a shop over there and was jailed for 30 days.

At that point, he made the switch from street punk to serious criminal. When he got back to Liverpool, he set himself up as a dealer. He befriended an older, white villain called Stan Carnall, and they started doing business in Amsterdam. Like all success stories, they had luck on their side. They were ticking along, doing one-off shipments of heroin, when they were approached by a newly formed cocaine cartel from South America that was looking for new outlets in Europe. The official story went that Curtis and Stan then linked up with the Cali Cartel's main salesman on the Continent – a 22-year-old kid called Mario Halley.

Back in the UK, Curtis had started networking with the trafficking elite and was soon partners with Brian Charrington, a former second-hand-car dealer from the north-east. Between them, they started shipping in the first 1,000-kilogram loads into Britain. Warren later became a household name – an anti-hero for the ASBO generation. Within months, he was recognised by all the major firms in Manchester, Birmingham, London, Cardiff and Scotland, and was the number-one player in the cocaine game – bar none.

To be honest, I wasn't too aware of the significance of all this at the time. Curtis was just one of a number of lads from around the barrio who was doing very well. However, my newly discovered partner Rodriguez was only too aware of Curtis's fame.

I'd grown real close to my tax accountant Sandy. Her boyfriend Rodriguez, a Venezuelan, turned out to be a gangster in London, although he was very low-key. And, apparently, Curtis Warren's reputation preceded him, even in the upper echelons of London's criminal society.

Rodriguez and I quickly became friends and partners. One day, Rodriguez asked me if I knew Curtis. When I told him that we used to do burglaries together as kids, it was as though I'd told him I was a personal friend of Tony Blair. Totally awestruck, he said, 'You personally know him? So you could ask him to do some work with you?' Who was he talking about here – Bill Clinton? Curtis was a solid platinum underworld legend, and I didn't even know it.

'I wouldn't like to, because it's not that kind of friendship,' I replied but Rodriguez forced, pressured and cajoled me into getting Curtis on board.

However, when I thought about it, I realised it could be the perfect scenario. If I could, I would score off Curtis and ship the drugs to Rodriguez to sell. I told Rodriguez that I would put up the money, but he would have to do all the work, for which he would get half the profits. It's a business principle that's worked for me ever since. Even today in my property empire, I will supply the cash to buy the land and the materials to build the houses, but my contractor partners have to supply the labour, and we split the profits between us.

As I thought this over, I realised that Curtis and I were very similar. Like me, he had a sixth sense. One time, he went to Burtonwood services to collect a £40 million consignment. On an itch of his nose, he allegedly turned his back on it because he had smelled a rat. Now, how much money do you have to have to be able to do that?

As it turned out, no one got nicked that day, and Curtis reportedly had to cover the £40 million loss himself. If you're in the drugs game, there is something called a 'yellow pedal' that usually gets the dealer off the hook in the event of a bust. Say, for example, that the £40 million consignment had been discovered by the bizzies. This would certainly have made the papers. Curtis could then show his international suppliers a press clipping to prove that the goods had been seized through no fault of his own. This clipping was called a yellow pedal, because the suppliers would often be shown a yellow charge sheet to prove that someone had been nicked and that they weren't getting ripped off. This meant that everything could be substantiated, and there was no bill to pay.

After the death of Andrew John – in a strange, grudging way – all our mutual friends were pushed closer together. Whatever the history had been between us, I knew approaching Curtis was worth a try. I had decided that Curtis Warren was to be my saviour.

17

IN LEAGUE WITH THE DEVIL: FWMD – FRENCHIE AND WOZZER MAKE DOLLARS

I phoned Curtis. 'Curtis, you all right?' I asked.

'Who's that?' replied the voice on the other end of the line.

'It's the long fella.'

'Oh, the long fella, what do you want?'

'I need to see you,' I said.

'See me about what? Do you want me to come to your house?'

'You don't know where I live, Curtis.'

'Yeah I do,' he replied. 'You've got those three swords over the mantelpiece.'

Even though we hadn't spoken for ages, Curtis was letting me know that he had me pegged. The subtext of the conversation was: 'You think I don't know where you live? Warning: don't try anything clever with me.' So much was said without being said. One of Curtis's key phrases was, 'Sometimes information is more valuable than gold.'

After the initial verbal fencing on the telephone, I told him that I was on bail, and it wasn't safe for me to meet him in Liverpool. I said that I was moving to Dublin in Ireland until things cooled down. Curtis said that he was frequently in Dublin doing business, so we agreed to meet the following week.

Toxteth's finest – the Young Black Panthers. *The Observer* magazine took a picture of us jumping off a wall at the Anglican cathedral. I'm top left, leaning over wearing a red tracksuit.

The European Cup in Poland.
Warming up before going into the ring.

Training at the Dojo in
Lodge Lane, Liverpool.
Trying to be Japanese.

Malcolm X – no sell out.
As a political activist, I was
a card-carrying member of
the Federation of Liverpool
Black Organisations.

Me and A.J. at my graduation
ceremony in 1988.

At the height of our powers, we
controlled everything. My mum (far
left), Denise Andrews, Andrew John
and a friend's daughters in 1989.

My favourite photo of Dee
on our honeymoon in 1990.

Daddy's delight
at Christmas.

Serious gangster flex.
Me and Andrew John.

Big Daddy shows
his tender side.
Abbey was only four
months' old at the
time of this photo,
but my daughter
changed me.

A recent picture but still as serious as ever.
(© Rohan Tait.)

Samuel L. Jackson came to Kirklands when he was making
the film *The 51st State*.

I've only been to prison once. This photo was taken on
the right side of the bars in 2007.
(© Rohan Tait.)

New Devil, New Danger. My take on the iconic Tony Blair
'Devil Eyes' poster. I use it to promote my political message to the
youth, which is 'put down your guns'.
(© Rohan Tait.)

The Devil's ride. Stephen French next to his new £100,000 Bentley in London's Docklands, June 2007.
(© Stuart Griffiths.)

'You all right, lad?' Warren asked.

'Yeah, I'm all right,' I replied. 'You OK? How's things?'

'Oh, I'm surviving. You?'

'Surviving.'

I then launched into a brief history of the blackmailing of the Chief. I told him all about the statements that I had made to get us out of the police station. The pay-off for telling him all this was that I wanted him to think of me as being a man who he could work with. However, this confession would later come back to haunt me.

Anyway, I told him that I had 25 grand left. He said, 'I'll do you a ki for that.' I asked for more on scrap, so we reached a compromise – buy one get one free. I was getting 50 grand's worth for 25 grand to get me up and running. After that, I'd have to pay for everything up front.

In a matter of days, I was back for more, and business boomed from them on. My out-of-town connection would bake up the gear so that we got £1,200 for the ounce. That meant we made 17 grand on every kilo. From April 1991, we started doing a kilo every three days. That was seventeen grand every three days – roughly thirty grand a week – and we kept that up solid and steady until the end of July. Bam, Bam, Bam. All I had to do was meet Curtis in Dublin, get the goods off him, organise the courier and send them out of town.

Now, the amazing thing about Curtis Warren was that he would actually serve me up himself. He was Interpol's number-one target, the biggest drug dealer in Europe, with NCIS, MI5 and Drug Squad tracking his every move, but he would still take time out to come and sell me a couple of kis in person. Normally, he would have sent a bottom-feeder around with such a paltry amount. However, this deal was special to him. He was back working the street again. This was two kids from the neighbourhood doing business together. No international phone calls, no helicopters in the jungle, no Swiss bank accounts – just two lads from Liverpool grafting in a backstreet.

He would arrive in his own hire car, park two streets away, walk up to the back door of the house I was renting and say, 'There you go, Stephen. Where's my money?' He would then take his dough and leave. It was as raw and up front as that. He actually believed he was untouchable. I guess he had his sixth sense to guide him.

We both had systems in place to arrive at my safehouse. To this day, I go around a roundabout four times, even if I'm just going out to buy a pint of milk. It's just habit. I once went on a private-detectives course and learned about three-car surveillance – the authorities' preferred technique. However, three-car surveillance is easy to spot if you know what you're looking for. I learned how to travel southbound on a carriageway and all of a sudden switch to a northbound carriageway. This meant breaking a few driving regulations, but if somebody mimicked my move, I instantly knew I was being followed.

I also had special mobile phones that allowed me to switch between several numbers without changing the handset. Curtis loved that. He never feared my physical prowess; he feared my intelligence when I showed him things like that.

Everyone in our network kept logs of suspicious cars and detailed descriptions of undercover officers – information that we assiduously shared and disseminated. One day, a dark-haired man from a police unit in the UK was hovering around near my safehouse. I had a kilo of cocaine on me that had just been served up by Curtis. He was trying to appear nonchalant, but I could feel him watching me to see where I was going. I knew that I needed to get off the road, because I was going to get nicked any minute. I walked towards a railway bridge, but there was nowhere to hide. It was a 40-foot drop from the bridge to the ground below. People actually used to commit suicide by jumping off it.

Suddenly, a bend in the road gave me the opportunity I needed. I was out of his sight for a few seconds, so I took full advantage. I jumped over the wall and dropped the 40 feet down to the railway lines. Martial arts had given me incredibly strong legs, and because I knew how to drop and roll, I could do it. You'd be amazed how far a young body can actually jump. I was a world-class athlete at that time, and I could actually vault a six-feet-high wall in a single go. One of my nicknames was 'Frenchie Lightfoot'. You're not catching me – I'm too fast, like the fucking wind.

I scrambled up the grass embankment and relieved myself of the parcel on the way, stashing it carefully. I knew that he hadn't seen where I'd gone. At the top, I slipped through a fence and deliberately came back into view. The whole daredevil exercise had taken less than 90 seconds.

As soon as I got home, they swooped on me. Whoosh. There were three unmarked cars and about seven or eight officers, all in plain clothes. 'Freeze,' they shouted. 'Get your hands up. We want to search you.' Some of them were Irish police, others were intelligence officers from the UK. They frisked me and searched the car but found nothing. They were completely perplexed.

'Where is it?' they asked.

'Where's what?' I replied.

'We know who you've just met.'

'Who've I just met?' I enquired.

Nine times out of ten, the authorities jump quicker than they should. With them, it's all a matter of timing: should we hit the suspect now, or should we do it a bit later? Then again, a few of us top criminals had a major advantage: a sixth sense that saved us time and again from total annihilation. Kenny Noye had it. Curtis Warren had it. And I had it.

I gave Curtis a call to warn him. We never talked on the phone – one ring on a mobile phone was the signal for us to both go to a pre-arranged phone box. I used to change my mobile phone every three weeks as a precaution.

Later that night, at around 4 a.m., I got dressed into my black SAS-issue combat gear. I crept into my backyard and carefully took the bricks out of the bottom of the wall, wide enough for my body to fit through. I'd learned that trick after watching a film about a gangster called *The General*. He had dug a tunnel out of his own garden, because the police were watching his front door.

He would go out and rob banks and then come back into his ken through the tunnel. I slithered out into the night, stayed off road all the way to the railway embankment, collected the gear and sold it for 42 grand.

Although I was living in Dublin, I frequently commuted back to the UK to see my family. If I was home, I'd stay in London and train at a very well-known boxing gym in the capital. I kept my training hours religiously, so Curtis would come to the club to see me when he was passing through London. Villainy goes hand in glove with boxing, right back to the Krays.

On one occasion, we were discussing my near miss with the police. 'That wasn't your heat,' Curtis said, 'that was my heat.' He then explained how the authorities were fast closing in on him.

We were standing by a wall outside of the gym and steam was coming off my sweat. 'Why do you do it, lad?' I asked. 'You've got hundreds of millions of pounds. I do it because I'm going to jail and I need the money.'

Another rule in *The 48 Laws of Power* states:

> Never outshine the master. Always make those above you feel comfortable and superior. In your desire to please and impress, do not go too far in displaying your talents or you might accomplish the opposite – fear and insecurity. Make your masters appear more brilliant than they are, and you will attain the heights of power.

I was doing this shit instinctively, without even having read the book at that time.

I said, 'Fucking hell, Curtis. How do you do it, lad? I've only had one bizzy on me, and my fucking arse is like that – gone. I don't know how you can cope with having a whole division on you.' A sick-looking grin spread across his face. Inside, I could see he was thinking, 'I can do something Frenchie can't and Frenchie is supposed to be the hardest bastard in Liverpool and far beyond.' I reinforced my point: 'You do this fucking 24/7, like it's nothing.'

He said, 'I've got enough money to stop and I wouldn't have to work again. But what am I going to do? Fucking sit at home and watch daytime TV? I do it cos it's something to do, lad.'

He was taking the patriarchal position with me, and I allowed him to, because I was making seventeen grand every three days from the geezer. I was trying to be useful to him, providing him with technology and so on, so that I could continue to curry favour in his court. I was trying to align myself with the king. It's what you're supposed to do as a courtier. You're supposed to align yourself around power but not make it too obvious. Machiavelli had written about it and now I was putting it into action.

Curtis then told me that his motives went beyond the money. He said, 'If I spent 50 grand a fucking day, I couldn't go broke.' He used to drop little lines like that on you to make you start counting up his money, but he never told anyone what he had outright.

I respected what he did, despite the problems I'd had with him over Andrew John. He had outwitted some of the smartest that the opposition had to offer. Also, he followed the rules of engagement: never grassed or compromised himself. I've had it said to me that Curtis Warren's a grass, and I think, 'Go and kiss my granny.' He's just anti-establishment and has been from the day he was fucking born. He was born kicking and screaming, but envious people have said that he couldn't have got to where he did and be as big as he did without being a grass. I would say to those people, 'No, he paid people to get there, and he had the bizzies in place.'

We could have gotten real big together, but there was a fundamental mistrust between us. He knew it was there, and I knew it was there, but we didn't talk about it. Two bulls can't live in the one pen. However, I've still got a massive, grudging respect for the guy. Later, when he went to prison, he did his bird without bitching and screaming. In contrast, when I was in jail, he spread this rumour that I had had a nervous breakdown. He said, 'Frenchie isn't a proper criminal.' That was because I had been to university, had a job and was doing things. My comeback was that I considered myself a twenty-first-century criminal, whereas they were still lagging behind in the twentieth century. The funny thing was that it was still only 1995. There were five years to go until the twenty-first century. I always was ahead of my time.

So, anyway, there we were outside the boxing gym, and I was having a little bit of a cool down. I asked him, 'If I want to start up again, can I come and see you?'

He said, 'Your money is as good as anybody else's, Stephen.'

When I paid him, I always ensured that my money was in five-grand bundles – never a penny short. Curtis loved that, because he counted every penny he got. I'd watched him count his money from the other dealers, and he'd explode if it was short. He'd say, 'That cunt. He gave me a bag with 25 grand in it, and there was only £24,980. The cunt kept £20 for ciggies.' That's how I knew he counted every penny of his money.

Curtis told me that one of his turn-ons was counting money. I've seen bundles of money the size of a couch – four-feet long and three-feet wide. He allegedly used to keep cars in inner-city streets, miles away from Liverpool 8, with bags the size of a man crammed with £10 and £20 notes in the boot. However, no one would look at these cars twice, cos they were bangers. I've seen him reduce the bulk of £100,000 in sterling to the size of a laptop by converting it into 1,000-guilder notes. This was a common practice among international drug dealers, who were always trying to reduce the physical size of their huge piles of cash by converting it into high-denomination foreign notes. A 1,000-guilder note was worth about £300, and Curtis was thought to have 1,000-guilder stashes all over Holland. According to underworld rumours, he had so much English money buried that there wasn't enough time to dig it all up when the notes changed, rendering millions obsolete. But fuck it. There was tens of millions more, reportedly wrapped up in businesses all over the world.

So, that was that. I had made a lot of dough, and I was ready to face prison. Bring it on.

18

LUCK OF THE DEVIL

While I'd been dealing drugs, I'd also been working on my case to try and 'persuade' the Chief into not showing up at court. I was hoping to do this by digging up more compromising information on the arranged marriages he'd been involved in. However, my team of DIY detectives couldn't find any hard evidence.

My barrister didn't know what I was doing behind the scenes, so he took one look at the case and said, 'The best thing you could do is plead guilty.'

I replied, 'The best thing you can do is take your fucking briefcase and fuck off. You're fired. That's not what I want to be hearing.'

The truth was that I was all out of puff, ready to throw my hand in. But one night I stayed up until five in the morning studying the legal papers, looking for a way out. Just as I was ready to turn in defeated and depressed, I noticed something strange. The bizzies had photocopied the Chief's passport, which had his full name on it. But on his statement they had got it wrong in the rush, as bizzies often do – they aren't very good spellers. Not only was it spelled wrong, but it was also back to front. In their ignorance of African names, they had put the surname first. So, all this time, we had been working off the wrong name. Fuck me.

I jumped in the car – wearing my trackies and housecoat – and drove down to the central registry office in Liverpool. I waited outside until it was open and was first in the queue to ask the civil servant if they had anything with the Chief's name on it. I waited around with a plastic cup of tea from the vending machine.

About an hour later, the guy called me to the counter and said, 'Sir, there must be some mistake. We've got this guy down as the groom in four marriages in the same name.' Fuck off! Mistake? Give it fucking here! I took the certificates and dropped £50 to the lad behind the counter.

Within weeks, using the correct name, my team and I had dug up a whopping 17 false marriages in which he'd been a groom or witness. This information was gold dust. I got copies of the certificates and sent them to the Chief. Then I got on the phone and said, 'Right. Are you listening, prick? If you come to court on the day of my trial, these certificates will be given to the judge and you'll be getting nicked.' The dickhead didn't know whether to shit or comb his hair.

On the day of the court case, the Chief didn't turn up. The judge slagged him off for leaving his ten-year-old kid at home, for disappearing back to Africa and for his previous history of heroin charges. To me, he said, 'Mr French, you're not guilty, and the charges are dropped.' My new brief then told me to get arraigned, which meant standing in the dock and saying 'Not guilty' so that I could never be charged with the same crime again.

The first person to congratulate me was Curtis Warren. That was Curtis all over. But, deep down, I was made up that he'd called. He had given me a glimmer of hope that one day I might be invited into his inner sanctum. I wanted to tell him there and then, 'I can take instruction. I can be part of a team. Everybody's got it confused about me. I don't always want to be in charge and be the leader. I just want to be liked and accepted.' However, I knew Curtis was just playing me – hinting at the paradise that could be mine, while at the same time able to snatch it away from me at any time. He was teasing me like a kid.

Curtis, like all powerful people, also showed me he could be totally ruthless. As he was shaking my hand, he was telling everyone I was a grass. People say there's a thin line between genius and criminality. Well, it was fucking true with him. It was true to a lesser extent with me. As I've said before, I reckon it's all to do with having no men in our lives as kids: being raised by women; no dad to show us right from wrong. I was a masculine man but had gotten everything from a feminine perspective. It's like a gasman fitting a leccie meter. He's going to wire it up wrong. Somewhere along the line, he's going to fuck it up and the house is going to blow up. I've looked for explanations for people like me and Curtis. Why was I so ruthless and uncompassionate? I'd rob a drug dealer, and as I was leaving I'd turn around, take my mask off and say, 'It's me, Frenchie. You know where to find me, don't you?' I was testing and proving myself. When I look back now, it's all crap. It's all bullshit. Nonetheless, I believed it at the time.

With Curtis, there was also an extra motivation. All he ever wanted was to be a hard case, a good fighter, like me and Andrew. Andrew and I were like the Krays, and he wanted people to fear him in the same way. However, that desire expressed itself in a different way. Rather than physical violence, he made connections with people who had money and access to huge amounts of drugs. He was one of the few people on the planet to make it pay on a billion-dollar level. Because he couldn't beat people with his fists, like Andrew John, he turned his mind to becoming an intellectual criminal. This is why the police would eventually be accused of having to break the law in order to catch him. Ironically, after he was caught, one of the main quotes used to describe his fabulous wealth was, 'Next to Curtis Warren, the Krays were pathetic minnows.'

The day after my court hearing, I flew straight to the Caribbean for a month-long holiday. I stayed at the Trinidad Hilton, and we had a massive party I met all my West Indian family and had a great time. When I got back to Liverpool, the first thing I did was go and visit Andrew's grave, because I hadn't been allowed to go to the funeral. I was shocked to find that he'd been buried in a pauper's plot. All the lads were millionaires and they hadn't done jack shit. I had a whip round from Curtis, Johnny Phillips and the rest and raised £10,000 for a headstone. The epitaph, written by my Dionne, reads, 'Andrew John. Father, son, friend, mentor, brother, relation. He was not one to turn his back and pretend he did not see. Forgive them for they know not what they have done.'

It was spring 1992. I was thirty-two and had just used up one of my nine lives. I should have been shot along with Andrew John, but, praise the Lord, I had been in jail. Now I was about to use up my second life. In March 1992, a nuclear bomb exploded in the Liverpool underworld – but I was lucky enough to be in a reinforced shelter.

To understand what had been going on, we have to rewind a couple of years. Curtis Warren had been under intense investigation for quite some time. I had felt a little bit of the heat over that one kilo, when I jumped off the bridge, but no one would ever have guessed how bad the heat was on him. In July 1990, Curtis's gang had been infiltrated by an informer. Remember the big-time car dealer Brian Charrington? Well, he'd been recruited by the North East Regional Crime Squad to keep track of Curtis's 1,000-kilogram loads. During the winter and spring of 1991, the Cali Cartel was preparing to send their biggest ever load to Europe – a whopping 2,000 kilograms – using a metal export company as a front. A cool 500 was going to Curtis.

In October 1991, as I was preparing for my court case in the new year, the load docked at Felixstowe. In the first week of November 1991, the ingots reached a haulage yard near Liverpool, where the cocaine was extracted using extra-long drill bits. At that point, the gang was infiltrated by a second supergrass by the name of Paul Grimes, ostensibly a scrap dealer who had been drafted in to dispose of the metal ingots once their precious cargo had been retrieved. Even with two telltale tits on the inside, Customs lost track of the load, and before they could swoop, Curtis sold his 500 for a £70 million profit.

On 12 January 1992, just a month before I was due in court, Curtis received a staggering 905-kilogram load, worth £150 million at street prices. A few days later, an 845-kilogram load arrived in Holland. On 29 March, just a month after Curtis had called me up to congratulate me on getting out of my jail sentence, Customs swooped in and arrested him and 11 others. The biggest bust in history. End of.

Just think, if I had been fully initiated into Curtis's crew, I would have been arrested too. All my criminal life, I had wanted to be on Curtis's team. Now I understood that I'd been frozen out for a reason. Nine lives, man. Someone up there was looking out for me.

It looked like the Devil was all on his own again, so I went back to doing what I did best – taxing. And I did it with a vengeance.

19

THE DEVIL IS IN THE DETAIL

After Curtis was arrested, my drug dealing opportunities dried up, so I started collecting debts for international drug cartels. My first clients were some hard-hitters from London who were owed £750,000 by a notorious Scouser drug smuggler called Paul Bennett. This wasn't a huge amount of money to them, but in the underworld debt recovery is all about the Japanese concept of saving face. These top cockney villains wanted to be able to tell their cronies at the next boxing do, 'That cunt Ben owed me three quarter of a million quid. I had him sorted by a black Scouser.'

The most accurate British gangster film is *Gangster No. 1*, which really encapsulates this culture. There's a scene in the film in which the main characters are all sitting around a table at a charity boxing match smoking cigars when one of them goes to the toilet. All the others call him a fucking cunt behind his back. Then they laugh and joke with him when he returns. That's what it's like.

I arranged to meet up with Ben outside Yates wine bar. As soon as I jumped into his Mitsubishi Shogun, my spider senses shot through the roof. Ben was only a skinny, scruffy kid from Norris Green. He was dressed in a bottle-green Lacoste tracksuit, was wearing trainers and had seven days' worth of growth on his face – he was unshaven and unwashed. I seemed to terrify him, but my instincts were telling me that he was bad for me. I would either end up dead or in jail. There was a dark and inexplicable force at work.

Someone like me has to be very careful around these sorts of guys. They will plot, scheme, trap and kill you. If that wasn't the case, the lions would be ruling the world instead of men. Men cage and trap lions, then feed them meat and kill them.

I've had seven attempts on my life, including four contracts on my head ranging from £5,000 to £30,000. I've had my house petrol bombed, I've been shot at and I've been stabbed. The reason why I'm still here is that I've always listened to my instincts. Sometimes, I'll get up in the morning to do some graft, but if there's a bad sign, I won't do it. For example, if I stumble over a chair or put a hole in my shirt with the iron, I won't follow through with my plans for that day.

So, all I said to Ben was, 'You know what? Forget it, lad.' Then I jumped out of his car. Later on, I found out that if I had pursued those funds, I'd have found myself in a lot of trouble. It turns out that they had a nice acid bath prepared for me.

The next debt I collected wasn't a drug debt. Brian Schumacher, who was one of my doormen, was owed a load of dough by a top boxing promoter after a fight in London. I went to another boxing match and got the promoter in the toilet. I said, 'You think we're all stupid from up north, don't you? We'll have you here and now, mate. You can bring who you want. You'll never walk again.' Consequently, he gave me the cheque. However, it didn't do Brian much good – he later went to jail for killing his stepfather.

During that time, I also took the opportunity to settle a few scores from the past. One day, my mate Kevin told me that he'd been beaten up by a club owner in town. 'What's this guy's name?' I asked.

'Tommy,' he replied.

The name sent a shiver down my spine. As you may remember, this was the same Tommy who had bullied and humiliated me outside a club when I was a kid. This was my chance for revenge. Tommy now owned a club with an ex-footballer. I told Kevin to pretend that he'd lost a 14-grand Rolex in the fight. I then went to see Tommy and could immediately tell that he was a yellow bastard. I told him that I wanted five-grand tax as compensation for the fictitious Rolex.

Tommy spluttered, ''Ere y'are, lad.'

I said, 'No. There's no "'ere y'are, lad" about it, Tommy. You slapped me when I was a fucking kid. I'm not a fucking kid any more. I'm a man.'

'Oh, is that what this is about?' he replied.

'Yeah, it's a little bit about that, and it's also about the fucking watch. You're *going* to pay.'

I hit him in the stomach, right into his big, fat belly. He doubled up and fell to his knees. His mate, the ex-footballer, went to make a move. 'Stand still,' I ordered. 'Don't even fucking move.' He froze, because I'd given him my monster stare. I grabbed Tommy by his hair with my left hand and said, 'I'll be back tomorrow at 2.30 p.m. for my money. Don't think about getting anybody down here to wait for me.'

The next day, I went bare knuckle, because I knew he was a shit house, and my spider senses weren't flagging anything up. I sucked the money out of them and emptied it on a snooker table to check the amount. 'Thanks, gentlemen,' I said. 'Nice doing business with you.'

The moral of the tale is this: don't stand on the young boys of today, because they will be the men of tomorrow – and they will come and find you.

Around that time, I had trouble from an unexpected source – in the form of one of my old karate teachers called Dylan. For years, I'd been harbouring a grudge against him. He was a big, fat cunt who didn't like niggers and hated me because what I lacked technically as a fighter I made up for with courage and heart.

One day, Dylan said to me, 'I'll say what no one else will say to you. You're only a champion because Alfie Lewis has trained you.' Alfie Lewis was the star of our club, the star of the country and five-times world champion.

I said, 'Mmm, I've been training with Alfie for two years. Dylan, you've been training with Alfie for eight years. How many world championships have you won? Or did you only get a silver medal? Get outside, you fat bastard. You're always picking on me, and I've let it go, cos your sons come into this club and Alfie's told me to leave you alone because he needs you for funding.'

However, he shit out of it, so I forced him to drop to his knees and apologise. Humiliation: it's a Japanese thing.

Later, his son came into the changing-rooms and said to me, 'He humiliates me on a regular basis. I've got no problem with what you did to him. I'm glad you did that to him, Stephen.' Then we hugged. Dylan's son ended up a terror in both the martial-arts and outside worlds.

During this period, not only was I avenging my past, but I was still collecting millions of pounds in unpaid drug debts. Whether they were Turkish or South American, the system was the same. I'd leave a message with their top boss, who would call back, screaming obscenities down the phone – how they were going to shag me, shoot me, burn me, what they were going to do to my wife, etc. I would let them finish their little diatribe and then give them some of my rhetoric in return, which usually made them think that they had bitten off more than they could chew.

Now, criminals worth their salt would usually go away and do their research on me before making further threats. The common response to their enquiries would be something along the lines of, 'Fucking hell. Frenchie? They call him the fucking Devil because he's that fucking ruthless.'

Nine times out of ten, I would get a phone call back: 'Er, er, sorry about that. I didn't realise.'

I'd say, 'Oh, you've done your research now? You've found out who I am? You realise now that you might get yourself sucked into some serious violence.'

It's all about tone and intimidation. The great Chinese military author Sun Tzu says, 'Best battles and all battles are fought and won in the mind.' Like when Tim Witherspoon knocked Frank Bruno out because Frank couldn't look back at him during the weigh-in.

In nine cases out of ten, the reputation is a lot bigger than the man. It's all about preserving the myth. I know just how to play up to it. I also know when to play it down. I've learned to utilise and read body language to my advantage. Most people give themselves away with a twitch or a look.

But there is one kind of debtor that it doesn't pay to pressure – and that's family. At various times, I've been owed a total of £36,000 by members of my family. However, I learned to always let the money go after one relative called Larry caused me great problems. After some argy-bargy, I went round to his house to collect the debt. Little did I know, he had shopped me to the bizzies and told them that I was going to be armed. Three police cars swooped on me and told me to get out of my car. Stephen, my son, was in the back. Two police officers came over and took hold of my arms. I'm still a big strong guy, but I was even bigger then, and I spun them round with ease. I then opened my car door and said to Stephen, 'Everything's OK. Don't worry.'

Suddenly, two officers grabbed my ankles and yanked them from underneath me. As my head hit the car, another copper scooped me from behind the neck, and I was rendered unconscious for only the second time in my life. I remember feeling a prickly sensation in my right temple, then I was out.

I woke up in the back of a base vehicle with an officer pointing a firearm in my face. He said, 'If this was South Africa, I could just waste you now. You'd be a dead man.'

I replied, 'Well, fucking go on then!' I then tried to bite the gun. 'Shoot me! Kill me! If that's what you want to do, do it!' I went into madman mode, but I was only acting, because I knew he wasn't going to shoot me. He would have had to endure a 12-month investigation if he had. He was just trying to see if he could make me piss or shit my pants – or start begging and crying for mercy. It was just like at the end of the movie *Angels with Dirty Faces* when Jimmy Cagney says, 'No, I don't want to die, I don't want to die.' Was he really a yellow rat or was he just doing it so that the kids didn't follow in his footsteps?

At the police station, they searched my son's bag and found nothing. At that point, the gun-wielding pig tried to be my friend. I brought up a golly from the pit of my stomach and spat it right in his fucking face. As far as I was concerned, the moment a police officer abuses the power vested in him he enters into the arena of the jungle and the cauldron of the Netherworld. And who's the king in the Netherworld? The fucking Devil, that's who. Just to drive this point home, I *told* him that I would hunt him down to his house and get him there.

I encountered a further example of police brutality outside the Cream nightclub. I quoted PACE at the police, and they jumped on me, beat me up and charged me with a public order offence. It cost me thousands to fight it, but, eventually, the judge proclaimed, 'Mr French has taken it upon himself to research PACE, and he's always dealt with the police in a rational manner.' Thus, I got my conviction overturned.

In my chosen career, high resolve was an essential characteristic for success. For example, one of my relatives called Tom started selling drugs to a dealer in Bradford by the name of Macdonald. Tom was owed about 50 grand off this guy, so he shot his house up a little bit and found himself in jail. It was my job to retrieve the goods. I didn't know anyone in Bradford, but, within two hours, I'd got hold of a guy called West Indian Phil. He thought he was a yardie, but in no time I'd kung fu'd his arse, putting a few moves on him, and he shit out the goods. He told me the money and drugs were hidden in a broom cupboard. This is the determination, tenacity and reserve of STF – Stephen Terrible French. Eighteen months later, someone gave Macdonald a grand to drop the charges.

It was around that time that I started to question my life as a drug dealer. I'd try and justify what I did all the time. I knew that I was selling death and misery: causing kids to be brought up by junkie mothers. Nevertheless, I would say to myself, 'Well, I don't import the stuff. I only sell it or tax those that are selling it.'

I used to justify my criminal actions by concluding that the whole world was corrupt, especially those at the top. For instance, I would rationalise that Queen Victoria had stolen the Kohinoor diamond from India, but, just because she was part of the establishment, it was considered to be OK. Now don't get me wrong. I've got the greatest respect for the monarchy. But, at the end of the day, the current Queen shits and pisses like the rest of us. To me, she is just a human being whose ancestors got ahead by being corrupt.

I was angry, frustrated and searching for something new. I didn't know where to turn. Alas, to fill the void, I made the common mistake that many people make when they are going through divorces and midlife crises. I threw myself into my work – the work of the Devil.

20

HELL'S KITCHEN

Every drug dealer in Britain expected Curtis to get at least 20 years.
After all, he was the perpetrator of the biggest cocaine haul in
history, according to the prosecution. But the jammy twat walked
– on a fucking technicality. The prosecution case fell apart over
the shady goings-on of the informer Brian Charrington. On the
steps of the court, Curtis allegedly turned to the Customs officers
who had worked for years to nail him and said, 'I'm off to spend
the £70 million I made off the first consignment.' His nickname
was 'Cocky', by the way. I was truly made up for him, but I still
thought that I'd had a lucky escape. The key point was that I had
seen the writing on the wall and had got out just in time. Even
though he'd got lucky with this case, I knew that it was only a
matter of time before they rammed it up him again.

In the meantime, Whacker had to go on the run to Holland
and Germany. Before long, he'd sourced a cheap and plentiful
supplier of weed. This coincided with me setting up shop for a
while in a very rich and exclusive part of Europe, where cannabis
was a rarity. I got him to buy 100 kilograms. I paid £700 a kilo in
Amsterdam and sold it for £2,000 a kilo in this European country
– £1,300 profit on a kilo.

The only problem was that for the next load we didn't have
any transport back from Holland. Once again, I was cajoled into
going to a recently freed Curtis to see if he could help – although
I hated asking him for anything.

Every king loves to bestow favours to his underlings. I could see the power trip he was on: 'Yeah, Frenchie. You're back at my fucking table again, mate. I've got to sort your problems out again.' Picture the scene: we were looking at each other and playing a mind game – continual and unspoken – that we both knew was there. On the surface, I was happy to pay lip service to him, but, deep down, the gratitude was a burden.

He scribbled down an address in Germany, close to the border with Holland, and said, 'Have your weed delivered to that address by 4 p.m. tomorrow and you'll have it over here in two days' time.'

Sure enough, our parcel was smuggled into a busy port in a container of motorbikes. Curtis's men then unloaded it into a van and parked it in a pre-arranged place. Later on, when I was given the keys, I summoned one of my £500-a-day men to go and pick up the van.

I said to him, 'We don't know if it's on top or not. Are you prepared to do it?'

He replied, 'What is it, weed? Yeah, I'll go and do it.' This was because nine times out of ten there was nobody watching. Also, if he got nicked, I'd give him a grand and his family would get looked after while he was inside.

These £500-a-day men have super spider senses, and they have a good look around before they open the van. They know how fucking hard it is to hide a full surveillance team, so they're often able to pick up on anything suspicious.

Anyway, the van was collected with the cannabis inside. The first thing I did was make sure everything was there. Whacker, the bloke in Amsterdam, had put it in the container, having wrapped it and given it a particular seal. Each crew has a different seal, and that is how you can tell where certain drugs have come from. Next was the weighing. I always made sure that I was personally present at the weigh-in. However, instead of 100 kilograms of weed there was only 95. That missing weed was worth ten grand of my cash, which equated to a new car and a holiday.

Somewhere along the line, someone had stuck down on us, just as used to happen after a robbery. Up until then, there had been trust and camaraderie between us. Nevertheless, this kind of underworld camaraderie is like Scotch mist. When it suits, it's there, and when it doesn't, it's not.

I had to make a call to Curtis to suss out what had happened to the missing weed. I'm a great believer in contractual law and ironing everything out at the beginning of a deal. So, in my mind, now that it had gone wrong, he owed me ten grand or five kilograms, because from the beginning I'd made a verbal agreement with him. However, if you ever started talking to Curtis on the phone about drugs, he'd just hang up on you, so we arranged to meet up.

Although I was doing business all over Europe, I regularly commuted back to Liverpool. At that time, there was a big gang war going on in the city. This meant that we couldn't meet in our usual haunts, as people were getting shot left, right and centre, so we met in the park. I told him the situation and said, 'Well, you know, you either give me five kilograms of bush or ten grand.'

Curtis said, 'All right, lad, I'll sort it out.'

Although the transport was a favour, he was still charging us the going rate – 100 times £250. That was 25 grand for the delivery. The way I figured it, even if he had to pay us off from his end, he'd still have been up by 15 grand. This was part of his day-to-day business. It was what he was into, what he did best. Not only was he an international trafficker, he was also renting out his transport. He had transport all the way from Colombia, or so the rumour went. He supposedly had lorries full of cocaine in England circling the motorways all day.

The ten grand didn't *really* matter. It was just that I didn't want him to get one over on me. However, I could afford to wait for Curtis to give it to me. In the meantime, I paid off my partners Rock Star and Whacker, who were in on the deal.

Most drug dealers live from hand to mouth. Take my partner

Rock Star, for example. One minute, he'd be driving the best car and so would his bird, and the next he wouldn't even have a pint of milk in the fridge. It was all fast money, so it was spent just as fast.

Eventually, I set up my own transport network, and we carried on shipping weed over from Holland by the tonne. Business was booming, but the ten grand thing kept nagging me. A perceived slight can distort your mind and send you crazy. When I was in Pentonville, Ski Gold yoghurts were a luxury. One day, a top drugs baron did me out of two of these yoghurts. In revenge, I decided to murder him. I spent a month plotting and planning his death, like it was a military operation – all because I was thinking, 'Does he think I'm a prick?' After he stole my Ski Gold yoghurts, I had my eye on the fucker. Now I was having similarly dark thoughts about Curtis.

The funny thing was, my wife used to work at Granada TV, based at the Albert Dock, right next to where Curtis had his docklands ken. Every morning when I was back in Liverpool, I'd take her to work at 8.30 a.m. and without fail I'd see Curtis leaving the Albert Dock. We'd give each other a wave and smile through gritted teeth. I'd give him a wave, whilst saying to Dionne under my breath, 'That fucking cunt again.' But, if truth be known, I could not help but like and admire him. He'd also wave, probably thinking that I was a cunt, too. He always looked at me in a nervous, suspicious way in case I was coming to the Albert Dock to do something to him. Curtis was always very aware that he could be kidnapped, tortured and robbed at any time – when all I ever wanted was to be on his firm.

One time, I bumped into him and said, 'If you're not going to give me my money, I'm going to get it by any which way, because nobody keeps the Frenchman's money.' If you owed me, you paid me. If you didn't pay me, you'd see me. At the end of the day, there was nothing that would stop me, short of a .45 in the head.

As well as this little niggle, I also had another nagging thought at the back of my head. All the time, I was thinking that I was better than this. I knew I could make money legitimately. Inherently, I knew I was worth more than picking drugs up from A, carrying them to B and selling them for X plus Y. All the while, I was questioning my self-worth. Whatever had happened to the world champ? I wasn't doing anything about it, but deep down I knew my current lifestyle was a dead end to nowhere. I didn't find it challenging. The treachery and betrayal had become a headache.

I also found the constant intrusion of the Old Bill disturbing. They regularly pushed my wife around when I wasn't there, and there was nothing I could do about it. When the harassment reached breaking point, I seriously considered taking a policeman out. I actually thought about saying to Merseyside Constabulary, 'Well, OK, let's go to war, shall we?' and then assassinating a copper.

So, like all men under pressure, I started to make mistakes – a lot of mistakes.

21

A PRESSING ENGAGEMENT

I received a tip-off that a drug dealer called Mona had 85 grand hidden away. Needless to say, I wanted it. Marsellus and I kidnapped Mona, which turned out to be a very pressing engagement. Mona refused to tell me where the money was, so I put the Morphy Richards on him. Marsellus held him down while I ironed his arse and his arms with a red-hot steam iron. But the real *coup de grâce* was yet to be delivered – a 90,000-volt stun gun applied to his feet, neck and ears. The fumes from the burning skin and hair made us both baulk. By the time I got to his bollocks with the iron and the stun gun, he was screaming like a bitch. When we got to his pubic hair, he well and truly shit out the money.

We also took his red Mercedes convertible off him, sold it out of town and subsequently bought a brand-new one with the dough. On the way back, I dropped Marsellus off near his house. I went 150 yards up the road, looked in my mirror and saw the police swooping down on him. I had managed to escape by the skin of my teeth.

Consequently, I found myself on my toes in Manchester. Most people think that if you go on the run, you have to go abroad. However, if you follow basic rules, you can stay hidden for years, just miles from your manor. Top criminals like myself – and solicitors defending a case – rely a lot on the apathy of the ordinary police officer. Basically, they're lazy bastards, and the only thing they care about is getting paid. I moved 30 miles up the road, lived under an assumed name, got myself a little flat and set up shop again in an Asian area called Rusholme. I also took the precaution of securing a safe house in Cleckheaton, near Leeds – just in case.

Any visitors from my old life simply had to cover their tracks when they came to see me. For instance, when Dionne came to visit, she would start off by leaving our house in Liverpool and travelling to my auntie's, who lived over the water on the Wirral. Dionne would park her car outside their house, with the police watching it. My uncle would then take her down the back garden and smuggle her into a secret car a few streets away. She would then jump on the train to a place in the countryside before switching to a bus to Manchester. If there had been tail on her, she'd have lost it by then. In the meantime, the main surveillance team would be left sitting in front of my auntie's house, thinking she was in there having a cup of tea.

One day, Dionne came to me with a message from Johnny Phillips. Like me and Marsellus, he was in the shit with the bizzies, and he wanted my help in straightening out a witness. A well-known man in the city by the name of David Ungi had just been gunned down in the street. David was white and the shooters were black, so the murder had triggered a massive gang war between the two communities. I was trying to build bridges through a white cousin of mine called Toby Marshall, who I'd saved from being killed by Johnny and members of his gang. The police couldn't link Johnny to the murder of David, but they were able to pin an earlier attack on him. They had a star witness, a guy called Bubble, who I knew very well. I made a deal with Johnny: if I leaned on Bubble and told him to withdraw his statement, Johnny would in turn lean on the witnesses against me and Marsellus to get us out of our predicament. Mona had snitched on us for torturing him with the iron. I hate grassing bastards who run to the police when it gets hard for them. Johnny came to see me in Manchester to go through the details. As a sweetener, he gave me a Colt .45 and 15 grand before he left.

I stuck to my side of the bargain and slipped back into Liverpool to threaten Bubble. I told him, 'If you go through with this, if you give evidence against Johnny, your life will be over. And even if I don't get you sooner, it will be murder for the rest of your life.'

The next day, a terrified Bubble withdrew his statement and told the police he hadn't seen anything. Johnny was off the hook. I didn't lean on Bubble to cause any offence to the Ungi family; I was doing it to get myself out of a situation. I was trading off one thing for another to solve my problems. Tony Ungi, the eldest brother, is a guy I respect a lot, and I would do nothing to offend him. And that goes for the other brother Joey, too. It was just a case of realpolitik.

The bad news was that Johnny (who was later killed by contract killers) was as full of shit alive as he was dead and didn't keep up his end of the bargain. To add insult to injury, he had the cheek to ask me for his gun and money back. I told him to go and fuck himself. 'Until you've done what you said you're going to do,' I said, 'that's my payment, cos I've kept my end of the bargain.' He knew that he owed me, big time.

The downside of being on the run was that it cost a lot of money to lead a double life. I had both a British and a Russian passport, which cost a few grand. Fake documentation to enable me to hire cars cost hundreds of pounds. I had to buy a different car every few months or get one given to me. Everything had to be bought in cash so that I wouldn't leave a trail. My safe house had to be paid for up front. Furthermore, I had to keep on the move, which meant a lot of hotels – and they had to be four or five star. I wasn't able to cook anywhere, so I had to eat out. You're talking at least £15,000 a week just to keep your show on the road, if you've got a certain kind of lifestyle. Out of that, I had to keep my family going as well – mortgages, new cars, holidays, the works.

To keep the money coming, I started once again to deal drugs at a prolific rate. I used every trick in the book to avoid paying for them, so I could make double the profit. I took counterfeit money with me to buy the drugs. Every week, I'd buy 50 grand's worth of blouse notes for £200 and use it to buy a couple of kilos of cocaine from sucker dealers. I'd put the money in a plastic bag and let them see the cash when I walked in the room. If they managed to touch it or feel it, I'd let myself down. However, just showing a man a washing bag full of money and saying, 'I've got my money, mate,' often put him at his ease. I'd crack a few jokes and be gone with the gear before they'd even cottoned on.

When I was feeling cocky, I wouldn't even bother with fake money. I'd just fill a bag with potatoes and leave the dealers with that. I'd buy ten kilograms of cocaine for the price of a sack of spuds. Some of them would moan and threaten me afterwards. At the end of the day, they were acting illegally, so it was an open playing field as far I was concerned – a gladiatorial arena in which only the fittest would survive. If you can't hack it, get out. Get yourself a nine-to-five. Don't come fucking crying to me cos I've taken something off you. Just come and try to take it back off me. That was my philosophy.

Nevertheless, even by taxing, I still couldn't keep up with my massive expenditure. I had a lot of money stashed away, but sometimes I couldn't get access to it. A lot of people owed me money, so I ended up constantly chasing them in order to keep the cash flow going. I'd been asking Curtis for my ten grand for months. Ten grand to Curtis was like a gnat's bite to an elephant – fuck all. However, for some reason, he still wouldn't give up the goods. I'd even been asking for my dough through his partner Peter Lair, who had a grudging respect for me, because we still had a connection through Andrew John. None of them would tell me to my face that they thought I was a cunt, but I knew they were saying it to each other behind my back.

Anyway, one day, Johnny came to see me about a solution. He was still feeling guilty about his failure to lean on the witnesses for me and Marsellus, and he knew I wanted compensation for it. He told me that he knew where £450,000 of Curtis's money was hidden. This was an example of the kind of treachery that was common in the world of drug dealers. Johnny had temporarily fallen out with Curtis, and anyone who fell out with Curtis always came round to my back door to see the taxman for retribution. They were always coming to see me saying, 'Oh, I fell out with him. He's such a prick, and he's got this here and he's got that there.'

I was only really interested in my ten grand – as a matter of honour. However, if there was a bonus £440,000 going, then I'd have that as well. So I started to plan how to rob Curtis's money. To be honest, I did this reluctantly. If he had kept to our agreement and paid me back the ten large, I would never have done him wrong. But he tried to dismiss me as a minnow when in truth I was a killer whale. I brought in a mate called Mick 'the Scorpion' to help. He was called the Scorpion because he was capable of deadly, extreme and irrational criminal betrayal. He got the name from an old parable: the story of the scorpion and the crocodile. The scorpion says to the crocodile, 'Take me across the river.' The crocodile is reluctant but is persuaded by the scorpion, who explains that he will not sting him because then they would both drown. So the crocodile jumps in the river with the scorpion on his back. Halfway across, the scorpion stings him. The crocodile asks, 'Why have you stung me? Now we're both gonna drown?' The scorpion replies, 'I'm a fucking scorpion, man. What did you expect?' That was Mick – everyone expected him to sting them. However, I understood his philosophy. If I didn't give him the opportunity to fuck me, he'd help me out.

We soon found out that Curtis had two minders looking after the money in the loft of a house – a doorman called Rory and an Arab lad called Abdul. The plan was to get Mick the Scorpion to dress up as a CID officer with fake credentials. He would then blag his way in. I would steam in behind him, armed to the teeth, take care of anyone inside and grab the money.

The stash house was round the corner from a pub called The Dart. On the night of the attack, I sent the Scorpion up to the door. I had my mask and gloves on, my tools to hand and was crouched down in a nearby car. I was coiled up like a spring. My adrenalin was flowing, and I was ready to fly. It was fucking show time.

However, when the Scorpion knocked on the door, all hell broke loose. Rory ran out of the house, shouting, 'I know it's you, Frenchie. Aaaagh!' He then ran down the street, waving his hands over his head, screaming like a banshee.

'Someone's fucking blew us up,' I thought. They must have known we were coming. Rory was terrified out of his wits, because he'd been tipped off that the Devil was coming for him. Mick and I jumped back into the car and got off.

At 10.30 that evening, my mother-in-law was putting out her rubbish. A voice shouted from the bushes, 'Are you Stephen French's mother-in-law?'

She turned round, shit herself and said, 'Why, why what have I done?' She expected to be shot dead.

A man appeared from the shadows. He put his hand in his jacket – and pulled out a plastic bag. 'Curtis Warren sent this for Stephen. It's ten grand.'

Would you believe it? The cunt had finally paid me back.

22

THE DEVIL'S SCORPION

Despite our failure to tax Curtis's men, Mick seemed to think that he had what it took to work for the unofficial Inland Revenue. He'd been cultivating a couple of drug dealers in Liverpool and wanted me to help tax them. They were hard-hitters, who only dealt in five kilogram loads – extreme killers, armed to the teeth. However, they trusted Mick so much that they would invite him round to their stash house. During one of these visits, Mick had even managed to take copies of their house keys, using plasticine, and had his own set made.

The Scorpion was ultra intelligent, ultra confident, 100 per cent focused and had a great personality to boot. He kinda reminded me of Michael Manley, the one-time prime minister of Jamaica. He could slip into yard talk better than I could. He knew everything there was to know about weed. The Scorpion was international – he'd done jail in France, Holland and Belgium. He wasn't a fraidy cat.

It was supposed to be a straightforward job: in and out – plain sailing. The plan was to tax the dealers then lock them in the house to prevent them from following us. On the day of the graft, Mick – armed with a bag of confetti money – went to buy five kilograms of cocaine off them as planned. I waited outside, dressed head to foot in my traditional black clothes. I then put my bally on and got into character. Four minutes later, I went in after Mick. Following his footsteps, I carefully opened the door and crept down the hallway. I knew by their voices that they were all in one room, weighing the gear.

I booted the door in and jumped into the room, larger than life. 'Nobody fucking move,' I shouted. I immediately glared at the two dealers. Their eyes went wide with fear. All they could see was my .45. 'I'm here to relieve you of your drugs. Give me the parcel and nobody'll get hurt.'

I scooped the gear up then pointed at Mick. 'He's with me,' I said. 'He's in on the tax. He's the one you find if you want to do anything about this.' Mick wasn't bothered by this, and it served as a psychological distraction – I had enough heat on me already. Then I threw Mick the door keys that he'd given me to get in and said, 'Lock them in.' This covered our escape.

Our getaway car was a 1.3 litre Corsa. It was all we needed, because no one, in theory, could follow us. In practice, it didn't go quite like that. I had only driven a mile when I looked behind and saw the people that we'd just robbed in hot pursuit. I turned to Mick and said, 'You didn't lock the fucking door, did you?' He sheepishly told me that he'd forgotten.

'Well, there's no time for recriminations now. We've got a serious fucking problem on our hands.' I'm a very serious individual and can keep cool under pressure. I would *never* forget details as Mick had just done. I've often made the mistake of thinking that others are of the same ilk as me. Mick had certainly talked a really good fight before the graft, and I'd really believed he'd known about taxing and the importance of remaining calm under pressure. However, his flaws were becoming clear to me.

Nonetheless, being a professional, I always made sure I had a back-up plan. I would often trawl the streets of Liverpool, planning a contingency to every eventuality. One of the lessons that I'd learned was to use the urban topography to my advantage. I'd once come across a place called Ash Grove, a cul-de-sac. I'd studied it carefully and realised that there was just enough room to slam on in a car. At the bottom, there was a seven-foot wall, and if you could get over it, you were away. Being a world-class athlete, I could vault over this wall in one go. No one would believe it, but one night I'd actually tested myself on this wall and made it. Obviously, most people couldn't do that, so my reckoning was that if I was ever being chased, I could use this advantage to get away. Whoever was following would have to retreat. By the time they'd sorted themselves out, I'd be halfway to Spain. If necessary, I would lay down some light suppressing fire from the Colt to keep them at bay.

I wasn't interested in the Corsa. That could stay in the cul-de-sac. I stopped the car, got out and threw the bag containing the gear over the wall. I then gazelled it and landed nimbly on the other side. I was home free. Not only had I four or five yards on them, there was also a seven-foot wall between us. Nobody was going to catch me. I could run faster than Kip Keino – a great Kenyan runner who used to run in his bare feet.

I looked back when I was about ten or fifteen yards from the wall and spotted Mick with only his elbows and red face visible. He looked like that famous piece of graffito 'Kilroy was here!'. He couldn't for the life of him get over. By that point, I'd lashed off my balaclava and was on show. However, I quickly realised that Mick would be dragged down by these geezers and beaten to within an inch of his life. They wouldn't even have the intelligence to interrogate him and find out where the stuff had gone, who his accomplice had been, etc. They would just set about him like animals. However, I had a ting on me. We had started this mission together, so we had to finish it together. I was duty and honour bound to go back over the wall.

My instincts were screaming at me to keep on running. 'You've got everything you need,' I told myself. 'Fuck Mick. Get back to Cleckheaton. You've got a hundred grand's worth of gear to keep you going.' Nonetheless, the ancient Japanese code of Samurai and my sense of honour wouldn't let me do it.

Unmasked, I jumped back over the wall and punched one of the dealers. 'Get the fuck off him,' I said.

'Frenchie, Frenchie, it's you. All right, Frenchie. We'll back off.'

They put their hands up in a gesture of 'We don't want no trouble' and started to back off. Even during the small beating, they'd managed to fracture Mick's leg. I picked him up. He'd suddenly become Mick the Prick in my eyes. 'Get over the fucking wall,' I said.

Later, we retrieved the car and drove back to Cleckheaton. The danger now was that the dealers knew who had robbed them – I was expecting a call at any moment. Mick was giving it the big 'I am', saying, 'No matter who they are, we're not giving any of the gear back.'

Cleckheaton is a little village near Leeds and Bradford. It's like the place in the 'I'm the only gay in the village' sketch, except in my case I was the only nigger in the village.

As predicted, the phone went. It was Peter Lair. He said, 'All right, Stephen. The five kilograms you took is ours. Those two fellers were selling it for us, and you're going to have to give it back.'

Every fibre in my body wanted to tell him to go fuck himself. I didn't owe him anything. However, at the same time, he had been passing messages to Curtis on my behalf, so I did feel beholden in that respect. I had to weigh up the pros and cons. If I didn't cooperate and Lair couldn't find me, he would go after my family, my friends and my son. Make no mistake, Lair, whether he liked me or I liked him, was not a guy to be messed with. He was a fellow dreadnought, a street fighter the same as me. In fact, Lair and I had been circling each other for a while, and I knew this incident could be the trigger for an almighty showdown between the pair of us.

While I was deciding what to do, Mick was still saying, 'We're not giving it back.'

I said, 'If you'd have got over that fucking wall, we wouldn't have to give it back. But because you're a fat cunt, I had to come back and save your fucking arse.'

Mick hadn't realised I regretted going back for him. I could have sent the coke down south, got a 20 grand deposit straight away and waited for the rest of my money. I could have stayed in hotels again and the £500-a-night suites. My name could have been Michael Winner – a film director – and I could have stayed where I wanted.

Instead, I was stuck in a shit hole of a house in Cleckheaton, with no money, a guy with a broken leg and Peter Lair on my case. I knew I had to give the goods back – not out of fear, but out of respect.

That was the one and only time that the Devil ever refunded a tax – and I did it to maintain the status quo. To this day, Lair and I still haven't had that street fight.

23

MIRACLE ESCAPE

In spite of a few tax setbacks, I was still a free man – even though
I was on the run. My motivation to stay on my toes was simple.
Marsellus had just been given 15 years in jail for his part in the
torture of Mona with the stun gun. If I got caught, I could expect
the same treatment. I was still living in Rusholme and had come
into contact with an Asian guy who kept bugging me about a
deal: 'Do you wanna buy some heroin? I can get top grade direct
from Pakistan.'

I kept saying no, to give him the impression that I wasn't
interested, but all the time I was grooming him for tax purposes.
He kept on and on, and I could tell he was really excited. I could
see it was a challenge for him to get in with the mysterious black
Scouser who was knocking around his manor.

In the end, still feigning reluctance, I agreed to help him out by
offering to shift some of his gear for him. On the surface, I whined
and moaned and told him, 'Oh, go on then. Just this once, as a
favour to you, I'll buy some.'

He brought me a sample of his brown, and I sent it to my boy
in Scotland for testing. That night, I got the call from my man who
said, 'It's high purity. Buy it. It's champion.' I arranged to meet
the Asian guy in his lock-up garage opposite his shop to buy one
kilo off him for £15,550. I only bought the one to make him feel
relaxed and happy. If I had asked for more, he might have felt a
bit out of his league. Slowly, slowly, catchy monkey.

A few days later, the Asian guy said, 'I've got a couple of kis. D'you want them?' I could tell he was getting a hard-on about being in the underworld. It must have been a change from getting up at 4 a.m. and having to chat to the gobshite community-care types who hung around his newsagents in the morning. He was thinking he was Tony Montana. So, in the end, I agreed to buy a couple of kilos from him for 30 grand.

About a week later, he told me he'd just received a delivery of ten kilograms of heroin. I said, 'Well if I'm gonna buy ten, I may as well buy twenty, but you have to give me a better price.'

Greed had now got the better of him, so he came back and said, 'OK, £250,000.'

I said, 'Look, if I want 20, then we do the operation in the garage again.'

He replied, 'Well, OK, but you've got to come by yourself.'

I got some counterfeit money and put it in a big washing bag. I then went to his garage and showed it to him, and he showed me the gear. Now, 20 kilograms is quite heavy to physically run with, so I had the car parked right outside.

The last thing the Asian guy expected was a tax job. He knew my name and where I lived, but what he didn't know was that my name was bogus and the flat was rented. Still, he had brought an Asian bodyguard, just in case. I started haggling over the price and gesticulating with my hands, as you do when you're bartering. 'Look at that hand there – look at my left hand,' I said, pretending as though I was indicating at some part of the transaction. As his eyes followed my left hand, I whacked him with my right. It's one of my little tricks – an old one, but it still works. The Asian guy went down, and I kicked his bodyguard with such force that he flew across the room. I grabbed the gear, and before I knew it I was in the car and away.

I crept back to the flat to get some of my stuff and sent the heroin to Scotland for sale. Wholesale, it was worth £250,000. Ounced up and danced on, we would enjoy a total return of half a million. I slipped back into Liverpool to find a safe house for a few days, before I went out of town to get my dough. On my way there, I bumped into Johnny Phillips, of all people. He dropped a bombshell. Apparently, I was going to be on *Crimewatch* the following week as the poster boy for Britain's most wanted man. There would be warnings out saying how dangerous I was and how I shouldn't be approached, etc. Johnny reckoned the police would find me. 'Things are going to hot up for you,' he said. 'If I was you, I'd get off.'

Now, when a thing like that happens, you know it's time to leave. I'd been walking round Manchester being a happy-go-lucky Scouser, but now everyone in the country would know my face. As I had little time, I bought a direct flight from London City Airport to Rotterdam. There wasn't even enough time to get one of my blag passports, so I ended up using my own. I was panicked, to be fair. I phoned Rodriguez, who was in Scotland with the gear. 'Sell the gear for £500,000,' I said. 'Take £100,000 for yourself, and you can give me my end next time I slip back into the country.' I picked up five grand cash for spends from my kitty in Liverpool and headed for a new life on the Continent.

At first, everything went well. I breezed through check-in and security, had a continental breakfast at the leather-trimmed bar in departures and chatted with the exotic business travellers from Milan and Munich. Everything was how it should have been on a glamorous business trip to a new and exciting life. I got on the plane with the five grand stuffed down my drawers. The air stewardess smiled and flirted with me, then announced there would be a slight delay. No probs. I was still buzzing from the champagne livener I'd enjoyed at the bar. I settled back to read my *Daily Telegraph* and the obligatory in-flight *Newsweek*.

The next minute, I felt some pressure on the back of my seat. A voice came into my ear: 'All right, Stephen. It's DC McDougal here. We've got a van outside on the runway. You know where you're going, don't you? And it ain't Rotterdam.' Fuck. The bizzies had caught up with me. So near, yet so far.

The game wasn't over yet. I immediately looked around to

assess the lie of the land. What about the escape exits? As I lined him up for an uppercut, I thought about jumping from the emergency exit. However, I've got an edict that I never assault a police officer in an official situation, especially if he was being fair. If an officer knew my ID, I never assaulted him, because ten years down the line it could come back to haunt me. So, instead, I told him I'd go quietly.

You have to be quite thick-skinned not to feel embarrassed about being escorted off a plane full of passengers. It's the stereotype of the big black criminal being shackled and led away in front of a gossiping, slightly fearful white crowd, loving the drama of it. But I had actually conditioned myself not to care – to keep the focus on my next move. You can't be worrying about what the man in the street thinks about you. You've got to be thinking about how you're going to get from A to B – and, most importantly, how you're going to avoid incarceration. However, at that time, the only conclusion I could come to was that I was fucked and facing 20 years.

When I got back to the Liverpool nick, a solicitor called Enzo Scarri came to see me. 'I've been sent to you by one of your friends,' he said. 'You'll be going home tonight.'

'Bollocks,' I thought. 'Not in a million years.'

I said, 'If I'm going home tonight, you can have a grand out of that five grand the bizzies have taken off me.' Now, I didn't know what this guy had in mind, but I was prepared to give it a shot. Enzo refused the £1,000 but still came up with a plan.

He quickly flipped through my legal papers and started reading the statements about the pressing engagement with Mona. After I had burned Mona, we had stolen his Mercedes and driven it up to Scotland. During that journey, I'd got stopped by a police car for speeding. I had given them a false name, Peter Purlough, backed up with a matching ID. Apparently, the copper who had stopped me had said in a statement that the man driving (me) had a distinguishing mark on his forearm. He'd gotten mixed up – my distinguishing mark was actually on the back of my arm.

Enzo said to me, 'When you go upstairs to do the ID in front of the copper, say fuck all and just show them the inside of your forearms. Don't show them the outside. When they ask to see the outside of your arms, refuse.'

Lo and behold, that minuscule technicality got me off. When *Daily Mail* readers complain about fancy lawyers working the justice system with the odds stacked in favour of the criminal – they're fucking right. And God be with them.

The police were fucking furious and rightly so. They were determined to get me back inside, so they even tried to pin the speeding offence on me. Then, at the magistrates' court, the copper who had mistakenly identified me bumped into me on the stairs. My lawyer argued that he had contaminated the case, and it was as good as binned. However, before it was dismissed, the magistrate wanted to see the mysterious distinguishing mark for herself. Instead of just letting me go, she looked me up and down. She explained that she had to examine my body for tattoos and scars – just to make sure. She came round from the bench, and I could hear her breathing heavily. I was 33 with a body like Adonis. I reckon all she wanted to do was to have a perv of me. She was an elderly white woman who most probably had fantasies about black criminals. It was quite amusing to say the least, and she probably wouldn't have complained if I had turned her around and bent her over. Of course, I didn't, but she let me off anyway.

When I got out, the first thing I did was visit Marsellus's family. He was doing 15 years, and his bird was in bits. They were skint. Furious, I dug out my trusty Morphy Richards and headed towards Mona's ken to get even with him for grassing us up.

I got hold of Mona on the phone. 'Listen, you cunt,' I said. 'I'm coming to iron you again. This time I'm going to do your face. You deserved to be burned the first time, and I'm gonna burn you again. You've put Marsellus in jail, and you've caused me to go on the run for a year.'

A few minutes later, he called back. 'Stephen. Back off. We'll pay you compensation.' Music to my ears. I slammed on the brakes, did a U-ie and headed to the gym for a massage. The next day, 40 grand in cash was dropped round at Marsellus's bird's house. Not enough to see her through the sentence, but better than a boot in the face.

As I was working out, it struck me that I had had a very lucky escape. I could see the writing on the wall – one day my nine lives were gonna run out. Ever since Andrew John had been murdered, I'd been in touch with my own vulnerability. Now it was beginning to go deeper – existential. I started to question my own mortality – my own morality.

For fuck's sake, what was all this shit for?

24

THE DAY OF THE JACKAL

Like in any other business, when you have accrued wealth and power in the underworld, people start approaching you with 'investment opportunities'. With the reputation I had, individuals would come to me with their get-rich-quick schemes, in the hope that I would throw a few quid behind them. It would often be fellows I didn't even know!

'Stephen, a man of your stature,' they would say in their pitch. 'A man of your money could easily pull off a deal like this. If we just do this, or we just do that, we can all make a lot of dough.'

Nine times out of ten, the schemes would be rejected, but every now and again something with serious potential would appear on the horizon. It was a bit like that telly programme *Dragons' Den*, except that the 'candidates' coming before me and my partners weren't budding inventors – their proposals didn't involve a self-cooking-egg machine or a new type of underwear. These people were hardened fucking heroin traffickers and cut-throats of every description. Their schemes usually involved underwriting drug deals, tying someone up and torturing them or blowing up a house with a hand grenade. Venture capitalism for sure, but hard-core villainous at the same time.

One thing that definitely differentiated our dragons' den from the telly version was that if you tried to double-cross our little panel of experts, you wouldn't be getting out of the fucking den. Never mind a telling off from Duncan Bannatyne – you would be stripped naked, sexually abused with a broom handle and singed by the full force of the Devil's flames on the hairs of your balls – from a red-hot Rowenta. We were real fucking dragons – no back chat was tolerated. It was a true test of a man's entrepreneurial spirit to come before us with a business proposal.

Our crew was doing pretty well financially. We were working out of an office called Wear Promotions, which served as a front for all our illegal activities. On the panel of our little firm was the cream of the criminal elite in the UK. On my right was Whacker – international dealer extraordinaire who had recently returned after being on the run. And on my left was the Rock Star, the legendary underworld taxman, drug baron, enforcer and general all-rounder. We had a boardroom where we would hold court, entertaining a steady stream of freelancers and their hare-brained ideas. One such guy went by the name of 'the Jackal'. He'd been on the periphery of the firm doing odd bits and pieces, and no matter how much he took the piss you couldn't help but like the guy, cos he had the gift of the gab. He could sell snow to Eskimos and sand to Arabs – he was that kind of guy.

One day, he came into the dragons' den and told us that he had a Turkish connection. That meant only one thing – heroin. 'I can get cheap gear out in Turkey,' he said. 'But the only problem is that I haven't got the funds to buy it, nor the means to get it back here. That's where I need your help, Stephen, with your contacts and all that carry on.'

I sat there thinking, 'Well, we've obviously got some good contacts in Europe and South America, but we haven't got any transport from Turkey. That's not one of our areas of operation.' Just like one of the real dragons, I was ready to declare myself out and give it a pass. However, like any good businessman, you can't just make decisions unilaterally – you've got to consider the other directors.

The Rock Star was in the boardroom with me. At that moment in time, he was going through a dry spell and was a skint dragon. The Jackal's Turkish connection could just be the key to getting a bit of pocket money for him, so we decided to take a punt. We told the Jackal that we'd be prepared to dip our toe in the water. No big parcel – no 100 kilograms or anything like that – just a few bits to start off with. We told him we would put up a kitty of 20 grand as our part of the bargain. That would get us four kilograms of top-grade Turkish heroin. By the time we got it back home, it would be worth 25 grand a kilo, so you're talking a 100-grand return on the original 20-grand investment. That was a 400 per cent profit.

I reckon if drug dealers went on the real *Dragons' Den* asking for money to fund shipments of gear, the dragons would be falling over themselves to sign up. Who could blame them?

Anyway, we green-lighted the Jackal deal and started to sort out the details. Whacker and me put in ten grand each. Although the Rock Star had no money, we would let him ride free, as he was a mate. Originally, the Jackal had wanted us to fund the purchase of the heroin and organise the transport back from Turkey, but we negotiated hard with him. We agreed to put the money up for the gear, but it was his problem how he got it back to us. Take it or leave it. He wasn't going to a get a better deal anywhere else.

The Jackal came on board. He said that he had a route worked out to Turkey and back. Our end was to get him the money and a suitcase with a false bottom. It was going to be a brazen job. Basically, he was just going to crash the borders – mule himself up and go for it. If he wanted to do that on a ten-grand hit from me with a 40-grand return, well he could go right ahead. I was prepared to throw that stone, because it was a good deal for me.

This guy wasn't called the Jackal for nothing, and it wasn't because he was a dog – the underworld equivalent of a low-down rat. It was because he was as devious and had as many personalities as the character played by Edward Fox in the film *The Day of the Jackal*. He was a slippery guy – an extremely cunning fellow who could outwit anyone. Peter Foster had nothing on this guy.

So, we knew we had to keep an eye on him. We knew that at any given opportunity he would try to fuck us. He knew that we knew, but he was playing the old gambit, the one they always rely on: pretending to fear the wrath of the Devil. 'I wouldn't try to fuck a man like you, Stephen,' the Jackal would say.

When I heard something like that from a criminal, I knew that they were thinking about fucking me. It's like when a guy says to you, 'You can trust me.' Immediately you start thinking, 'Oh, fuck that, he's going to have me off at the earliest opportunity.' It's like when a football commentator says, 'Neither team looks like scoring today,' and the next minute somebody whacks the ball in the net. It's that kind of scenario.

Anyway, we gave the Jackal the money. He headed off to Turkey, did the deal and called us to say that he was on his way home. I don't know exactly what happened in Istanbul, but he called us from Paris to let us know that everything was OK – that he'd got the goods and was just waiting to get from France to the UK. So far, so good.

We waited for the next call. Sure enough, the next time he checked in with us he was in Kent. Good news. He was making good progress and everything was sound. As far as we were concerned, it was a done deal. Or was it?

Instead of relaxing, I knew that this was exactly the time to watch out for any shenanigans. Look at it from his point of view. He'd just landed back on sovereign terra firma and all the hard work had been done. He'd been carrying a suitcase worth 20 grand, and its value had suddenly shot up to 100 grand just by virtue of its location. Better than that, he was still 300 to 400 miles away from us and the drop, so he wasn't exactly in our airspace. From experience, I knew that this was the point when temptation might kick in – this 300- to 400-mile window in which he might see an opportunity to fuck us.

Lo and behold, he phoned us again and terrible things had happened to him. He'd been dragged through a hedge backwards and only had one kilogram left out of the original four. He gave us some cock-and-bull story about being in a safe house where three of the kilos had gone missing, but he'd managed to save us one by the skin of his teeth.

Over the years, I've learned with experience never to tell anybody that they're a liar over the telephone. Especially if they think you've bought the story and they are willing to come and bring you something to limit the damage. Let them come to you. Don't say, 'You're a fucking lying cunt. I know you haven't been robbed. You've got the gear, and I'm going to kill you,' because they'll go to ground. Play the dumb nigger: 'Is that what happened to you? Bad one, la.' Give them sympathy: 'Well, the world is a terrible place, kidder. I'm not surprised so many unfortunate circumstances have befallen you.' Be reasonable: 'Well, if that's what's happened to you and you've saved a kilo, then at least our exies [expenses] are covered.'

I knew that was exactly what the Jackal was thinking: that he'd give us the original value of our investment back so that we could sell it for 25 grand. We'd get our twenty-grand investment back plus five grand on top for a little drink. We wouldn't have been out of pocket, and he'd be thinking, 'If they're not down, they won't be that angry.' He was banking on us quickly forgetting the escapade and moving on to the next candidate. That was the reasoning behind it. I can't even remember the whole story he gave us, but we brought it on board for the time being and got together for some crisis talks.

I said to the Rock Star and Whacker, 'He's got the gear, right? He's going to bring us only one kilo, but I say we take it and accept everything he says.'

The Rock Star said, 'No, no, fuck that. Stick a fucking gun in his mouth, and he'll tell me where everything is.'

I replied, 'Well, maybe, maybe not. The gun might go off, he might die and then we'll never find our gear. We don't need to do that. All we need to do is copy what the police and Customs do to us. Set up surveillance. Follow him and let him take us to the stash. He'll lead us to it, I guarantee you. He'll go straight to whomever he's working with, and they'll have the rest of the stuff there.'

The Rock Star gave me one of his long, hard looks, which meant he was not actually in agreement with my decision not to beat the Jackal up immediately. But he trusted my judgement as far as the bigger picture was concerned, especially on financial issues. In the past, in a crisis situation like that, he had tended to take his own counsel. He wouldn't listen to me because he thought I was a bit reserved and too apprehensive to go in all guns blazing. Now he was willing to defer to my more businesslike way of handling things.

In a football analogy, I'm a defender. In a boxing analogy, I'm a counter fighter. The Rock Star was the exact opposite – an attacker. He always went on the offensive. It was the only way he knew.

He gave me one of his long looks and said, 'OK, Stephen, but you fucking better be right. Simple as that. You better be right.'

I looked him straight in the eye and said, 'That's my money, isn't it? And I'm going to be right.'

I got the Jackal to come to our offices. He came into the boardroom and put the one kilo onto the table whilst delivering his tale of woe. After each twist and turn in the story, we would say 'Bad one, bad one' and 'Get away'. All the time, we were feigning compassion, as though we were three fucking Rupert the Bears.

Anyway, after the heart-rending finale, which finally accounted for the mysterious disappearance of the gear, we all put on a brave face, and I said, 'Anyway, all is not lost. We'll sell this kilo, get our exies back and you'll even get a little drink for all your trouble. We'll get between 22 and 30 grand for this single kilo, so there's a few grand to go round.'

The Jackal looked at me, watching my every move and trying to read me. As he was older than me, I knew he'd pick up a molecule out of place. You've heard of double devious, well this guy was quadruple fucking devious. Nonetheless, I am a good poker player. I enjoy going to the casino and was getting pretty good at cards at that time, so I kept my poker face on. None of us were about to give anything away.

Throughout the meeting, I was thinking about the surveillance we had set up outside. As soon as the Jackal left us, he would be trailed to his next destination. Then it was game over. The surveillance team consisted of the Rock Star's brother, a friend of Whacker's and some of my counterparts. The plan was to trail him in three cars, using a rotation strategy. That meant the Jackal would always have a different car behind him. Even for someone as on top as him, it would make it difficult for him to suss us out.

In the end, it transpired that he had gone to a tower block in the Everton Brow area of Liverpool. As soon as he went into the building, our surveillance team deployed a foot patrol to follow him.

If you're going to follow a black guy who doesn't want to be followed, use white people – it's common sense. Better still, use a white woman or a single white mum with a baby. Just get her into the lift behind your target, have her sit there petting the baby and get her to see what button he presses. Then you've got his destination. End of story. She can then press the button for a floor higher than him. Women are the best for following drug dealers, because men tend to dismiss them. They're looking for geezers all the time. You see a bird pushing a pram and it doesn't even appear on your radar. Police use the technique on a regular basis. They get their families to sit in the back of the car when they're trailing you. I've had it done to me. You clock the car and think, 'There's a guy driving, but there's his bird, and he's got the kids in the back. He's not following me.' But they are – Special Branch tactics.

When we used the same techniques, I called it surveillance reversal – using the measures that were used on us but to our benefit. It's all well thought through stuff, but I consider myself to be a bright fellow, so there's no problem on that score.

Our spy observed the Jackal getting out of the lift on the fourth floor. As the door closed, our single mum also noticed that he'd gone into flat 23. Done deal. As soon as she rang through with the info, I phoned the Rock Star and said, 'I guarantee the gear's going to be there.'

The Rock Star started jumping around, saying, 'I'm fucking going in now. I'm bursting the ken. I want to see his face.' The Rock generally took things worse than I did. All I was interested in was retrieving the goods. I didn't want to beat anybody up, if at all possible. Of course, I had a heater on me, just in case. As far as I was concerned, the Jackal was just one less person to share the goods with once I had them back. Under the rules of engagement, he was no longer entitled to anything.

To save a drama, I phoned the Rock Star to stall him. 'OK,' I said. 'Tell you what. Leave it for like half an hour, and we'll go in together.' I knew full well that I would be on the plot in the next 15 minutes. All I wanted to do was get the stuff and get off without any problems.

When I'm going into a potentially hairy situation, I always have a right-hand man with me. In this case, my right-hand man was an old pal called Wallace. He could lean on a steel door and it'd immediately fall in. We got to flat 23, and I listened through the letterbox.

I said, 'He's in there, Wallace. I know he's in there.'

'Are you sure?' he replied.

'Yeah. Deal with the door.'

Wallace was six feet one inch and around twenty-two to twenty-four stone – a man mountain. The door flew off its hinges and fell down flat on the floor. We were right over it and inside the flat within one and a half seconds.

When you burst a ken, it's like American marines storming a house in Iraq. It's all over in seconds, and you rely on your speed, aggression and mobility to catch your target totally off guard.

The flat was a typical high-rise abode, with a long corridor behind the steel-plated front door. Inside, there were internal doors on either side of this long hallway and a living room at the end, like the cross on a capital 'T'. We started to kick open the doors.

The bedroom on the left – clear. Bedroom two on the right – clear. Kitchen – clear. Living room at the end – clear. It was a fucking mystery. The Jackal had done it again. He'd outfoxed us.

But hold on. There was one place left to search – the khazi. Wallace and I slowly moved towards the door. I tapped it with my toe, and it creaked open slowly. Lo and behold, there he was – the Jackal himself – sitting on the toilet, like an emperor on his throne, having a shit.

The best news was that right next to him – resting on the side of the bath – was a briefcase containing the missing three kilograms of heroin. Nothing had yet been said because of the extraordinary nature of the situation. So far, the Jackal had just looked up at me with a quizzical look in his eyes. Then he spoke: 'Fucking hell, Stephen, it's you.' I knew exactly what had been going on. He'd been sitting there, having a shit and nursing the three kilograms, thinking, 'I've done it. I've pulled off the perfect stroke, and I've got the 75 grand. I've had one over on Frenchie. Oh, this is lovely.'

Not quite. Rewind a bit. Imagine you're on the toilet, having the best shit in the world, with three kilograms by your side, and you're thinking how great you are. Suddenly, the door crashes in, and seconds later the guy you've just fucked over is looking at you sitting on the khazi. I was laughing as the shit poured out of his arse in terror, and there was nothing he could do about it.

I'd been in situations like that many times before. In my experience, the first thing a guy would try and do is make a run for it – jump right through a window, anything to get away from the Devil. However, there was nowhere for the Jackal to go. Wallace was standing behind me in the tiny bathroom, swaying from one foot to the other like King Kong, and I looked like one quarter of the Four Horsemen of the Apocalypse. There was no way out.

I pegged my nose with my fingers to avoid the smell, leaned over the bath and scooped up the gear. 'Thank you very much,' I said. 'That's mine.' I handed the gear to Wallace and told him to take it to the car.

At that point, the Jackal thought his life was over. He had studied the book of underworld revelations and knew that the Devil always took revenge – mercilessly. I took out my Colt .45. Already, I could see the scenes-of-crime pictures flashing through the Jackal's head: grimy bathroom, blood-spattered B&Q tiles and shit all over the place – a horrible and degrading death. What a way to go!

I took a step towards him. His lip quivered; his eyes were wide open. The smell of fear had now replaced the fumes from the faeces. I cocked the gun and leaned over his right shoulder as though heading for the back of his head. Instead, I followed through to the cistern, scooped up the toilet roll with the barrel of the gun and handed it to him. 'You'll be needing this,' I said. 'Because you're in deep shit.' With that, I was gone.

In the meantime, half an hour had passed. The Rock Star phoned me. He was all pumped up. 'Are we ready to go, lad?' he asked.

'I've already been in and done it,' I said. 'I've got your gear, and I'm coming home with your share.'

The beauty of the Rock was that once he was sure the money was secure, all his aggression would subside in an instant. His attitude would change, and he would say, 'Well, who are we selling it to, and when am I getting my money?' This was where Whacker would come into his own and was why I liked him so much. We would give the gear to him, and he would have our dough 48 hours later. This was because Whacker was one of those kids who could knock everything out and get the cash in dead quick. Everybody loved him for that.

These days, the Jackal and I are mates again. We always have a laugh about that little caper. To this day, he tells everyone, 'I once tried to rip Frenchie off. But he caught me with my pants down.'

25

THE DEVIL'S GHOST

Over the next couple of years, the underworld dragons' den proved to be a big hit. We had a 75 per cent success rate on our graft and our reach extended globally. One day, a gangster called Skateboard put forward a proposition to harvest some super-strength skunk in Holland.

Skateboard was of mixed race, about four or five years older than me and had been an international drug dealer all his life. I'd got to know him when I had sorted out a problem for him using the ancient art of serious violence. He was a rich kinda guy – we're talking millions – with a lovely big house in an exclusive part of the country. However, like all shrewd operators, he wanted to share the risk on any new venture.

The deal was this: I would put up all the money while he'd do the work and provide all the technical know-how. He asked for a £100,000 capital investment up front to set up an industrial-scale super farm in a disused aircraft hangar in Holland. He promised it would churn out a bumper crop every ten weeks. State-of-the-art technology would ensure that the harvest was of high purity and production-line quality.

Some of the other board members were wary about us putting so much money in while Skateboard contributed nothing. Nonetheless, I am a lot more business-minded than most villains, and I was of the opinion that it was like any new development in production – usually built with someone else's money. I could see

Skateboard's rationale. If the worst came to the worst, it wouldn't be him making the loss. I wasn't doing the work, but I was taking the financial risk, the way banks do. I was prepared to do that if the project materialised and I got 50 per cent of the profit plus my investment back. To me, it was just a few mobile-phone calls made from the comfort of my bed.

The extra beauty about the proposal was that it was perfectly legal to grow skunk in Holland. There were low operational costs, as all the Dutch electricity would be fiddled by a pair of Scousers over there, and all the nutrients were being shipped in from the Third World for buttons. The labour was provided by sweatshop-cheap Eastern Europeans. To grow it cost us fuck all, but a kilo would wholesale at three grand over here – £100 to £150 an ounce at retail. Good money for weed.

We got the operation up and running and flooded the country with skunk. Within a year, my return had reached half a million quid. However, profits soon began to diminish – not because of the bad press surrounding skunk in the UK but because Skateboard had begun to slack off.

When a business matures, it often needs a troubleshooter to tweak it and put it gently back on track. The only problem is that I'm no Sir John Harvey-Jones. When it comes to motivating managers, my problem-solving repertoire doesn't extend much further than my old friends – kidnap, torture and blood-freezing violence.

I used my intelligence network and found out the reason why Skateboard had been neglecting my interests. Apparently, he had been investing some of the capex I'd put up into a new Class A venture, which was giving him an even better return, so I asked him for my £100,000 back. He started to splutter and stammer, and um and ah, and I soon realised he didn't have it. However, I didn't show him my displeasure or concern. My poker face concealed all that from him. Instead, I started hatching a plot to get my money back.

Not long afterwards, I got talking to him about his new cocaine venture. He told me a shipment had just come in. I said, 'I'll buy five kis off you for £125,000.' Then we shook on it. At the next meeting, I brought my new right-hand man Wallace on board and told him he could have anything we taxed over and above the value of my initial investment – £100,000.

Skateboard bounced into my office to collect his money. Instead, I tied him to a chair and whispered in his ear, 'I've asked you for my 100 grand, and you haven't given it to me. You're going to call your runner now to get the money.'

He said, 'I can't be doing with that.' Slap. I gave him a heavy-handed wallop on his face. This cut his mouth, and he started to bleed.

I said, 'Look, you think you can use my fucking money and do something else with it. If you had given back my money when I asked you, you wouldn't be having this problem. You better fucking make the call now.'

Anyway, he made the call and a young white kid came down with the cash. As far as I was concerned, I was in the right and a line had now been drawn under the matter.

The next morning, I heard a banging on my front door. I looked out the window and saw two South American brothers called Julio and Hector. Julio was the elder brother, the brains, and Hector was a street fighter who thought he could fight anybody.

Dionne was at work, so I opened the door in my dressing gown. 'Come in, gentlemen,' I said.

Immediately, they got down to business: 'That cocaine you took off Skateboard is ours. That's our five kis, and we want it fucking back. We know what you've done. You've set him up. You've been feeding him money for weeks and weeks, and then, all of a sudden, you've just snatched all the gear off him.'

'Is that what he told you?' I asked them as I slowly walked towards Julio. He jumped back at every step I took, watching me like a hawk. 'Look, Julio,' I said. 'If I'm going to hit, I will declare it. I'll say, "Defend yourself now, because it's on." So you don't have to worry about me going to steal it on you or sneaking up to hit you, because that's not my intention.' I scratched my bollocks. I could see that Hector wanted to attack me, but I reckon he was overawed by my reputation.

I then said, 'If you'd have knocked on my door and said, "Excuse me, Stephen, can we have a word?" and told me that this was your coke and what Skateboard had done, I might have considered giving it back to you.' Obviously, I wouldn't have done this – it was just a line I was using. 'Instead you've accused me of feeding Skateboard for weeks so that I can rob him of 100 grand. How disrespectful is that? You haven't asked me my side of the story. You've just decided that I taxed him. So get the fuck out of my house. You're getting fuck all back.'

I went into my kitchen drawer, pulled out my biggest knife and chased them like a pair of naughty schoolboys. 'You've been banging on my door like you're fucking somebody. Get the fuck out.' However, I knew that Hector would hold a grudge over this and that I'd have to watch him, as he might try to test me in the future.

I was back in bed when the doorbell went again. This time, there was a female at the door. It turned out to be Skateboard's missus. She pleaded poverty, saying that her husband had been foolish, losing all their money, and the 100 grand I had taken was his last bit of dough.

I could see that Skateboard had spun her a line, so I told her that her husband deserved it. As far as I was concerned, that was the end of the matter. However, not long after, I received a call out of the blue from Mick the Scorpion. He said, 'You're never going to believe what I've been asked to do to you. You're going to laugh your head off. I've got something for you.'

We met at Café 53 in Bold Street. As soon as I sat down, he gave me 15 grand in cash and a Toc (Tokarev) automatic – an eastern European, 13-shot, 9-mm automatic handgun. He said, 'I've been given those two things to kill you. This is the gun, and the cash is the down payment for a contract killing. And when you're dead, I get another 15 grand. The job's worth 30 grand altogether.'

'Who's put the contract out?' I asked.

'Skateboard and the Colombians,' he replied.

The Scorpion had never forgotten that I'd gone back for him that time after the bungled tax job. He told me that he had always been indebted to me for not leaving him there to be slaughtered by the animals. He said, 'I always remember what you said to me, Stephen: "You think I would leave you lying there when there's room on my horse for two?" That was the kindest thing anyone has ever done for me, and I'm now about to repay you.'

He pulled out a Polaroid camera. I asked him what it was for, and he said, 'To go with this.' He put a tube of lipstick on the table. I looked at him and thought, 'A Polaroid camera and a woman's lipstick?' I'm a pretty sharp geezer, but I still hadn't twigged.

Mick grinned: 'We're going to fake your death, get the other 15 grand and reap sweet revenge on the man who wants you dead.'

I thought, 'What a good fucking idea.'

We went off to a derelict house on the outskirts of Liverpool. Mick told me to roll myself in the dust to make it look like I'd been roughed up. Then, using the lipstick, he put a heavy dot on my head – to resemble a bullet entry wound – and a little trail of 'blood' on my face. Both of us had been in these situations plenty of times, so we knew exactly what a Tokarev bullet to the head looked like. We also knew about the finer details of the consequences of a kidnap, torture and shooting – bodily fluids leaking onto the floor, sweat, dirt and grime, and scuffed up hair and clothes.

Remember those fake pictures in the *Daily Mirror* of the Iraqis being tortured by British soldiers? As soon as I saw them, I knew that they were fake – mainly because there was no dirt or sweat on the hooded man. Those pictures would never have got past even the most basic of underworld checks. If only Piers Morgan had been a gangster, he would have known. So, I arranged myself into a pose I had seen in a picture of a man I once knew who had been shot. From memory, I copied the way his mouth had hung open with his teeth kind of exposed – rat-like. Then Mick took the picture.

About a week later, the Scorpion went to see Skateboard to tell him that the job was done and to collect the balance of 15 grand left on the contract. Being a shrewd businessman, Skateboard said, 'Where's the proof? I haven't read about it in the papers.' Reading about something in the papers is like a receipt or an invoice in the underworld, and it's often used as evidence that someone has carried out a task. It's the same thinking behind the yellow pedal.

Mick had thought it all through. 'Because I buried him under the floorboards of an out-of-the-way house and nobody's found his body yet,' he replied. During the previous week, when I was supposed to be dead, I had made sure I'd stayed incognito and wasn't seen out clubbing or anything like that.

The Scorpion continued, 'But I took the precaution of taking a Polaroid picture for you, so you can see for yourself. I know you'll be happy to see it. I wanted to show you it before I destroyed it. Then I want you to pay me my fucking money.'

As he was looking at the picture, a smile appeared across the soft cunt's face. He'd actually gone for it, believing I was a dead man. 'Nice one,' he said. 'I'll meet you in the Greek restaurant tomorrow night, to collect the 15 grand.'

The following day, I told the Scorpion, 'Make sure you get him in the restaurant sitting with his back to the door, so he can't see who's coming in.'

That night, the Scorpion arrived at the Greek on Borough Road in Birkenhead. I waited outside, watching the proceedings through the restaurant window. Sure enough, Skateboard handed over the 15 grand. Then, over a kebab and a haloumi salad, they started to celebrate the demise of the Devil.

As soon as the handover took place, I quietly slipped into the restaurant. I could see that the Scorpion had spotted me out of the corner of his eye. He was a great actor. If he'd gone to Hollywood, he would've got an Oscar. He didn't flinch and Skateboard didn't notice a thing, as he was facing the other direction as planned. He was laughing and joking about how he was going to be the king of the underworld for having toppled the Devil.

I walked up to his right-hand side and just stood there. There was a mirror on the wall, and when he looked up he saw me dressed in black and wearing silver shades and my best Colgate smile. He jumped up like he'd seen a ghost.

'We are each our own devil, and we make this world our hell,' I said, quoting a bit of Oscar Wilde that I'd picked up especially for the occasion. 'So, Skateboard, you want me dead? Well, I'll take this 15 grand then.' I gave the money to the Rock Star, who I had brought with me for the laugh, and said, 'And you now owe me another 25 grand as a fine for trying to have me killed.'

The Rock Star said, 'Is that it? Aren't you going to do nothing to him?'

I replied, 'No. He's a waste of time. A joke. A waste of space.' I turned to Skateboard, 'If you carry on messing about in the real underworld, you're going to get killed, your brother's going to get killed, your wife's going to get killed and your daughter's going to get killed. You don't belong in this world. You've been fined 25 grand. Pay the money and I'll forget all about it.'

He then said to me, 'Stephen, Stephen, I haven't got that money.'

'You can pay it in instalments,' I replied. 'Pay me any way you want. But you'll have to pay the lot.'

Two weeks later, Skateboard had paid the amount in full. All in all, I'd made about 40 grand out of my own death. Talk about turning a negative into a positive. Is that not fucking super or what? What business guru or motivational speaker could teach you to pull one like that out of the hat? I'm a master at it.

If someone screws me over, I will let them go free if they pay me the fines. Like in the judicial system, you've atoned for your crime. I'm not going to make you pay a fine and then fucking punish you. I'm not going to fuck you twice for one crime. That's just not fair, is it?

To this day, Skateboard is still selling skunk and doing his little bits of bobbing and weaving around. I saw him the other week at the traffic lights, and he pretended not to see me. I could tell he was terrified – he just tried to keep looking straight ahead, the way you do when you're too embarrassed to make eye contact. However, as we pulled off in our cars, I knew he wouldn't be able to resist a quick look in my direction – and I had prepared myself for this. When he glanced at me, all he could see was my head lolling to one side on the head rest, with my mouth hanging open and my teeth sticking out, like in the film *Goodfellas* – and just like in the Polaroid.

He nearly crashed his car. What a hoot!

26

THE DEVIL'S COURT: THE CASE OF THE CAVALIER ATTITUDE

Followers of Islamic Sharia law will tell you that it is man-made and of lesser value than the will of the prophet Muhammad. Fair enough. Greek-based Western philosophy dictates that no man is above the law. Common sense. Followers of the dark arts will understand that in hell there is only one rule – the law of the Devil, and his word is final.

One day, I started to ponder the philosophy behind the judicial system. The only reason that I got away with being a taxman was because the underworld was beyond the reach of the long arm of the law. No one's going to tell the bizzies that they've had 20 kilos of coke robbed off them, are they? However, tax law is only one part of a whole body of legal thinking, imposed on society in order to govern the way we live. So, I got to thinking, 'What if I extended my tax laws to regulate all kinds of underworld behaviour? Not just confine them to the profits of drug dealing. What if I invented a *whole* judicial system for villains, punishing things like antisocial behaviour, fighting and theft?' The law laid down according to Stephen Terrible French and imposed by the Devil Judge himself – just like in Skateboard's case. Justice would be done, and, more importantly, I would cop for all the fines – kind of like what speed cameras do.

With this in mind, I set up a kangaroo court with wide-ranging powers and began fining villains for every transgression imaginable. Whenever I felt the need to beat someone up for letting me down, I would simply fine them instead. Of course, I charged extortionate rates, like all the best legal eagles, and soon became very rich in the process.

I'll give you an example of a typical case that came before me. All rise for the Devil Judge – his court is now in session. One night, I was having a quiet drink in a nightclub called Plummer's with John Reilly, a mate of mine – a short guy with the heart of a lion. Suddenly, a damsel in distress came over to John and asked him to help her, as she was getting beaten up by her boyfriend. Now, it's never a good idea to get involved in a domestic, especially when the victim's boyfriend is there with his three mates and has just seen the girl come over to get help from one big nigger and one little nigger. They didn't know me, and I didn't know them. Nonetheless, by the end of the evening, they *would* know me, and by the next day they'd never be able to forget me.

John went into his back pocket and got her a 20-quid note. He said, 'The best thing that I can do for you, love, is to get you a taxi home. You can't be fucking coming over to us. Go away.' My spider senses immediately switched on when I saw the four lads taking umbrage at us having given the girl money. So, discretion being the better part of valour, I said to John, 'We should get off, mate. These are only four run-of-the-mill lads, but I can't be arsed.'

As we were leaving via a steep embankment of stairs, one of the individuals took a running jump from behind me and landed on my shoulders, piggyback fashion. I could see the gang's rationale – take the big one out first. The geezer on my back wrapped his legs around my waist and strangled my neck with his hands, furiously trying to squeeze me out.

There are two things that you can do in this situation: you can struggle and try to pull his arms off you before he renders you unconscious; or you can go with the flow and use your opponent's momentum against him. I chose the second option. The weight of him landing on me had made me stumble forward down the steps into the street. As we moved forward, I reached behind me over my own head and grabbed him by the scruff of his coat and neck. Then, in the same movement, I sharply bent double and pulled my attacker fiercely over my head as hard as I could. With this move, I was able to slam my assailant very heavily onto the concrete, WWF-style. He was unconscious immediately.

On seeing this, one of the four musketeers in the charge behind him took off up the street like Speedy Gonzales. That left two opponents, and I liked those odds. I pushed one of the remaining men into the middle of the street's oncoming traffic, leaving Johnny to deal with the last one. The fight should have been over within ten seconds. I knew what I was going to do – one karate kick to the head and the guy was going down. However, pride comes before a fall, and as soon as I raised my leg I somehow slipped over on the steel tips of my £400 moccasins and found myself sat squarely on my arse. But opponent number two didn't take advantage of this situation. Instead, he danced around me, trying to get in a position to kick me in the head. I started spinning on my back like a break-dancer, trying to keep my head away from his feet as I planned my next manoeuvre. Next, I did what my mate and five-times World Champion kick-boxer Alfie Lewis would later call a Scorpion kick. I threw my weight back onto my shoulders, stiffened my legs and flicked my feet directly out and up. My head was resting on the floor, my shoulders were at a 45-degree angle from the ground and my feet were pointing towards the sky. Bam! I'd hit him right under his jaw, lifting him off his feet and forcing him to stagger backwards.

The kick was enough to knock out an elephant, but all that it seemed to have done to him was fuzzy his mind and weaken his legs. However, it gave the Frenchman time to get back on his feet again. I looked into his eyes, and he looked into mine. He was ready to fight. I told him, 'You know you're in trouble now, don't you?'

He replied, 'Yeah, I think so.'

I attacked him without mercy and whacked him unconscious. I then turned around and saw Johnny struggling with the other guy over by Plummer's. The guy was kind of on top of Johnny, with his back towards me, so I gave him a roundhouse kick to his ribs. I heard the bones go pop, and the geezer fell off Johnny and started rolling on the floor, screaming. I kicked him towards his two mates. The geezer who had jumped on my back was just about coming around. They all staggered off down the road but then, for some reason, waited there.

It then came to my attention that I'd lost a gold chain and a Buddha that I wore around my neck. But I didn't have time to hang around, because I could already hear police sirens on their way, and I had a gun and £10,000 in cash on me. The first individual – the piggyback guy – was still on the floor, so I started to look around him for my gold chain. Instead, I came across a key to a Cavalier. I knew that it was a key for a Cavalier because I'd just bought my wife a brand-new SRI model. I looked around and saw a Cavalier parked near Plummer's. I realised that it was their car, which was why they were still hanging around at the end of the road.

I said, 'Come on, John, we've got wheels. Let's get off before the bizzies get here.'

The next day, the telephone rang. It was a guy called Ginger Jones, the first cousin of Peter Lair. 'Stephen,' he said. 'About the Cavalier you took last night. That's my lad's car, and we've got some graft to do, so we need it back.'

Like a judge in a court, I replied authoritatively, 'Four of them attacked me last night and spoiled my evening. I'm fining them two grand. If you want the car back, it's going to cost you that amount.'

'Ah, you can't do that to us, lad,' he replied. 'We're old mates. What you going on like that for?'

While I was speaking to Ginger on the telephone, Johnny Reilly was dancing around in the background like a banshee, saying,

'Let's just fucking burn it. Burn it, Ste. Set it on fire. Fuck them. They tried to do us in. Let's set the car on fire. We don't need their money! Set the car on fire!'

However, I was thinking more like a businessman. 'Sorry, Ginger,' I said. 'I can't help you.' Then I put the phone down. About 15 minutes later, Peter Lair phoned me up. Apparently, Ginger had gone up the ladder and asked Lair to have a word with me. Now, as you may remember, Lair and I had history between us. Everyone was dying to see us fight so that they could see the outcome. He was about six or seven years younger than me, but I was bigger and better trained than him. Nonetheless, he was perfectly polite and reasonable on the blower. He didn't tell me that if I didn't give the car back, there was going to be trouble. He wasn't telling me what to do, he was asking me, and there's a world of difference.

However, I still didn't give a damn. 'It's not your car,' I said. 'If it was your car, Peter, I'd give it back to you, but it's Ginger Jones's car. He wants to make fucking money off it today, but last night his boy and his boy's mates wanted to stamp all over me. They came unstuck because they picked the wrong nigger to fuck with. So, now it's a two-grand fine, and the lad that I kicked in the face has to come down in person, cos I want to know how he survived that kick I gave him.'

Lair replied, 'OK, Stephen, I'll tell them.' Peter would have done exactly the same thing. If we were to get it on, it would have to be for a good reason. There was grudging respect between us.

We met at a 24-hour garage that had CCTV, because everyone wanted to be on camera to be safe. The lad I'd kicked in the face was there as I'd requested – the left side of his jaw looked like he'd swallowed a cricket ball. His face was kinda hanging on his shoulder, because I had caught him with a solid double Scorpion kick, which was the equivalent of getting springboked by a donkey.

He looked at me very nervously, genially even, and said, 'You're good with your feet you, aren't you?'

I tapped him right on his sore jaw and said, 'How the hell did you stay awake after that?'

He took the index finger of his right hand and ran it under his nose, meaning that he'd been snorting cocaine. Charlie had kept him awake. Then I took his two grand off him. Before he got off, I gave him my verdict: 'It's OK to have a Cavalier attitude to life, but when you go too far you have to pay the price.'

That was the moral of the tale. Case dismissed.

27

THE DEVIL RIDES OUT

I started buying huge amounts of hash direct from Morocco.
Mohammed Abdul, my contact, was your typical Moroccan guy
who dressed as though he wanted to be European – he wore a
1980s suit with rolled-up sleeves, a shoelace tie, a stud earring,
patent leather shoes, the whole works. However, when he took me
up into the hills, he looked like a different guy – he wore a long
kaftan, Muslim skullcap and flat sandals, the earring was gone,
and he had a small goatee. From that point on, I looked at him
with a new-found respect. From the reaping of the plant to the
pressing, crushing and oil making, Abdul showed me the whole
process of growing hashish from start to finish.

On one of our trips to Morocco, the Rock Star and I stayed in a
hut in the middle of a really poor area, being bitten by bugs the
size of your fucking nuts, even though we had enough money to
buy everything around us. I could see dead people slumped in
the gutters. One night, I was lying in the hut unable to sleep. My
spider senses started tingling like an alarm bell. I looked across at
the Rock Star and saw that he was awake, too. As a precaution,
we hightailed it out of there at around about 1.30 a.m., and by
2.30 a.m. were safely ensconced in the Tulip Hotel at the top of
the hill. This place only accepted American dollars and locals were
refused entry. We were safe and sound.

We later discovered that Abdul had planned to double-cross us
and have us murdered in the mud hut that night, taking the money

and hashish for himself. However, his little plan had backfired. The next day, he was found floating in the local canal.

With Abdul gone, I needed another contact, so I started dealing with a tribal man whose name will go to the grave with me. Thanks to him, we eventually got 80 kilograms back to Liverpool. But the stuff was cursed. Some fucker robbed it from our safe house. As soon as I discovered the theft, I got on the tom-toms, letting everyone know that it was my gear and whoever took it better give it fucking back or there'd be trouble.

It wasn't long before we found out the name of the thief – a guy called Cruze. Of course, he denied everything, so I took him to the 13th floor of Macmillan House and hung him out of the window by his ankles. He was dangling upside down with the blood rushing to his head, and he was screaming like a girl. He pissed and shit himself – the smell was fucking horrible. Still, I got my drugs back, and we let Cruze go free. After that, I binned the Morocco scenario. The moral of the tale is that the road from Casablanca to Marrakech is a bumpy ride and not worth the hassle or the money.

I continued with my ventures a little closer to home. I started going to London to watch the big fights. The hotel I would stay in seemed to be a prime location for a monthly drug-dealers' convention. Loads of us would stay there – firms from Scotland, Manchester and all over.

One night, we were all drinking in the hotel bar. A dealer from Amsterdam started to boast about how *huge* he really was. Foolishly – very foolishly – he let slip to one of the lads in the bar that he had £100,000 in cash stashed in his room. Now this feller was a well-known hard-hitter, so he wasn't banking on any of the London villains or the Mancs having him off. Not only did the firms fear his reputation, but they also relied on him for gear. They weren't about to shoot themselves in the foot by thieving from him.

But when I found out about it, there was only one outcome. I made my way over to the Dutchman, bought him a few drinks and got him pissed up. Then, when he turned in, I bid him goodnight and went straight into action. I collected my bally and gun from my room. I then tapped on his door and pretended to be room service. When he opened it, I put the gun to his head and backed him onto his bed. I then blindfolded and hog-tied him with tape.

Within minutes, I was back in my room with a suitcase full of £100,000 in Dutch guilders. Breakfast the next day was frantic, with the Dutchman, his henchman and his allies trying to find the culprit. I sat at his table with my muesli and commiserated: 'Bad one, la. Who would do such a thing?'

Of course, he didn't know it was me. However, a few of our mob asked me, 'Was that you, Frenchie?'

I just looked at them and said, 'Me? Do that? What do you take me for?' We all shared a little smile.

I remember another incident in our nation's capital. There was this godfather type in London, whose wife was having an affair with a celebrity hairdresser. She told the hairdresser that her untouchable husband kept £320,000 under their kid's bed – that pillow talk is a killer. So, her fancy man tipped me off.

Wallace and I put the godfather's mansion under surveillance using Gulf War-surplus ex-SAS infrared night-vision goggles and remote-listening devices. Because I've got manners, I waited for the wife and kids to go out before Wallace and I broke in. I then crept up on the godfather while he was shaving. The Devil appeared in his mirror like an apparition and gave him the shock of his life. The money wasn't under the bed like we had been advised, and he wouldn't tell us where it was – at first. Unfortunately, the Tefal iron then came out. Eventually, we found the money in the cellar – and that's where we left him.

On jobs such as this one, a clean-up man always came in after we had departed to remove all physical evidence from the scene of the crime. This precaution was left over from our armed-robbery days when a clean-up man was responsible for petrolling the car and overalls. In this case, the clean-up man actually had to wash the victim down while he was still tied up, spending four hours cleaning the house from top to bottom. That's how careful we were.

When we got back to Liverpool, Johnny Phillips came to me with some more Inland Revenue work. It turned out that a distributor nicknamed Smokin' Joe Frasier had ten kilograms of Charlie on him and two hundred and fifty large. If I cut the dope, it equated to a half-million-pound deal, which was good work. The tax went like clockwork, until we got back to Johnny's shop on Granby Street to divvy up the winnings.

The shop was in a basement and was full of space invaders, slot machines and that kind of thing. Johnny turned up with two white boys and had a sick grin on his face. My spider senses started tingling. I knew it was all on. Predictably, the three of them pulled blades and told me that they were keeping everything and I was getting nothing. I raised my two hands outstretched in front of me and said, 'Look, lads, it's like this. If you want to keep the gear, you can keep the gear and you can keep the money. It's no big deal. No one needs to cut me. Just stay back with the blades.'

Encouraged by my quick surrender, Johnny then said, 'I always knew you were a shithouse. I always knew you were yellow.'

I said, 'You got the drop on me, man.' Then I put a sad look on my face and said, 'But what you've got to remember, Johnny, is that I'm a little bit cleverer than you.' And with that, I whipped out my trusty 1940 Luger from the small of my back and pointed it straight at him. 'Oh dear!' I said. 'Only a soft cunt like you would bring a knife to a gun fight. You think you're man enough to take my stuff and not pay me?'

When he saw the Luger, the look on his face was priceless because he'd actually sold me the gun in the first place! I turned to him and said, 'I'll let you walk out of here, because I feel sorry for you. I'll tell you what I'll do with you. Pack everything up – *all* of the cash and *all* of the gear. I'll take everything, and we'll call it a day.' I had turned a negative into a positive once again.

The irony of the situation was that he had tried to rob me at knifepoint, but I had ended up robbing him with his own gun! How sweet was that? It was a nice little earner, too, and the most beautiful thing of all was that Johnny had made the mistake of thinking I was yellow. As for the two white compadres, it didn't really have anything to do with them, so I let them go. It was just a power game between me and their boss.

The whole matter was sorted with the steel of my word and the strength of my character. It was beautiful man, absolutely fucking beautiful.

28

SYMPATHY FOR THE DEVIL –THE EPIPHANY

On 6 August 1994, my wife went into labour. At the time, I was in Walthamstow doing a deal – buying and selling huge amounts of Class A drugs that would destroy lives and decimate communities on an *industrial* scale. I could try and pretend I didn't know or care about the consequences of my actions, but deep down I knew, all right. I knew that the super-powerful poisons I was trading in could turn pregnant mothers into prostitutes and fathers into thieves, their children abandoned, battered and abused amidst the crack fumes in the living room. Dignified lads would be converted into horrible bag-heads, with shit coming out the back of their baggy-arsed kecks. Young girls who once played with dolls would be getting their disease-ridden bodies shagged silly by old fellas for the price of a ten-pound rock.

Anyway, I was determined not to miss the birth, because several years before I'd missed the birth of my first son Stephen in almost exactly the same circumstances – I'd been doing a drug deal. A wave of guilt and shame flushed over me. Nothing had changed in the intervening years. I was still a drug dealer. I was still the Devil. And now it looked like I was going to be bringing a second child into my hell. I jumped into my brand-new Lexus and did the journey back to Liverpool's Oxford Street maternity hospital in two hours and sixteen minutes.

On 7 August 1994 at 7.10 a.m., my daughter Abbey was born. I actually saw her leaving her mum, and, I have to admit, I didn't find it a pleasant experience. It was touch and go, cos the cord got tied round her neck and the midwife had to take the baby off somewhere. My mother-in-law Sylvia, who was a fierce defender of her family, followed her to see what was happening. When they took the cord from around her neck, she spluttered into life and suddenly we had a tiny new baby. For months, we'd been having arguments about whether she'd look like me or her mum – how dark she'd be, which of our features she would have, etc. When she came out, she was the spitting image of her mother with eyelashes you could sweep the carpet with. She was beautiful. When I held her, I'd never felt love like it before, and I knew there and then I couldn't be the Devil any longer.

From a moral point of view, how could I look this human in the eye if I was responsible for the misery and deaths of so many like her? From a personal point of view, not only did I have to stay alive, but I also had to stay free in order to make sure that this little bundle of joy got the start in life she deserved. It was a true epiphany – that's the only way I can describe it. I filled up with warmth, love and happiness, and a single tear rolled down my left cheek. It was kind of sentimental and fuzzy – it was fuzzy wuzzy.

From that moment on, I became a different person. I vowed I would get out of the drugs game and avoid any confrontation that could lead to trouble. The epiphany happened in an instant, but I'd been building up to it for a while. In all honesty, I felt guilty. The drugs had affected all communities but had destroyed the black ghettos in particular. I had started off in the Young Black Panthers. My brother Shaun had founded the Federation of Liverpool Black Organisations. We'd dined with King Gustav at his place in Sweden with hope in our hearts. I had fought racist doormen to let black lads in. We'd been strong, fit and clear of thought. After the riots, we'd had the choice to build something positive out of what had happened. Instead, I was a drug dealer, and Shaun's life was in turmoil. Somehow we had chosen the wrong path.

When drugs started coming into the community, people sold them and made money. They weakened our militancy. Drugs made us apathetic and turned us against our own. We started killing each other. In America, the black male under the age of 25 is an endangered species. They're killing each other at a prolific rate, each murder going unreported. It's started to happen here, too.

When I was a drug dealer, I would try and rationalise my actions. The more money we made, the more power it gave us. It gave us a sense that the whole community was getting strong. But then the real effects started to kick in. Drugs gave us a false sense of security. That was the eternal contradiction – the drugs were making us strong in one way but killing us in another.

I never set out to harm anyone, but I couldn't deny that my actions had a hand in poisoning my own community. I was caught up in my own duality. If the truth be known, I did it partly because my feet were bigger than my stepbrother's feet. As a child, I was forced to wear his shoes, because his dad would buy shoes for him and my dad liked to back horses and play cards. I had to force my feet into his small shoes, crushing them. To this day, my wife laughs at me because I like to save on the leccie. My mother would leave us sitting in the dark until she could get some money on her book for the leccie. I don't say these things to curry sympathy or for respect. I say these things as a matter of fact.

There were other more practical reasons why I wanted to go straight. Drug dealing was getting harder, and the bizzies were catching up. Marsellus had got 15 years, and I knew they were gaining ground on the bigger fish – like me, Curtis Warren and all the rest. It was time to move on.

A few months before my change of heart, my solicitor had told me that my best quality was my ability to read when the writing was on the wall. A lot of villains get shown the writing on the wall but don't read it. He said, 'If you carry on the way you're going, you're going to get 15 to 20 years rammed up your arse.' After Abbey was born, he said, 'If you're not careful, the next time that you'll see your daughter she'll have a daughter herself.'

That's what straightened me out. It wasn't fear of other gangsters. It wasn't fear of getting older. It was fear of incarceration. I knew everything that jail had to offer, because I'd spent four months on remand. The only thing I didn't know was the long-term effects of incarceration. Individuals who say that they'll do a long stretch spinning on their dicks – and in the underworld we all know who they are – are either liars or insane. For anyone reading this book and thinking about being a crook – the downside is jail. Jail is a waste of your life, a waste of your time, a waste of your space. When you go to jail, it's like you've died, and when you get out of jail it's like a resurrection. You can start your life again. I know guys that are 40 and have spent 18 years in jail. It's no good.

Even the old-school guys from the 1970s couldn't cut it in the end. One was a villain I knew called John Haase. I had the utmost respect for him, because of his raw courage and bottle. He was a one-man army, and he feared no one. He spent most of his young life in prison for armed robbery. When he came out, he got onto the drugs bandwagon and made himself a lot of money real quick. When they arrested him, they found around £200,000 under the bed – just a small part of his financial empire. Nevertheless, when I went to visit him in Long Lartin prison, it was clear that jail had got to him. That was in 1993, a year before my epiphany. I remembered thinking, 'If he can't cut it, what chance do I have?'

PART THREE

THE STRAIGHTGOER

29

ON THE SIDE OF ANGELS

Going straight wasn't as easy as all that. I had a lot of money stashed away, but I needed to invest it in legitimate businesses in order to get a regular income flowing. However, my first ventures were disasters, and I lost a lot of cash very quickly. To make matters worse, one of my cash hoards from my previous life had been captured. Money had been lost and robbed, and money I was owed from big drug deals never materialised. In the past, I would have used extreme violence to right these wrongs, but I was determined not to go back there. Astonishingly, I virtually went broke. I got down to a house – which still had a mortgage on it – a car and nine or ten grand in readies. Panic stations.

The hardest thing was to avoid temptation. My mates – who were still grafting – would call me up and offer me 20 kilograms of cocaine or give me a tip-off about a drug dealer I could rob. If I had given in, I could have made £100,000 in a matter of hours. By teatime, I could have been rich again, but I'd had enough and just kept looking at my baby while I was on the phone to these people. I'd be knee-deep in nappies with Richard and Judy on the telly in the background, Abbey on one arm and the handset wedged between my ear and shoulder, and I'd think, 'No, I don't want to go to jail.'

The problem was that I didn't know how to be anything else other than a taxman. Then I had a bright idea. Why not try and apply some of the skills and techniques I had learned as a gangster to the business world? That was how I found myself in the world of *legitimate* debt recovery, loan arbitration and security negotiation.

My first job was to help save Cream, the world-famous super club. The security firm who ran the doors – let's call them Ozone Security – were making life difficult for Stuart, one of the owners, so he came to me to get them off the door. Ozone were pretty hard-hitters and had been investigated for four murders and linked to countless other shootings and maimings. So, I said to Stuart, 'I'll get Ozone to a meeting, and all that you've got to do is back me up.' The job was all about front, because at the end of the day it was me against 14 roid-head, killer doormen.

I got my game face on and bounced into the meeting. Once there, I made sure that I looked all 14 of them in the eye and said, 'Stuart doesn't want you on the door any more.'

The Ozone boss sneered at me and said, 'Why?'

'Because I'm taking over, that's why,' I replied.

Now, what they shoulda done was pick me up and throw me out the window there and then. However, they knew that if they did that to me, they could get themselves sucked into some serious ninja violence – if I decided to take a step back into the dark side. You see, they didn't know I was going straight. They thought they were still dealing with the Devil.

I could see some of them starting to make moves. But I knew my Devil stare could freeze a man's blood. I watched the dissenters – the ones I could tell really wanted to machete me – and said, 'There's no point in behaving. Yous are off the doors – end of story. You know what I mean, lad? That's it. It's the end. You've had a good run, but I'm doing it now.'

Amazingly, they swallowed it. They put their tails between their legs and just got off. The path was now free for me to take over the door. However, Stuart still wasn't happy. He didn't know I had turned over a new leaf and feared I would cause him the same problems as the Ozone lot. He panicked and asked my old friend Alfie Lewis to do the contract.

By then, Alfie had a well-established security firm that trained police officers, and he had a squeaky-clean reputation. He came to see me to sort out what was a rather delicate situation. He said, 'Look, Stephen. He's offered me the door, and I'd like to take it.'

I simply replied, 'Brown envelope, Alf. Brown envelope and I'll move aside. Simple.'

He said, 'Well, how much do you want?'

'Well, I've got rid of Ozone, and Stuart has got his club back.'

At that time, Cream was killing it, taking hundreds of thousands of pounds per week and millions more in official spin-offs. However, the real money was being made front of house, with the door team selling Ecstasy. Obviously, this was done covertly, and the owners and managers of the clubs had no knowledge of the illicit trade. Nevertheless, some of the doormen had become multimillionaires. One of my mates was making fucking 30 grand on a Saturday night. It was only after Leah Betts died in November 1995 that they clamped down on it. Nonetheless, I was going straight and wasn't interested in making 30 grand a night, so I told Alfie and Stuart to make me an offer. A few days later, they paid me 20 grand to step aside – not a bad fee for a 15-minute meeting. That's when I realised I could make a lot of money using my brain and my tongue, as opposed to a gun and a knife.

However, the pull of the ghetto was strong. No matter how much I wanted my life to be peaceful and pure, there were always demons trying to drag me back into hell. Often, it was only the petty squabbles of everyday life – family disputes, fallings out, etc. In the past, I would have dealt with them like a gangster, but the next bit of work I did – although only small – taught me a gigantic amount about how to collect a debt without resorting to criminality and how to resist the pull of the ghetto.

My nephew Daniel has got a bigger heart than King Kong, but he's also got killer eyes. In the early 1990s, a few pioneers tried to set up 'head shops' in Britain, Amsterdam-style coffee bars where you could smoke weed and purchase all the technical apparatus you would need to grow a skunk farm. Daniel went into business with partners from Anfield called Norman and Owen, one of whom was the son of a well-known old-school face. The police quickly closed the shop down, and Norman was arrested. Even so, Daniel reckoned Norman owed him 17 grand. After a year of trying to collect his debt, Daniel came to me for help. In the past, I would have gone in straight away – all guns blazing – if only to save face for the family.

The first thing I asked Daniel was, 'What is your settlement figure?' I knew he had probably exaggerated the actual figure he was owed. Sure enough, we arrived at four grand as a satisfactory amount. I went to see to Norman in my very scary black uniform. I allowed him to list the reasons why he thought he didn't owe the money to Daniel. All the while, I wasn't even listening. You have to be dogmatic, otherwise you find yourself being led up the garden path.

Then I said, 'Are you finished? I've listened to what you've got to say, lad. Here's my card. This is who I am. You owe our kid ten grand.' This was simply the opening gambit. Remember, I was ready to settle for four grand.

The next time I went down, I took Daniel, and we opened talks in their kitchen. I said to Norman and Owen, 'I don't give a fuck who you are. I don't give a fuck who you know. You're going to pay this money, and you're going to pay it before you go to jail.' Then, in the interests of fair play, I bollocked Daniel as well: 'I've told you about messing around with these white guys. They just think you're a dumb nigger. They'll turn you over as soon as look at you. Stick with your fucking own.' It was all role play. I was saying this in front of them for effect. As a sweetener to Norman, I then said, 'I know you're going to prison soon for the head shop. One of my relatives is in there at the moment. You can either have a good reception when you land on K wing or a bad one.' I could see him thinking, 'He's cornering me on the outside, and he's cornering me on the inside. What the fuck am I going to do?'

The next day, I decided to switch the pressure from Norman to his partner Owen. This was a good debt-collecting tactic, just in case Norman decided to go to the police. Owen was a businessman who didn't want any aggravation. I said, 'Make me an offer, and I'll go away.'

A little later, I received a phone call from Alfie Lewis. 'Stephen, you're going to have some problems over this debt that you're trying to collect.' He mentioned the name of a notorious crime family who had agreed to throw in their lot with Norman and Owen if it all went down to the wire.

I told him, 'Well, Alfie, you know me. Tell them I don't give a fuck. I don't care who they are.'

'Well, I know that, Stephen. I'm just phoning you up to let you know who's involved. If you need anything, give us a shout.'

At that point, both sides were preparing their nuclear arsenals, polishing the warheads ready for mutually assured destruction. It was Cuban Missile Crisis time. It would soon escalate into a fully fledged gang war – if someone didn't bring the matter back to the table.

Forty-five minutes later, Owen called me up. I said, 'Look, I'm not getting a penny out of all this. My nephew's a pain in the arse to me. Your partner's a pain in the arse to you. We need to sort this out, lad. What d'you say?'

He said, 'I'll give you three grand.'

Remember that Daniel had said that he'd settle for four. I told Owen to make it four and we'd have a deal.

However, he replied, 'No, I'm giving you three.'

I couldn't be seen to have been bullied, so I went away, sat Daniel down and said, 'Look, they want to give you three grand. No guns drawn. No aggravation. My advice to you is to take the three.'

'Man, the Stephen of old would've got 50 grand,' he argued, trying to pour scorn on my attempt to go straight. He was trying to use emotional blackmail to get me to step back over the line. I had to point certain facts out to him.

'Look, you've been on this for 12 months and got fuck all,' I said. 'I've been on it for a day and you've got three grand. Shut your fucking mouth and take the money.' I phoned Owen back and said, 'That's a deal.'

I understood that the biggest worry for Owen would be looking like he'd lost face by giving over the three grand. So I said to him, 'You'll hear a lot of bullshit designed to wind you up, so I'm going to send you a text message, and I'm going to sign it with my name. When anyone says to you that the Frenchman's stood on you or made a show of you, you show them it.' I'd covered all bases. The text said:

> Thanks for your cooperation and your help in sorting out this problem between your partner, who's a pain in your side, and my nephew, who's a pain in my arse. You had no debt. You had no responsibility to pay it, but you've shown the maturity of a man, and you've paid three grand in order to save everybody's face. If, in the future, the Frenchman can do anything for you or any favours for you, do not hesitate to ask. Also, when Norman lands on K wing, he'll be looked after. I'll make sure that he gets a good reception.

Twenty-five minutes after sending that text to him, I got a phone call from Alfie Lewis, laughing down the phone. 'I've seen the message you sent him, you cunt,' he said. 'He's done nothing but fucking show it to everyone in Anfield.' Of course, I knew that he would. I knew that people would say to him, 'The Frenchman came and you melted. You collapsed.' However, with that text he was able to defend himself and say, 'No, I didn't. Here's the message I got off Frenchie. Me and Frenchie, we're mates. There you go.' He'd be able to big himself up with his crew and say, 'As far as I'm concerned, that cunt French owes me a favour. What's three grand to me? It's that fucking knobhead partner of mine causing all kinds of fucking problems. Frenchie hasn't told me to give him the money. He hasn't made me give him the money. He has asked me. He's not telling me what to do. He's asking me what to do.'

In that world, being told what to do and being asked what to do is a universe apart. If you're told what to do, you're a boy. If you're asked what to do, you're a man.

Around that time, I had another revelation. Up until about 1995, you could've termed me anti-white. The truth was that I never really had much time for white people. I knew a lot of white guys and did a lot of deals with them, but, deep down, I'd always believed there was an insurmountable divide between us – never the twain shall meet. That was until I came across a young man called Christian Mark Nesbet, who changed my view of a whole race.

30

UP FROM THE ASHES

There was an old-time comedian called Michael Bentine, who was in the RAF during the war. He joked that he always knew when a pilot was going to be shot down on the next mission, as he could see the tombstones in his eyes at breakfast. Well, on the reverse side, I had the ability to spot people with lights in their eyes – winners. And Chris Nesbet was one of them. He was a guy with bright, shining beams behind his retinas.

Chris had a simple vision. He'd worked as a surveyor in a massive building corporation and had noticed that businesses were obliged to spend millions on security for their sites – on unreliable gangsters who always let them down. His dream was to set up a clean, efficient, gangster-free security company and take the world by storm.

Chris set up his first company with a man known as the Pugilist. Not the best idea. By the time I caught up with him, Chris was on his arse. He was sleeping on his mum's couch, his house was in danger of being repossessed and, worst of all, he was driving a Rover. Chris and the Pugilist didn't have the best relationship – and there was fuck all Chris could do about it.

Enter the Frenchman. I was desperate to buy into Chris's utopian dream. I had a chat with the Pugilist, and he brought me on board. My first job was to go and collect a ten-grand debt from a furniture shop. I entered the store and immediately asked the skinny proprietor to give me the keys. He said, 'I beg your pardon?'

I replied, 'My name's Stephen French. You owe our clients ten grand for rent. I'm seizing the goods in the shop.'

Meanwhile, Chris was bombing around with a calculator, adding up the price tags. The owner then piped up and tried to threaten me: 'I know a few faces. I'm going to make a few calls, and you'll be dead within an hour.' To be fair, he was connected to some very bad firms, but when he went away and did his research it was clear that he was told, 'If the Devil is in your shop, the best thing you can do is give him the keys and leave.' So he did.

The itinerary in the shop amounted to 50-grand's worth of pine: beds, wardrobes – everything you could possibly think of made of fucking pine. We decided to flog it in a half-price sale and invest the 25-grand profit in our company and vision for the future – all for a little growl at some prick. That was good business as far as I was concerned.

The beauty of the situation was that it was all legitimate business – tax paid. Again, it all came down to utilising the skills I'd learned at the Inland Revenue – reputation and psychological intimidation. My unique selling point was that I could make debtors think that the moon was going to fall out of the sky and land on their house if they didn't pay. My favourite phrase was, 'If you double-cross me, you'll be seeing me in your fucking dreams. You'll be seeing me in your nightmares. You'll be seeing me when you're asleep.' Often, they had something to hide, so I was playing on the 'guilty act, guilty mind' theory. Of course, I would only say this to debtors who threatened me – and Chris never knew that I said things like that.

Anyway, we had this whole heap of pine, so the first thing we did was bring our partners down to have the pick of what they wanted. My wife chose a bed and wardrobe and basically kitted our bedroom out in pine. Chris's mum and the Pugilist's bird did the same. All equal. Therefore, it came as a great shock to learn later that the Pugilist had been sneaking pine out the back door and keeping the money for himself. At first, I didn't believe Chris when he told me. I said to him that my loyalties lay with the Pugilist, as he had brought me on board in the first place. However, I also understood company politics. If the Pugilist fell on his own sword, the path would be clear for me and Chris to propel the company out of the small time and into the blue-chip world where it belonged.

The idea of catching the Pugilist in the act appealed to my Machiavellian nature. Whether you're planting bugs for the White House or stabbing your co-worker in the back over the water cooler, you have to get deep down and dirty. People don't climb the greasy pole by being kind and making grand gestures. They slide up it, propelled by backbiting and base human behaviour.

Chris said to me, 'The Pugilist has been selling the beds incomplete without any fitments. To prove it, just go and knock on the door of someone he's sold one to and tell the person that the Pugilist forgot to give them the fitments. If they take them off you, we know he's been selling beds. We can then confront him with the evidence.'

Soon after, I found out that a gangster had bought a bed from the Pugilist. I knocked on his door and said to the gangster's moll, 'I've brought the fitments round for the bed that the Pugilist sold you.'

'Oh, yeah,' she said. 'The bed's upstairs. We still haven't put the wheels on it.'

The gangster realised what was going on and screamed at his bird, 'What the fuck are you saying to him?' However, he knew the game was up.

To be honest, I was very upset and emotional about what had happened. I took the Pugilist for a drive, told him to get out of the car and said, 'Let's fight.'

He said, 'I'm not fighting with you, Stephen.' He wasn't frightened of fighting me – he would've had a go. However, he said, 'I like you too much. I'm having some problems and that, and I'll just leave the firm.' He was embarrassed about the situation.

Come Christmas, I knew he was struggling financially, so I dropped a couple of grand off for him and his family to get them through the day, because, believe it or not, I was developing a social conscience – and he had a lovely young family.

The path to glory was now clear. Chris and I set up a holding company called CDS Management, which stood for 'catering, development and security'. The key to running a successful security company was dealing with the 'intangibles', such as fights with other security companies, death threats and hand-grenade attacks – day-to-day occurrences in the cut-throat world of the security business. That was my area of responsibility; Chris had no idea that any of this went on.

We immediately won a big catering contract from a Japanese car company to feed their workers. That took in two grand a week in cash at 60 per cent profit. The debt recoveries also started to fly in. With the surplus cash, we started building housing estates. If I had only known how easy it was to make money legitimately, I never would have chosen the path to evil in the first place!

However, some of my old compadres weren't as good as me at staying ahead of the law. One by one, they began to fall by the wayside, purely because they ignored the writing on the wall. Curtis Warren moved to Holland to distance himself from his sidekick Johnny Phillips, who was in a hell of a lot of trouble over the David Ungi incident. However, in 1996, the Dutch police linked Curtis with approximately £125-million worth of cocaine and jailed him for 12 years. I hear he spends a lot of his time behind bars trying to stay ahead of currency changes. According to some sources, he's got a lot of money buried all over Europe, and every time they bring out a new £20 note or new note in a foreign currency he has to get his minions to dig it up and change it over. He's lost a lot of money that way.

31

SELLING YOUR SOUL TO THE DEVIL

Over the next few years, I became Britain's numero-uno legitimate debt collector. I recovered millions and millions of pounds' worth of debt that had been previously classified as dead and totally irretrievable.

Every debt has a life of its own. At every twist and turn, people change sides and lie, motivated by greed and dishonesty. I don't suppose things have changed much since the times of the Medicis in the Middle Ages or the Hawala bankers in Arabia. Here is a typical example of how people would act when faced by the debt collector.

One day, the multimillionaire director of a successful car dealership came to see me. He and his two partners had made their fortunes by importing used cars into Britain and flogging them off cheap. As always, greed had got the better of them, and the other two had ripped off my man to the tune of 90 grand. I told him my terms: 50 per cent commission. From then on, it was *my* job 100 per cent. There was to be no interference, and Chris knew nothing about it. It was a strictly freelance operation.

My mate C.J. – a well-respected face from London – and I paid a visit to the garage. It was a nice set-up in an upmarket satellite town known for its infatuation with rugby. Let's call the co-directors

Laurel and Hardy, because one was short and fat and the other was tall and slim. I politely introduced myself, and in a businesslike way explained that I had been assigned to collect their ex-partner's 90 grand. Predictably, they became very irate. Before I knew it, Laurel had driven his car across the entrance to the car park to block me in and had called the police. He grinned at me smugly, thinking that because he was an upstanding businessman in the community and I was a big black man in a predominantly white area, the bizzies would back him and run me out of town. I relaxed onto the bonnet of one of his cars and wearily said to him, 'You're going to live to regret this. You've been very silly here today.'

'I don't think so,' he retorted. 'After the police have had their way with you, I'm gonna have you finished off. You don't know who I know in the underworld. I happen to know a lot of the main faces. You're finished.'

I replied, 'Well, if you know anybody who's anybody in that line of work, then they'll know me, and I'm telling you that you're going to live to regret doing this.'

The police soon turned up, but I had a number of tricks up my sleeve for dealing with that type of situation. First, I always wore a suit, tie and, most importantly, shiny shoes. This impression tended to throw the bizzies off-kilter, forcing them to deal with me civilly. Second, I produced a letter of authorisation from the client to prove that the debt was real. Third, I always made sure that I didn't threaten anybody. There's a very thin line between demanding money with menaces – which is a serious criminal offence – and enforcing a legitimate demand, which is perfectly legal. I was an expert at enforcing a legitimate demand. In fact, to this day, I think I'm still the premier expert in the UK, which is why I officially operate under the auspicious title of 'problem-solver extraordinaire'. I'm known by that name in the City of London, the debt recovery departments of many blue-chip companies and in half of the financial centres in Europe. I'm a man who can solve problems.

Within 15 minutes, the police had gone, and Laurel's face started to change, because he knew he was in deep trouble. He ran inside his office and phoned his gangster protectors. Now, in fairness, his contact was a senior member of a very powerful and dangerous UK crime family. But so fucking what.

As Laurel was talking to the gangster, his face started to relax. I could hear the gangster reassuring his gobshite ally, thinking that if he scared me off there'd be a bit of wages to be had. The gangster then told Laurel to put me on the phone.

I grabbed the phone off Laurel and said, 'This is Stephen French.' I immediately heard the pause. I knew that he knew who I was, and I knew I had won the battle. I continued, 'This is nothing to do with you. I'm going to get the fucking money, and if you want to line yourself up with these pricks, then I ain't interested.'

A little voice squeaked up and sheepishly said, 'Could you put Laurel back on the phone, please?' I then heard the gangster say, 'You're on your own.' Laurel went ashen-faced and began to shake.

I said, 'You think that you know faces in the underworld, do you? Well, now you're facing the Devil. How does it feel to be selling your soul?' Laurel and Hardy caved in and agreed to hand over the full 90 grand the following week.

However, as sure as night follows day, I knew that the second I left they would be on to the co-director they had screwed over. They would apologise profusely, take him and all their birds out for Chinese, and try to kiss and make up. The next day, they'd go and watch the rugby in the directors' box and then hit him with the old, 'We've had a few differences over the years, but it was all business. We're three white middle-aged businessmen who've started off with fuck all and done very nicely for ourselves, thanks very much. So, why are we letting this nigger get involved in our business, trying to destroy what we've worked for all these years? Fuck him off and let's just sort this thing out between ourselves, like the fat cunts we are.'

Before half-time, Laurel and Hardy would have talked their old mate round and found out about my 50 per cent commission, thus realising that their mate would only be getting 45 grand out of it anyway. They'd say, 'We'll give you 30 grand, and we'll all be mates again,' no doubt promising a future partnership.

Lo and behold, a few days later, I found out from my sources that my client had indeed naively decided to realign himself with Laurel and Hardy, thereby cutting me out of the deal and treating me like I was a fucking Muppet or something – a mistake with a capital 'M'. I called up my client and organised a meeting with him. I was really nice and cosy with him. I explained that it was all bullshit, and they'd fucked him once, so they'd do it again. 'Don't realign with them,' I said. 'Stay with me, and I'll reduce my commission to 30 per cent.' This convinced him to come back over to my side. However, I was well and truly fucked off with the effrontery of it all, so I made an executive decision: I was taking the fucking lot. Nobody was getting any of the gravy. To be honest, I had been looking for a reason to fuck them all as it was, and now he had given me one and played right into my hands. He'd wavered. That would cost him.

Collection day soon came around. My spider senses started to tingle as soon as I woke up. However, it didn't feel as though it was a warning about the Old Bill or anything like that. They were tingling as if to forewarn me that these fellas might try something. I could see a vision of an upstairs office and had a sensation that the danger might come from above. As I was cleaning my teeth, I grabbed my .38 – my great equaliser – and put it in my jacket, just in case.

However, when me and C.J. got there, the lovely money was ready for counting. It was all going swimmingly. Nevertheless, I felt my attention constantly being drawn upwards. 'What's upstairs?' I asked.

'Oh, nothing,' they told me. 'Just a storeroom.'

I suddenly got an overwhelming desire to go upstairs. 'I want to go to the toilet,' I said. On the way to the 'toilet', I found a set of stairs and crept up to a room at the top of the building. When I opened the door, I saw two of the biggest fellas I'd ever seen in my life sitting on a bed. These guys must have each been six feet five inches and twenty-five stone. They had an array of weapons on the floor, as well as some tape and a couple of chairs. They had planned to beat us up and then tie us to the chairs.

I wasn't going to fight them, so I pulled my gat out and said, 'You fuckers sitting there, get fucking downstairs, now.' I then marched them down the stairs, like two huge baboons, booting them up the arse to make them get a move on.

'Who the fuck are these?' I asked one of the businessmen. 'What are they for?'

The biggest thug said, 'Please, mate, we're just rugby players from the local team. You're not going to shoot us, are you?' It turned out they were two professional players.

I turned to Laurel, 'You brought these pair of pricks for me. You think these guys frighten me? The two of you get on your fucking knees now.' Laurel and Hardy got on their knees and started begging for their lives. I told them that I was going to fine them an extra five grand for this outrage. I then got the two gorillas to strip off. They stood there like a couple of naughty schoolboys.

C.J., who had a broad south London accent, said to me, 'Fackin' shoot the cants. Let's fackin' fill 'em full,' but he was just playing the game. He didn't mean any of it – it was just a bit of psychological terror to keep everyone under control. Within sixty seconds, Laurel had appeared with an extra five grand. I made him sign a piece of paper, and then I turned to the rugby lads, 'Good luck with your game on Saturday.' With that, I got off.

I'd arranged to meet the original director at McDonald's to give him his share. When I got there, the greedy twat took one look at my bag and greeted me like I was his best mate. I pulled out a tenner and said, 'Go and get yourself a burger and cup of tea while I sit down and get sorted.'

He was cracking jokes with the burger flippers, steadying little kids with their drinks and practically helping little old ladies across the road. It was the best day of his life, and why not? He'd just had his revenge on his old business partners and earned 63 grand to boot. When he finally sat down, he started tucking into his dinner and asked, 'Have you got the money?'

I replied, 'See that hamburger? Enjoy it. Cos it's the most expensive fucking Big Mac in history. That's all you're fucking getting.' C.J. had waltzed in behind me to get a Filet-O-Fish. He looked at the stunned director and said, '90 grand for a burger? Bit toppy, innit? You should have got a meal deal, mate.'

With that, I shouted to the lad at the counter, 'I'll have mine to go, please,' and I left, sipping my Coke.

I drove to a relative's house and gave them the bag of money. When I had a large amount of cash on me like that, I'd put the dough in a safe house and head out of town for a few days, just in case the Old Bill turned up. However, fortunately for me, the rugby players obviously didn't want to pursue the matter, probably because they were so fucking embarrassed.

That was a good pay day. In the end, I took 50 grand and gave C.J. 45. I knew he was an all-the-way nigger, as he had stayed with me and had covered my back. After all, the Devil – legit or not – needs his helpers.

32

YOU CAN TAKE THE DEVIL OUT OF HELL, BUT . . .

My security company quickly became very successful and landed a number of lucrative contracts to provide guards to building sites and commercial premises all over the UK. At its height, the business employed the cream – ex-bodyguards for the Saudi royal family, ex-servicemen and ex-coppers among them. Valued at £7.5 million, we seriously thought about floating our company on the stock exchange. However, there was a downside to being a successful businessman – the politics. There was sniping and backstabbing from the competition, the customers, the local council and the police. It was just a part of the culture of the business I was in, and I needed skin like a crocodile's to deal with it.

All the top builders who I did business with were Freemasons, and they used to get the gossip about me from the top bizzies. The talk at the top table was, 'We've got to bring that black cunt down. He's just getting too big for his own britches.' It was sour grapes. The police hated me doing well, because it looked like I had beaten the system, and I made more in a month than a lot of them made in a year.

But, to be totally honest, I hadn't actually cut all my ties with the underworld. I still knew all the major firms, and if there were problems between them, I would often help bring them together and arbitrate a solution without any bloodletting – a kind of underworld counselling service. RELATE for gangsters who'd fallen out of love.

For instance, one day, two of the most feared crime families in the country had a tiff. One was a huge multimillion-pound nightclub-owning dynasty, and the other family were prolific importers – both spearheaded by ultra-violent men. They were on the brink of nuclear war. Then I stepped in, told them to call off their submarines and brought them around to my attempt at the Oslo Peace Accords. After that, my stock went up, and I began to get a reputation for arbitration.

No one wants war – war is bad for business. War costs. A lot of the big firms had studied the gun war that had followed the death of David Ungi. Although David was just a businessman, gangsters had taken it upon themselves to start killing each other, and the police had flooded the streets with armed response vehicles. I'm not suggesting that the Ungi family were involved in drugs in any way, but David's death led to unrelated gangs killing each other. And who could move heroin around the city when there were bizzies everywhere? War interfered with trade. The cheaper alternative was me. I could counsel for both sides and strike a deal that would keep everybody happy – if they adhered to the terms. Everybody could then move on.

I actually liked that role. I was still a face, without being an active one. There was also another key factor: power, the ancient and irresistible addiction. Power, however petty and insignificant, is a turn on. When you walk into a nightclub for free with eight or nine big men in tow while every other cunt is shuffling about in the queue with a long face wondering if he's going to get in, that's power. It's not power on the same level as Tony Blair, who could send all those troops to Iraq to kill women and children. His power was on a macro scale, mine was on a micro scale. It was personal power. The power to say you can do this or you can't do that in my own little world. Whatever the practical differences, you bet your bottom dollar that the *feeling* was the same.

However, not all of the arbitrations went smoothly. For example, C.J. went off and formed his own security firm with another mate of mine called Kieran Packet, but they soon fell out. C.J. was scared to roll around with Kieran, but Kieran was equally frightened. A powder keg of a situation developed, so I agreed to arbitrate. A meeting was set up in a disused warehouse down the dock road. However, relations deteriorated from the outset. Suddenly, C.J. put a gun to Kieran's head and in his cockney accent said, 'You facking cant.'

To be fair, Kieran didn't flinch and said, 'What are you going to do with that? Are you going to fucking shoot me?'

It was a red rag to a bull. As if in slow motion, C.J. started to squeeze the trigger. 'No!' I cried and jumped up from my chair, whacking his hand down towards the floor. There was a massive bang. The gun had fired, but the bullet had miraculously missed Kieran's head. Instead, it had lodged in his hip.

Kieran was badly injured, so he had to go to the ozzie – there was no two ways about it. This meant the bizzies getting involved, which was just what the top brass had been waiting for – me to fuck up. Irrespective of whether I had been there to referee or not, it would look like I had gone there to help C.J. shoot Kieran. The bizzies must have been rubbing their hands with glee, saying, 'I knew if we gave him enough rope, he would hang himself one day. It's just one more nigger for the jail house.'

However, as always, I didn't wait for events to catch up with me. I hit on a genius idea and surrendered myself to the police. I circumvented the whole car crash by telling them the truth: that I had been there to keep the peace; that I hadn't known C.J. had a gun; and that by whacking his hand, I had actually *saved* Kieran's life. I even made myself out to be a hero. Talk about turning a negative into a positive. The bizzies at the station were fucking flummoxed. I was released without charge, and C.J. went on the run. Kieran made a statement against C.J. and stuck with it. C.J. eventually got caught and was sentenced to eight years.

When we built our office, I insisted that a back door be put in behind my desk. Chris asked me, 'What do we need a back door for?' But I insisted, even though I could see he still didn't really understand my reasons.

Not long afterwards, we started getting hassle from a gangster called the Psycho from over the water. He didn't know I was involved in the business, and he started smashing up our sites and asking for protection money. One day, the Psycho came into the office, slammed his two hands on Chris's desk and said, 'Are you Stephen French?'

The blood drained from Chris's face. I knew straight away that the Psycho had won that fight. I stood up from behind my desk and said, 'I'm Frenchie. I want everybody fucking out the office except him.'

Psycho walked over towards me. It was obvious to me that he wasn't a trained fighter, because the first thing he did was launch a haymaker from South America. I intercepted him with a swift right hook and smashed him on the mouth, splattering his teeth and blood across the wall. Suddenly, he didn't want to know any more. I kicked him up the hallway and said, 'Get this piece of shit out of my place.' Chris didn't know that any of this was going on.

However, he made one more pathetic stab at revenge before he left the premises. He keyed my Lexus 300 Sport down to the metal and then went to the police station to report me for GBH. By the time the police arrived to see the blood-smeared walls, I had flown out the back door, over the back wall and disappeared. That was the reason I needed a back door – in my line of work it was essential. It was a Friday evening, and I knew it was a bad time to get arrested, because I'd be locked up until Monday morning. So, I phoned up CID officers and asked them not to put a warrant out for me, saying that I'd come in on the Monday to sort things out.

The officer gave me attitude and said, 'Don't tell me what to do. If I want to put a warrant out for you, I will.'

I said, 'I've got the resources to disappear if you put out

a warrant. You'll never be able to catch me, so it's best if we cooperate. I'll see you on Monday.' That gave me two days to remedy the situation. I had to find the Psycho to force him to withdraw his statement. I soon found out that he was drinking in a pub with a couple of his friends. So Aldous Pellow, a mate of mine called the Pig and I set off to find our man. We were all big lads, and when we walked into the pub it went silent. I walked over to the Psycho, dropped one of his teeth into his lager and said, 'You know what to do, and you know when to do it.'

The next day, he withdrew his statement. Deep down, something was telling me that bit by bit I was getting dragged back in.

33

AN EXPLOSIVE FAMILY

If there is one story which symbolises the breakdown of the black community in Britain, it is this one. Just over half a century ago, three young men from the West Indies set out on a voyage together in search of a new life. One was my dad Henry French, the second was Nathaniel Earl and the third was Papa Jaafan. They were friends, brothers and comrades who sailed to Britain on the same boat, weathered the same storms and pulled each other up by the bootstraps until they eventually found their feet in a new land. When they were older, they would laugh about the old days in the shebeens around Granby Street, quietly proud that they had made a better life for themselves and their children.

Two generations down the line, the love between the three families had imploded. All three grandsons had moved down to London to make their fortunes in the drugs game. Now they were at war, locked in an everyday ghetto conflict of drugs, guns and death, without any respect for the family history. It was 1997. I was thirty-eight years of age with a three-year-old daughter. My adopted son Danny was 17 and had already been in trouble with the police on several occasions. Through my connections, I had managed to keep him out of jail.

One of Nathaniel Earl's grandsons was called Lito Earl. Lito's parents were decent, law-abiding folk. Lito, in contrast, worked for a white drug dealer who happened to be the husband of a very famous pop singer. One day, a member of a rival gang shot

Lito, and he ran to the police, like a rat. Later, in a classic case of Scouse perversion, the gunman paid him £30,000 to drop the charges, which he duly did. On hearing about Lito's good fortune, our Danny naturally wanted a cut for himself, so he started to plan a taxing expedition with a few of his mates. One night, Danny and his mate Harley Jaafan, the grandson of Papa, kidnapped Lito and took him to a secret abode. Danny whispered into Lito's ear, 'You're not keeping that fucking money. We're taking that money off you because you're a rat. Hand that fucking money over.' Like father, like son.

Not surprisingly, Lito Earl didn't have the 30 grand on him, so Danny got on the blower and repeatedly called members of Lito's gang to get them to come up with the £30,000 as ransom money. These phone calls set off a chain reaction through the ghetto. It wasn't long before I got a call. A guy called Lance Holman – acting as special emissary for the Earl family – phoned me up and said, 'Look, your Danny has kidnapped Lito Earl. His mum's talking about going to the Old Bill if her son isn't set free. Can you sort it?' I was particularly annoyed by all this hassle, as it was a Friday evening and I had been all set to go out for a nice bowl of soup down the Marbo (a Chinese restaurant) with Dionne.

I knew from experience that the first thing I had to do in this type of situation was to nominate an emissary for myself – someone who knew the parties involved and could mediate on my behalf. Therefore, I nominated a drug dealer mate of mine called Neo. Next, I phoned Danny, but, predictably, he had switched his mobile off. So I called up one of his mates and told her, 'If you get hold of Danny, just tell him to let the lad go.'

I spoke to her again a few hours later, and she said, 'Danny spoke to me, and he doesn't know what you're talking about. He hasn't kidnapped anybody.'

Did he think I was brand new or what? Other dads tell their kids off for forgetting to put petrol in the car. Here I was trying to sort out a kidnapping as though it happened every fucking day. Within hours, I'd got hold of all my connections on the street to try and find out the location of Danny and his gang. Once I knew where they were, I could SAS the ken, rescue Lito Earl, give our Danny a slap on the wrist and hand Lito back to his mum before she called the bizzies. Then I would be free to enjoy a nice Chinese meal with my wife.

Well, you know what they say about the best-laid plans. The Earl family lost their nerve before I could act and went to the police. In response, the bizzies launched a sting operation to nail Danny and his mates. First, the police taped all the ransom conversations. Second, they planted a stooge to pose as one of Lito Earl's gang and agree to the £30,000 ransom. Finally, they put £30,000 worth of traceable money into a bugged bag and sent it to the kidnappers in a taxi.

However, our Danny was too cute. He had the wherewithal to separate the money from the bugged bag. The police ended up losing track of the cash and the kidnappers – and they blew their top. Imagine if the papers had found out – the shame of losing £30,000 to a bunch of rag-arse kids would have been huge!

Under pressure to save face, the bizzies redoubled their efforts, using cell-site analysis to try and track the location of the kidnappers' mobile phones. However, Danny kept moving Lito and his kidnap team around the ghetto from safe house to safe house. Eventually, there was nowhere left to hide, so, as a double bluff, they opted to go to the London HQ of the Jaafan family, hoping that the police wouldn't cotton on. All they needed was a few hours to dispose of any evidence, get Lito Earl to agree to a cover story, clean him up, give him a cup of tea and tell the police it had all been a big misunderstanding.

However, the bizzies were hot on the trail. Twenty armed officers raided the Jaafan house and caught Danny in the bathroom. At first, the bizzies were more interested in finding the £30,000 of traceable money they had lost. However, they soon found the cupboard was almost bare. Only ten grand remained – the rest had disappeared.

That night, I got a phone call from the police station. 'It's me, dad,' Danny said. He sounded very subdued and forlorn, and I knew it would fall on my toes to find a solution to the mess he found himself in. It was not the first time I had been obliged to get my adopted son out of a tricky situation, and I toyed with the idea of washing my hands of him altogether, but my conscience soon got the better of me.

I got together with Harley Jaafan's dad William, and we came up with a plan. We each agreed to come up with ten grand as a bribe to Lito's folks to drop the charges – half the money up front and the rest when the case was dismissed. If Lito withdrew the statement of the kidnap allegation, only the ransom tapes and some police statements could be used as evidence in the trial. However, if the statements remained in place and they were found guilty, they stood to get between ten and twelve years. The statements made by Lito and his parents were the most damaging for Harley and Danny. But I knew from various sources that Lito and his family were shitting themselves at the thought of having to face the Devil. They knew that if they went ahead with the court case and put my son in prison, there would be serious repercussions.

From experience, I realised that they would be looking for a way out. I also knew that 20 grand was a lot of money for people like Lito's mum and dad. I'm not saying I'm anything special, but to me ten grand isn't a great deal of money. To me, it is just a half-decent holiday in the Maldives or somewhere – nothing mad, just one of those all-inclusive deals. Dionne's *got* to go to a place like that. There's no fucking her off for two weeks in Portugal or anything like that.

Anyway, my intermediary Neo arranged a meeting between me and Lito's parents in a well-out-of-the-way pub in Wales. Being a cautious individual, I had invested in some state-of-the-art ex-KGB anti-surveillance equipment. I was feeling a bit apprehensive in case Lito's folks had gone to the bizzies about the proposed rendezvous. I could easily have been driving into a trap. If truth be told, I was gambling on the French fear factor, letting my reputation do all the work and relying on them to make a deal without any fucking about.

When I got to the pub, it was quite busy. I scanned the room and spotted a little couple sitting together in the corner. The mother was black and the father was half-Chinese. They looked very frightened indeed. They had no idea who they were supposed to be meeting. Neo had just told them to be there if they wanted everything sorted out. I went over and told Lito's folks that I was there to sort out the problem. I then asked them politely to search me – to convince them I wasn't some police stooge all wired up. Then I whipped out my bug detector to give them a quick scan.

Lito's mum said, 'Look, we don't want no trouble with Stephen French.' She used the third person as though I was some kind of reverential being. 'During the kidnapping,' she continued, 'we tried to get a message to you so you could persuade your son to release Lito. If that had happened, we wouldn't have gone to the police.' She then whispered, 'We don't want to go to court.'

We cut a deal. The next day, I got Neo to drop ten grand to them as a deposit. By accepting it, they had joined forces with the Devil in perverting the course of justice. However, the case dragged on, and after a few months the charges still hadn't been formally dropped. This was partly because Lito had foolishly carried on his drug-dealing activities following the kidnap and had ended up on remand, and partly because Neo had failed to make regular contact with Lito's old dears. Later, I discovered the reason for Neo's lack of assistance. It was all down to bad blood between him and Danny.

Apparently, Neo had been driving past Danny's house one day with two kilograms of heroin – worth around forty grand – in the boot of his car. Suddenly, Neo realised the bizzies were on to him. He pulled over, got the gear, vaulted the fence into Danny's back garden, knocked on the kitchen window and asked Danny to hold on to the drugs. If Danny had been caught, it would've got him ten years in jail. Later, Neo only gave Danny £500 for his troubles. Danny found this paltry amount disrespectful, considering he had just put his neck on the line for a mate, so he plotted to tax Neo. Neo became aware of Danny's plan, approached me and I put the blocks on the tax.

Anyway, I knew Neo was playing me over the whole kidnap debacle, so I cut him out of the picture. As usual, I had to sort the mess out by myself. First, I went to see Lito's mum and dad again, and said, 'I'm telling you, when the police have finished with this case, they won't be interested in protecting you, but they might be interested in investigating your murder.' I was using a bit of theatricality and dramatics to put the frighteners on them.

Lito's dad said, 'Are you saying you're going to kill . . .'

I said, 'No, I'm only saying that the police might be interested in investigating it.'

Second, I got one of the top dogs in the same prison as Lito to send him a message from me: 'Your family has got French's family in jail. You'd better let young French go.'

This had a huge impact on Lito. Imagine that you're in jail and one of the top guys has just come into your cell and made a threat like that. As soon as I got word my message had been delivered, I made a call to young Lito. Bang! The whole thing fell apart there and then.

When Danny's case got to court, all that was left as evidence were the tapes. Unfortunately for the officers involved, they had failed to follow the correct procedures when recording the tapes and the case was dismissed.

However, that wasn't the end of the matter. William Jaafan ended up blaming me for the whole situation and reneged on our deal to provide the rest of the bribe money to Lito's parents, thus owing me ten grand. I wasn't particularly bothered by this. I was just glad to have my adopted son home. Nonetheless, one of my allies used this conflict as an excuse to settle an old score with the Jaafan family. He had a go at William about what a dirty trick he had played by not paying up as originally agreed. In response, Jaafan threatened him with a gun, and full-scale urban warfare ensued between my firm and their family.

One day when Grandmother Jaafan got into her car, it exploded, and she lost both her arms. It turned out that someone had planted an improvised explosive device made of Semtex next to the car and remotely detonated the bomb. Grandmother Jaafan had looked after my dad and Nathaniel Earl when they had first come to this country. From Windrush to urban warfare in just two generations.

34

HELL'S ANGELS

In spite of my determination to go straight, I was well and truly on the slippery slope. To make matters worse, I still couldn't resist hanging around with my underworld crew. We called ourselves the Herd. At full strength, our gang comprised 30 of the biggest, toughest geezers you have ever seen. The mentality of the Herd was that we did what we wanted, and if you tried to stop us we'd trample you.

It was great to go on a night out with the Herd. We'd go to a club and watch the whole place disperse in fear, leaving just us standing there. It appealed to my dark sense of humour.

Undisputed king of the Herd was the Rock Star – the Bengali tiger leading a herd of rhinos. But instead of trying to eat them, he was running alongside them. The Herd boardroom consisted of me and Franny Bennett, a fearless individual who could knock a man out with a single jab. The other main players were Paul Munro, an unbelievable street fighter and number-one jockey; two brothers called Chris and Russell; Quincy Sumner, a massive drug runner; and bringing up the rear were the Stevyns family, three brothers who ran a large security firm.

The firm was broken up into subdivisions. One subdivision might deal in weed, another in coke or heroin, and there was a little subdivision that did nothing except go out for a good time and the occasional fight. When the Herd was in a club, the doormen and club owners would send over free champagne and all that carry-on. I'd always bought into the underworld concept of respect.

One night, Chris and I went to a place called Bar Nine for a business meeting. The doorman, a gangster called Wally, knocked me back because he didn't recognise me. From then on, it became a personal challenge for me to get into the club by any means necessary. Bang! I whacked him with a right hand, and he fell to the floor. Suddenly, there were eight doormen around us. At that point, Chris turned the colour of boiled shite. I was bouncing round, not going anywhere. The rest of the doormen started to come towards me. I took my right hand and slapped it on my right-hand arse pocket as though I had a gun hidden there. Still bouncing around, I said, 'First one in is getting what I've got for them here. You know who my fucking crew are. I'll have the fucking lot of yous.' I then stormed inside.

In the toilets, I was surrounded by Wally, another doorman and Wally's brother Jake, a big hitter with huge muscles. I warned them, 'I might be here by myself now, but I ain't by myself.' That was the beauty of the Herd – you were never on your own for long. I could see Wally had never been hit as quick and as hard as I had hit him, and his whole confidence was shaken. 'Anyway,' I said. 'There's three of yous. It's the best fucking odds you're ever going to have, so you better fill me in now.' I was outnumbered, so I was playing a game of poker and bluffing them – this was when I always came into my own. If you want to be a king, act like a king. I said, 'I'm going to the fucking bar to have a drink.' Jake just looked at me helplessly, like a chicken with its head chopped off.

I went to the bar, ordered a beer and drank it in a nanosecond, because I didn't want to give them time to get their courage back. Then Chris and I left the club. No sooner were we outside than someone pelted a bottle at me. It should have been all on. However, I had proved that I was no coward by getting one drink, so the mob knew not to make a serious attack.

I consider myself a warrior. I've answered the call to arms every time the horn's been sounded. When things get heavy, you'll find me suiting up my armour. You won't find me lagging at the back. I'm always at the front, mate. And I have the scars to prove it.

Not long after this, the Herd decided to stampede over to Las Vegas to see a Frank Bruno fight. I did a little shopping and forked out the equivalent of £200 on a pair of shades. One night, we were at a nightclub in downtown Las Vegas when I spotted John and Casey, two drug dealers from Liverpool who ran a security firm. Franny had never met them, so I took him over to introduce him. On the way over, I bumped into a lad called Philip Mackendrick, a professional boxer from Liverpool. Phil asked if he could have a look at my new shades, so I gave them to him. Before I could stop him, he had crumpled up my new glasses. He was Charlied to death and was just trying to show off and be the big man.

He was standing to my left, and my right hand was furthest away from him. I switched my hips, threw back my left hip, came across with my right hand and cracked him with my Sunday punch. He rolled, hit a table and then came back up. It wasn't until later on that I realised he had been high on cocaine, which gave him the ability to take a tremendous amount of punishment. He rushed at me and grabbed me around the waist. One of his allies then spun an arm around my neck, choking me. Franny Bennett pulled that lad off me and quickly rendered him unconscious.

I ran across some tables and drop-kicked Phil. Down he went again. Then, just before I could finish him off, the Las Vegas security arrived – one Hawaiian and one Samoan. These seven-feet giants picked me up like I was a rag doll and carted me to the exit. On my way out, I grabbed a pillar, because I didn't want to be thrown out of the club, but these guys just picked me up again and turfed me out.

I was livid, like a crazy man. I found out that Phil and his crew were staying at the Las Vegas Hilton, so I rounded up the Herd and headed over there to get my revenge. As soon as we arrived at the hotel bar, one of their crew launched a bottle of whiskey at me, but I ducked just in time. Unfortunately, one of the Herd got the full force of the bottle, and it knocked him out. I went for Phil, but he legged it. Before we knew it, the police arrived, so we had to flee the scene.

When I got back to England, I sent word to Phil that he owed me a grand for destroying my shades and my suit. In fairness, he paid the debt, but I knew there was still bad blood between us. Two weeks later, my brother Shaun, the Pugilist, who was now my pal again, and I all headed over to Everton Park Sports Centre to watch a boxing match. I knew that Phil and his Park Road crew would be there, so I took an equaliser with me as a precaution – an eastern European 6.7-calibre handgun.

Sure enough, Phil was sitting in the bleachers with his crew. He said, 'All right, Frenchie? Can I have a word with you?'

Once we were in the loos, he started moaning, and I could see he was waiting for an opportunity to put his famous left hook on me. I pulled the gun out and stuck it in his fucking throat. I said, 'I'll fucking kill you, lad, I'll kill you. You're not in my fucking league. Stop fucking around and acting the goat.' Once I was back outside, I said to his Park Road crew, 'Before he tells you any shit, he's just swallowed big time in the toilets.' By this I meant that his arse had gone and that he had deferred to my greater power.

The Pugilist, Shaun and I then left. When you've done something like that – humiliated someone – you don't just sit there and give them the chance to get themselves back together. You get off.

35

HELL FIRE

I was now slipping back into my former life at a horrific rate. I was on a ride I simply couldn't get off, and I began to lead a double life, although Chris had no idea that I was up to my old tricks again.

The Rock Star asked me to collect a £200,000 drug debt, which one of his distributors called Dwight had run off with. Rock Star had been chasing him for two years. I knew Dwight was a slippery geezer, so I devised a trick to get him to meet me. He was involved as a witness in some case – the grassing bastard – and I pretended that I wanted to pay him lots of money to drop the charges. However, when he arrived, he was greeted by me and the Rock Star. I pounced on him and got a blade to his neck. To cut a long story short, the £200,000 turned up. I took £50,000, the Rock Star took £50,000 and we sent £100,000 on to Whacker's wife to tide her over for Christmas while her husband was in jail.

But that wasn't the end of it. Dwight initiated a guerrilla war against my legitimate security business. He started stealing white goods from sites we were protecting. I went to confront him, but he ran away. The next day, Dwight and 15 of his friends, armed to the teeth, arrived at one of my sites just as I was in a meeting with Chris, who was still blissfully unaware of this side of my life. Although I was seriously outnumbered, experience as a seasoned campaigner had taught me how to handle that kind of situation. I told them that even if they crippled me, I'd have my brothers push me in a wheelchair so that I could find them and blast them to death. Astonishingly, Chris and I walked away unscathed.

That same night, someone blew up Dwight's car. It was fair retribution for trying to embarrass me in such a fashion. My pride and ego were still a little bit dented, so I plotted to cut off one of Dwight's ears as well. Fortunately for the little scally, I ended up bumping into Marsellus, who had recently got out of prison, and he persuaded me to leave it.

My return to the underworld took a deadly serious turn. In the year 2000, the police informed me that there was a £30,000 contract on my life. 'Here we go again!' I thought. I said to the officer, 'Fair enough. Now can you tell me who it is? King Kong or Mickey Mouse?' In other words, were they seriously dangerous people or just kids messing about? The bizzy was not at liberty to say.

Within hours, I'd found out that the man who had issued the contract was a guy called Derek Sweeney, a member of a nightclub security crew from Everton – a staunch nigger-hating gang. The Herd and I were being blamed for firebombing his house, an incident in which his two daughters had been tragically injured.

I got hold of Sweeney's right-hand man and said to him, 'Look, I sympathise with what happened to Derek's family, cos I'm a father too, but somebody's just thrown my name into the hat. If you check my MO, you would know that when I have a problem with someone I go and sort it out face to face.'

The guy said, 'Don't worry about it, Stephen. I know that's not your style. I'll sort it out.'

I took him at his word and said, 'As you know, I would normally kill a man who put a contract out on me, but because I'm a father myself and I understand I'm going to let it go.'

However, the dispute escalated, and Herd houses were firebombed in revenge. My mate Neo had an asthmatic child who needed oxygen to help with breathing problems. Once the petrol bomb made contact with the oxygen, the house exploded. They all just about got out with their lives. Franny Bennett's house was also firebombed. And a house which they thought was mine was attacked, too.

Then, one night, I heard a crash downstairs. I looked out the window and saw flames coming up from below. I spotted someone running away and thought it was probably a junkie. Dionne was babysitting all the young girls in our family but had luckily taken them to her mum's for the night. As I walked down the stairs, I thought to myself, 'This means war.'

I called a meeting with Sweeney via his right-hand man, who said, 'He wants you to meet him at Littlewoods, as it's all camera'd up.' As Sweeney approached, I saw that he was only around five feet four inches and about five stone soaking wet. The first thing I did was turn my back on him as a mark of disrespect. If he'd wanted to, he could have stabbed or shot me, but I knew as soon as I saw him that he didn't want to have it with me. I looked at him and said, 'Derek, you've put £30,000 on my life and you've petrol bombed my house.'

'I wasn't responsible for your house,' he replied. 'I'm telling you that wasn't me. It's down to somebody trying to mix it between us.' There was a possibility that this was true, but I didn't believe him. He then said, 'Anyway, I don't care whether I live or die.'

I said, 'What about your two kids that survived the fire? Do they care whether you live or die? Because I've got a daughter who cares whether I live or die. Now, I've heard that you're a good little 'un and that you can go hammer and tongs. Well, I'm a good big 'un, and I can kick you up and down the length of this fucking street and beat you to a point where you're just about alive. If you don't believe I can do it, let's go, lad. Let's go.'

All the time I was talking to him, I was looking into his eyes and into his soul – the Devil persona and the dark looks were in full effect. Usually, when I was like that – breathing down someone's neck with smoke coming out of my nostrils – my target melted like fucking butter in front of a fire. This is no brag, just fact. I said, 'These are my words of iron. I didn't burn your family. I don't accost wives. I don't accost any family member. I keep it just between me and my enemies. You can check my track record. If I'd a problem with you, I would've attacked you there and then on your doorstep. I wouldn't have set your fucking house on fire.'

I could see he was beginning to realise that my words of iron held great truth. As one family man to another, I made him a deal. 'Look,' I said, 'the job on my house has been superficial. There's not really any great damage. So I'm prepared to draw a line here and now. You don't step over that line again. If you do anything to me ever again, I will come for you with everything I've got, and I won't stop until you're in a box. It's up to you. Do you want to make a deal with me?' Derek agreed that he would withdraw the contract on my life and swore that nothing else would happen to me or my family. True to his word, nothing else did.

It was around the time of all the firebombings that the Herd slowly started to disintegrate. One incident in particular signalled the beginning of the end for our crew. Two carloads of us were ambushed by a rival door crew over a misunderstanding. Lads with balaclavas and pickaxe handles ran over and started attacking the cars. I was sitting in the back seat by the window when one of them smashed it in and started waving a bat at me. Our driver panicked and drove off, not giving us a chance to fight back. One of our crew by the name of Wanda was left behind, and they stamped all over him. Later, we found out that our attackers were from a security firm from Everton called Dynamite Security – all bad racists with something to prove. Of course, there had to be some retaliation for this attack.

Soon after, one of Dynamite's mob called Shelley Birkenstein was shot in a nightclub. I knew nothing about it – it was someone else in the Herd who set up the contract. Ironically, Shelley was a mate of mine, even though he was part of the other firm. The other twist in the tail was that the shooter was a guy called Hassan. When he went back to his Herd paymasters for his fee, they murdered him. After that, it was evens. But the upshot was that there was too much heat on everyone, and the Herd scattered.

On top of all of this, the Rock Star and I fell out because of a dispute between our families. My nephew Grantley had been shot in the head by a kid who was best friends with the Rock Star's brother. It caused a great division between me and the Rock Star, forcing us to take opposite sides. We spoke about it on long early morning walks to try and find a solution. But when more shootings took place, I knew it was time for everybody to head for the hills. At that time, I had around 18 grand in cash lying around the house. I called the Rock Star and said, 'I know that things are a little bit tight with you at the moment, so I'm giving you nine grand so you can get off. Pay me back when you can.' I moved over the water and the Rock Star to southern Europe, and we kind of lost touch.

To this day, he still hasn't paid me back the nine grand. People have tried to poison my mind against him, but I believe in my heart of hearts that we will always be friends and brothers, and that we can one day pick up where we left off. The Rock Star's my last connection with Andrew John. He was Andrew's protégé and like a little brother to me. He is a tremendous person in his own right. I've got a lot of time and great respect for him.

36

PROBLEM-SOLVER EXTRAORDINAIRE

Like an alcoholic trying to stay on the wagon, I steeled myself to give up crime for a second time. I threw myself into building up my security company. Chris manned the desk, and I was the problem-solver extraordinaire dealing with the intangibles. A typical intangible involved dealing with corrupt contractors nicking loads of gear and trying to cover their tracks by blaming our firm.

One time, a site agent tore a strip off me after £40,000 worth of white goods went missing. I suspected it might be him, so I went to his house that night. The second I saw his face, I knew he was guilty. I said, 'If you've got the goods, I will take them back and won't shop you to your bosses. If you refuse to let me in, I will come in anyway, and if I find the goods, I will blow you up.' If someone behaves like that towards me, I have full licence to treat them like the worst bitch in the street. Gratitude is a burden but revenge is a pleasure. It felt good to get my own back.

The business grew. I had 500 lads working for me, and we were hired to do security for a £200-million office complex. I told my guards that I would give them a £500 reward if they called me whenever a thief tried to bribe them into turning a blind eye. One day it paid off, and I got a call from one of my guards. Apparently, he had been approached by a lad from one of the haulage firms who wanted to nick £10,000 worth of cobblestones from the site. Acting on my behalf, the guard agreed to let the lad into the site at midnight to collect the cobbles. Little did he know that I was hunched down by the checkpoint, lying in wait.

The lorry pulled up and the driver said, 'I'm here to collect the cobblestones.' That was my cue. I launched myself at the cabin like a gazelle, jumped across to the driver, smacked the keys out of the ignition and took the lorry hostage.

When I jumped back out of the cabin, the driver came out after me. He was a bit of a big lad, so I gave him a kick straight into his guts that doubled him over on his hands and knees. I then got him by the hair and said, 'You've chose the wrong nigger to try and rob, mate. This is Stephen French's site.' I then fined him £5,000 and confiscated the wagon as collateral. Later, the big brother who owned the haulage firm threatened me with all his gangster connections if I didn't give the lorry back.

I said, 'Listen, mate. I don't care if you're connected to King Kong himself, cos King Kong's got fuck all on me, you understand? If you want to come here, I'm ready. Talk is cheap.'

Finally, the elder brother paid me £3,500 and we shook hands. I believe he made his younger brother work off the debt in the end. As promised, I gave the guard his £500 reward, Chris got £1,000 (although he had no idea where it had come from) and I spunked my £1,000 in the casino. I also gave the site agent £1,000 as a gesture of goodwill and to remind him of my part in the whole affair. In the event that he was on another multimillion-pound project, the chances were that he'd hire us again, as we had shown ourselves to be a trustworthy and honest security firm. That's why I had the most jobs and the most exclusive contracts with builders. All I was doing was a good job and going above and beyond the call of duty when necessary, without impugning anybody's reputation. These stories illustrate how battles can be won without firing a single shot. It's what I like to call good captaincy – good piloting of the ship. Isn't that what you want? No casualties and total victory? Can it get better than that? No, it can't.

Our security business Chrymark Security soon reached a turnover of four million quid. But I was missing the action and craving my former life. I resisted, but in the end I substituted crime for another addiction – cocaine. It was bad. It took over my life for about a year, and I went low. To make matters worse, Chris had managed to break two legs messing around on a motorbike. We took our eye off the ball, and the security firm began to suffer. Then we fell out over a property venture. While I was in my cocaine stupor, I suspected Chris had gone behind my back on a property deal. First, I found out that he had used our company funds to help buy a £4-million property development, although it was only a small amount for a deposit that he later paid back. Second, I believed that the deal had only gone through because my contact owned the building. And third, Chris turned to me to save the day when the deal was about to collapse.

Meanwhile, Chris had been named Entrepreneur of the Year at an awards ceremony for local businessmen. I congratulated him and telephoned his mum and dad to tell them the good news. However, during his acceptance speech, he failed to mention me at all. One of the lads with us nudged me and said, 'You deserve that award as much as Chris does.' That was something that stuck with me.

Chris really began to distance himself from me. I was still in a cocaine stupor – my home life was in tatters, and I was very ill. I knew I had to come off the stuff. Within 21 days of stopping, it was out of my system, and my head began to clear. I started to get very suspicious about Chris and his secretive behaviour. As it turned out, I discovered that he had two new business partners and had completely cut me off. Disappointment, betrayal and despair – all superseded by furious anger – coursed through my body.

I'd always promised Chris that I'd never use violence against him, so we agreed to sell Chrymark. I settled on a fee of 250 grand for my share. I also wanted a share of the property portfolio, so I went to my solicitor to get his advice. It turned out that Chris had also paid a visit to Enzo, but my solicitor's loyalties remained with me, and he told Chris, 'You danced with the Devil. Now it's time to pay the piper.'

Chris accused me of blackmail and threatening his father, which was totally untrue. The police heard about the tension between me and Chris, and stopped me from flying out to watch Liverpool in Istanbul in the 2005 Champions League final. They thought I was going to damage Chris, who also happened to be going. Eventually, he agreed to pay me £1.3 million. Despite the conflict, I've got a lot of love for Chris, even though we are still poles apart.

In 2005, I switched my interest to property development full time, which is something I am still involved in today. I play the stock market and the Lloyd's insurance market. At my leisure, I still do debt recoveries, arbitration and act as a security consultant. I work when I feel like it and on average earn £250 an hour – more on a good day. Sometimes I can earn up to £5,000 for a half-day's work. And yes, the taxman's getting his. I ain't going to make the mistake of stealing his money.

Now let me ask you a question: would you rather risk your life sorting out some underworld mess with zero payment at the end or would you prefer to earn a truckload of cash mediating between two middle-class white businessmen, who at their worst might say, 'That's a bit strong, isn't it, old boy?' Exactly.

I'd finally reached a point in my life when I was happy and contented. I was rich, but no longer had anything to do with the underworld. The Devil was still inside me, but I had evolved into a totally different person. I finally had my demons under control.

First thing in the morning, I switch on my mobile and a message pops up: 'You are an unstoppable champion.' That sets me up for the rest of day.

EPILOGUE

SINS OF THE FATHER

On a hot summer's day in July 2006, I got some bad news. My son
Stephen had been shot. For a split moment in time, my whole
world collapsed. I had only spoken to him two hours before. One
of his mates called me to tell me that he was dead. I was grief-
stricken. Why had this happened. Was it God punishing me for
all those years of evil? Was it payback for being the Devil?

Soon my grief turned to anger. I had been going straight for
many years, and this would prove to be my greatest test. Would I
have to become the Devil again and avenge my son's tormentors?
I got my balaclava and headed for the woods to dig up the gun
I had stashed there for a rainy day.

Like an SAS soldier going into action, I prepared for war.
But as I was going through my mental checklist, I couldn't stop
thinking about Stephen's life. Growing up, he had continually
been in trouble. Signs of his criminal tendencies were there at
an early age. For example, I remembered getting a call from
my mate Brownie, complaining that Stephen and his mates had
been caught on camera robbing his shop. Brownie sold American
clothes. You know, the jeans round the arse and the big puffa
jackets – ghetto fabulous. I got the CCTV footage off Brownie
and paid for everything my son stole. Then, to keep him out of
trouble, I gave him a security job on one of my sites. For that,
he got a K-reg Renault 19, a petrol card and £350 a week. But he
never turned up. Instead, he pulled stupid stunts. For instance,

on one occasion he threatened a doorman with a gun. I had to say to the doorman, 'Look, he's my son. If you put him in jail, I'm duty and honour bound to do something to you, and I don't want to. So I'm asking you to take £5,000 and drop the charges.' Luckily he did. All Stephen's life, he had me to protect him from harm – and now this. Waves of guilt washed over me.

Apparently, three individuals – two on mountain bikes and one hiding in the bushes – had laid in wait to murder him. They had ambushed him and shot him. Now I had to make the biggest decision of my life. I had the power to plunge the ghetto into war over this and kill those responsible – blow their houses up and kidnap their kids. I even knew their families. They were decent folk who just sold a bit of weed. But it didn't matter. Now they were going to get it.

Within hours, my mate Marsellus, who was now out of jail, tracked down Stephen's aggressors. He phoned me and wanted to know what he should do with them. I could hear the yells and screams in the background. It was obvious that they'd already been seriously interviewed.

I took a deep breath. My whole future hung in the balance. Then, without flinching, I said, 'Hand them over to the police.'

'What?' He couldn't believe it. He continued, 'I'm reluctant to do that.'

'Let the authorities deal with them. There has been enough hurt and killing. It's got to stop.'

Marsellus pleaded, 'I don't want to do it, but, OK, I'll do it for you, Stephen.' He then delivered the culprits to the police station. That was when I knew I had truly turned a corner. I couldn't believe it myself. A huge feeling of relief washed over me.

Then, as if rewarded by God himself, a miracle happened. Stephen's mum phoned me up. 'He's alive,' she said. 'The wound is superficial.'

Stephen was alive! Luckily, he'd noticed movement in the bushes and had been alert enough to flee the situation, escaping with a bullet in the ass. I couldn't believe it. There is a God!

Eventually, I got hold of Stephen and warned him, 'No retaliations. No revenge. No more violence.'

At that point, I knew I had finally exorcised the Devil from my life.

POSTSCRIPT

This book is an account written by Graham Johnson. It is not an autobiography. As I stated in the preface, it is my opinion that the story you have just read could apply to any number of black males born in 1960s Toxteth, colloquially known as the ghetto since the 1981 disturbances.

At times, this book is funny, sensitive, harsh, brutal and vicious, but the central message is to lay down your firearms, embrace knowledge and education, and strive to make yourself a better person through employment, legitimately and legally. If this message reaches one person, the effort and energy that has been expelled to bring this project to fruition has been worthwhile.

This book is also a story about the city called Liverpool – the city of the Scouser. Black people have lived in Liverpool for 400 years. After the 1981 disturbances, now referred to as the Toxteth riots, the Gifford Report found that Liverpool was the most racist city in Europe. Fast forward and Liverpool will be the European Capital of Culture in 2008. As a result, this book is the story, from a black perspective, of how Liverpool has transformed from being 'the most racist city in Europe' to the venue for the European Capital of Culture and how the black diaspora has been intertwined with this development.

Later this year, Liverpool celebrates its 800th Birthday. The city is famous for being one of the world's great sea ports. What is not so widely known is that it was also the centre for what is

248

referred to as the Golden Triangle – the collection of slaves from Africa and their transportation to the West Indies, where they were exchanged for coffee, tea, sugar and other goods, which were brought to Europe and sold, the three-legged journey then starting all over again. To this day, the legacy of slavery can be seen in Liverpool. Parliament Street and Granby Street, famous thoroughfares in Liverpool 8, and Penny Lane, made famous by the Beatles song, are all named after slave traders who made their money and wealth in the traffic of human beings. And many of the historic buildings of Liverpool were made on the backs of black slaves. Racism was an intrinsic part of the Merseyside social fabric.

In the twenty-first century, racism still exists, although it is now a lot less overt then it used to be, thanks in part to legislation, political correctness and the development of a better understanding of different cultures from around the world. As for Liverpool being the most cosmopolitan city in the world, the jury is still out on that one.

My story has shown that I never allowed racism to hold me back, never allowed it to be a barrier, never allowed it to be a problem. That doesn't suggest that I was unaware of it, but instead that I decided I was going to do something about the institutional racism, the endemic racism, the guy in the street who called me a dirty black bastard. I decided to say, 'Fuck that shit. I'm not playing that game. I'm going to change the rules.'

A prime example of this was in the early to mid-1980s. There were several city-centre clubs that imposed an illegal ban on black people. The security staff would stop black guys and deny them entry into the clubs. My cohorts and I took over several of these establishments. The first one was adjacent to the Adelphi Hotel. Andrew and I went down, rendered four of the doormen unconscious and allowed young black guys entry into the club. We drank free champagne all night and left without paying. That is what I call 'rough justice'. The owners of the club contacted the authorities, who in turn contacted us. However, there was, of course, no evidence and no witnesses. It was as if nothing had happened, and we came out on top – as usual.

To the person who takes the moral high ground and says that I acted outside and above the law, I say that sometimes the law is an arse and sometimes the law does not encourage fair play. I specialised in fitting round pegs into square holes. I shouldn't have had to deal with a racist police force and an endemically racist community, but I adapted to my terrain and applied myself to any given situation. And I had the confidence in my own ability to achieve my goals.

A lot of people who know me well do not like me – they find me arrogant. Arrogance is a finger on the hand of vanity. Vanity is foolishness. However, what people generally mistake for arrogance is actually my strong self-belief. Self-belief is the key to success in any endeavour you wish to undertake. If one is the ying, then the other is the yang. Name me the champion of any sport and I will show you a person who has self-belief. Self-doubt, on the other hand, is a demon that lurks in the subconscious, waiting for its chance to pounce at the most inconvenient of times. The mark of a true champion is to identify self-doubt, confront it as the demon it is and tame it. I personally took self-doubt for a walk on a lead – such was my belief in my own ability to do what was necessary to get me to where I needed to be.

I have not always lived my life honourably or with integrity, but I have evolved into a person with both those qualities in abundance. Given the environment that I was born into and bad things that I have done, the fact that I am here today is testament to my self-belief and my ability to survive at all costs. I am a good man who is capable of bad things. However, I no longer bear ill will towards anybody. Instead, I aim to live my life out in tranquillity and harmony. But for those of you who wish to prod, poke and tease me, please do not mistake my kindness for foolishness. You will find an underlying strength that is unfathomable to the ordinary individual. I believe that I am extraordinary – I am the problem-solver extraordinaire.

I do not stand in judgement of anybody. And I am not trying to rationalise or dilute in any way, shape or form my past behaviour. To those people that I have offended or upset during the course of my life, I unreservedly apologise. However, to my enemies who called me the Devil, I have this to say: 'I never fucked a man who didn't deserve to be fucked.'

My philosophy on friendship is simple: it starts out as a clean sheet of paper with no marks or blemishes. If you do not mark that piece of paper, then neither will I. However, if you do mark the sheet, I won't cry and I won't moan. I won't even let you know I am upset until I am ready to totally cover and immerse the sheet and pay you back tenfold. I will let you know why I have acted and why I feel justified in doing so. Once again, if you are an enemy and you wish me ill, I say, 'Be careful what you wish for, because the Devil may come and get you.'

The fact that so many of today's young people are ready to kill each other at the drop of a hat is a sorry situation. What they don't understand is that the man to fear is not the man who is prepared to kill you at the drop of a hat but the man who is prepared to die at the drop of a hat. The man who is prepared to die at the drop of a hat and defend his honour and integrity is a man who lives without fear of contradiction. This is a rounded, well-adjusted and capable individual. This is the person I have battled to become.

But please don't misunderstand me. I do not consider myself to be invincible. Not even Achilles was invincible. We all have our vulnerabilities and our weak spots. I identified mine and lived without fear of any man on the planet. However, as a consequence of the life I once led, I realise that I could still one day be murdered. I do not believe that this will necessarily be my fate, but being an intelligent and logical individual, I know that there is always the possibility.

Now that you've completed the book, you've read about the many assassination attempts on me so far. One of the main reasons for telling my story was to emphasise the futility of a life of crime and to show the devastation that is caused to a family when one of its sons is violently taken away from them by gun murder – which is what happens every day in the black community. Gun crime is on the increase throughout Britain. How many more mothers and fathers are going to lose their sons?

I have been honest and frank about my experiences. Today I don't consider myself to be a Devil; I consider myself to be a warrior angel. I am involved in trying to get young men to lay down their firearms and pick up a bricklayer's trowel or plumber's wrench or a mechanic's wheel brace. Anything other than a gun. Organisations such as MAG – Mother's Against Guns – reveal on a daily basis the pain that is caused when a young man is shot, and I want to add to the good work that they are doing.

Because I am well-known individual in Liverpool, the police have come to me and asked me to arbitrate between warring factions in my community on several occasions. They have approached me with intelligence that certain people are in danger of being shot. Superintendent Lol Carr, who is in charge of south Liverpool, has called me several times to inform me that a situation is brewing. I have always tried to assist in finding a peaceful resolution without any bodies turning up and to find a return to the status quo. That is one of my roles now.

My intention in the future is to set up a training centre to teach the young men of my community, black or white, a trade so that they have a skill other than that of pistolero (gun man) or drug dealer – to learn how to provide for and protect their families.

Today, some people believe that nothing has changed in Liverpool since the riots. I do not believe this. For instance, I have changed my opinion of white people. I have also changed my opinion of the police force. Although I referred to police corruption and brutality in the account of my life that I gave to Graham Johnson, I have also come across some very decent officers: Peter Street from Bromborough Police Station in the Wirral and Superindent Lol Carr in Liverpool – a big man with a big heart and a great concern for the wider community – to name just two examples. When Liverpool lost Chief Constable Norman Bettison, we lost an honest, incorruptible and dutiful police officer. I was well aware of the changes that took place when he was in office. As a result of his tenure, the police force in Liverpool now seems a lot more interested in upholding the law rather than enforcing it, as was the case pre-1981. Although racism is undoubtedly still a problem in the police, at least there are now systems in place to complain about it. Racism still occurs and is especially obvious in police officers fresh out of training college, who have an overbearing attitude at times. Racism could be eradicated in these younger officers with more extensive training, more accountability and a longer probation period.

I now own four legit property companies and I am a commercial debt-recovery expert, but the jewel in my crown is my role as problem-solver extraordinaire – my security consultancy and arbitration company registered with the OFT. In business, I conduct myself with integrity and honour. I attempt to treat everyone with respect, with a view to receiving respect in return, thus enhancing interpersonal relationships.

One of my proudest achievements is that I run my own rehabilitation scheme for offenders, employing people that no other company would touch and giving the hard pressed in society a second chance. You'll be glad to hear that one of the people who has benefited from this scheme is none other than my old friend Marsellus, who is currently learning a skill after spending 15 years in jail.

A lot of my friends and colleagues will ask, 'Why the hell did you contribute to this book?' My answer is that it had a cathartic effect. I laid myself bare. In 2009, I will be 50, and I wanted to share my experiences about the futility of crime and the pain and devastation that it causes. This book is a platform to reach the young men of today, to teach them that there is another way.

My brother Andrew John was shot dead, my son Stephen was shot in the backside, my nephew Grantley was stabbed in the chest and shot in the head by a 9-mm pistol, losing the use of his left eye. Personally, I know at least 20 people that have been murdered. Go to any black community in the UK – Chapeltown in Leeds, Moss Side in Manchester or St Pauls in Bristol, to name but a few – stop a man over the age of 30 and I guarantee he will also know someone who has been murdered.

On 8 June 2007, A.J. had been dead for 16 years. Every year on this day, I meet his brother B.J. at his graveside at 12 noon. B.J. looks so much like Andrew it's uncanny, and we both say that not a day goes by when he doesn't flash into our minds. Though he's still alive in our hearts, he was ripped from us by a horrific and heinous crime. He was never allowed to fulfil his potential and to fully express himself in life. I assure you that this individual had even greater talent than me. Therefore, it is my hope and intention that this book will give me a platform to reach into the black communities up and down the land, and if I can stop one individual following the same fate as Andrew John, then it will have been worth it.

You may ask yourself how a man called the Devil can claim to have honour and integrity. Let me just say this: it is my wholehearted intention to increase the peace and to treat everybody whom I encounter with respect. With my honour and integrity intact, I leave you with this: at times the world can be a harsh place and harsh measures are needed to survive. But all you can do is strive to be a better person.

Stephen French
August 2007

GLOSSARY

79 kalookie – variation of the card game rummy

Babylonians – black word for police

bag-head – drug addict

bake – to turn powder cocaine into crack cocaine

bally – balaclava

bang on – spot on or accurate

barrios – neighbourhoods

bird – jail time

bizzy/bizzies – police officer/the police

blagger – armed robber or liar

blimp – glimpse/look

blouse notes – counterfeit money

blowing us through/up – when a police officer asks for criminal record information or a vehicle check over a radio

boxed it – when an action is complete; sorted

brown – heroin

bumped – refused to pay up

burst a ken – to ambush a house by bursting through the front door

bush – leaf marijuana

capex – capital expenditure

Charlied – under the influence of cocaine

chi – inner strength

chipping – cheating; specifically to hide profits from a partner

claret – blood

compo – compensation

crash the gaff – to storm a building

defo – definitely

dough – money

draw – cannabis

dollars – money

Ebonics – pertaining to black culture; something which is constructed using black influences

exies – expenses

face – well-known criminal

fessed up – confessed

fours, the – the fourth floor of a prison wing

gaff – house or place of business

gat – gun

gazelle – to run at speed or to jump high and far

gip – bother

go-around – fight

golly – phlegm

granny – used to refer to old ladies employed as drug mules

hash – cannabis resin

heater – a gun

Hoffman – run (named after Dustin Hoffman, who appears in the film *Marathon Man*)

intel – intelligence data

ironed or ironed out – killed/assassinated

jarg – fake or phoney

jockey – driver

jug – jail
kecks – trousers
ken – house
khazi – toilet
ki – kilogram
KO – knockout
la – lad
lash – throw
leccie – electricity
licks – punches or blows
mark – intended victim of a con or scam
mithering – annoying
MO – abbreviation of modus operandi
narco – narcotics
nice touch – successful criminal operation
noncery – paedophilia
on offer – vulnerable to arrest
on top – underworld emergency
one over the eight – drunk
oppo – partner/comrade
ounce out – split drugs into ounce batches
outro – escape route
ozzie – hospital
PACE – police and criminal evidence act
paper – cash
parley – meeting
pigs – the police
plod – police officer
punter – the victim of a mugging
put somebody under manners – to threaten a victim into following instructions; to make someone an offer they can't refuse

rattler – train
rep – reputation
roid-head – a steroid-using bodybuilder
rolling – mugging
scally – youthful miscreant
scooped – hit
score – to buy drugs
scrap – credit
screw – prison warden; job
shovel – jail
slam on – to bring a fast-moving car to a stop using a handbrake turn
springboked – kicked
squeeze somebody out – induce unconsciousness by compressing the windpipe
steward's – steward's inquiry, to get to the bottom of an incident
three-piper – foursome that includes three men and one woman
tick – credit
ting – black word for a gun
tippled – tipped off
town halls – balls
trackies – tracksuits
tranny – radio
tug – arrest
twat – hit
U-ie – U-turn
vidi – a look (from the film *A Clockwork Orange*)
white – cocaine
yellow pedal – a police document that proves drugs have been seized